A DEAD BAT IN PARAGUAY

a memoir

Roosh Vörek

© 2009, 2010 by Roosh Vörek
http://www.rooshv.com

All rights reserved.

Printed in the United States of America.

To my travel buddies

ACKNOWLEDGEMENTS

First and foremost I thank all the people who appear in this book. Without them there would be no story to tell.

The editor credit goes to a Miss J. Lynch, whose quick whip kept me focused and motivated in creating the best book I possibly could. I don't think she realizes how important her role was.

I thank my proofreader Wesley Moore. He fixed numerous errors that my brain simply couldn't catch despite numerous readings. I thank my friends Ron and James for help with the early edits.

Most of the book was written in Starbucks No. 07417 in Silver Spring, Maryland, which is now closed. I thank the friendly staff for allowing me to transform the corner table into my own personal office for twenty-five hours a week. I also thank my dozen or so coffee shop friends, especially Craig and Walt, for their constant encouragement.

Cover was designed by Al Garcia. Bat image used on cover was created by Nick Lobeck.

PROLOGUE	1
WASHINGTON D.C.	3
ECUADOR	25
PERU	69
BOLIVIA	105
SALTA & CHILE	125
ARGENTINA	155
URUGUAY & PARAGUAY	203
RIO DE JANEIRO	227
EPILOGUE	261

A DEAD BAT IN PARAGUAY

PROLOGUE

My stomach was killing me. If I fed myself a drop of alcohol or grease it would grumble and twist with pain, the result of infections with giardia, salmonella, and whatever I currently had, yet to be officially diagnosed. I was sluggish, beat up, and tired of the foam hostel mattresses, bedbug bites, illnesses, allergic reactions, bad sleep, and hundreds of hours of rough bus rides. I'm convinced the only reason travel is glamorized is because people rarely do it for more than a week or two at a time.

I stared at Delirio Tropical's café menu. Out of the dozen of salads waiting to be scooped by the young woman in the paper cone hat, I could only pick three. I hemmed and hawed at all the choices and held up the line until I could finally decide on something that I thought my new stomach would agree with. I remembered a conversation I had with a gringo where I declared that choice leads to unhappiness. With too many choices, I argued, you will be less satisfied with the ones you make because you'll wonder what would have happened if you chose something else. But unfortunately you'll never know.

I sat down at a counter facing a busy intersection. It would be only two more days until I returned home and this adventure would come to an end. A few hours ago I said my final goodbye to Mariana, but it didn't feel quite right. It was stiff, done early in the morning after breakfast. I took out my prepaid cell phone from my pocket, wondering what I should do.

I stared out the window and thought of how I was returning home poorer, carless, jobless, and unsure of what to do next. I tried to put together some meaning to the past six months and what it had done to me. What my bad travel luck had done to me. Just a month ago I was certain I was going to die.

A DEAD BAT IN PARAGUAY

WASHINGTON D.C.

I

I had known Bobby since college. He had an all-American look that girls loved and perfectly sculpted hair coated in big dollops of pomade wax. He was so desired by girls (he resembled Matt Damon) that I would get residual attention just by standing next to him. It was a nice little perk that came with the friendship.

One night, I followed him to a Georgetown University dorm party to meet with a friend of ours who knew a group of female undergrads. The girls Bobby and I had been meeting at clubs were difficult and flakey, so we were excited about the prospect of meeting easy college chicks, one year after we graduated with bachelor degrees from the University of Maryland.

At the party Claire stood out the most. She'd let out a hearty, belly laugh to our jokes, shaking the curly blonde hair that lent her the nickname Golden Curl. Her two girlfriends weren't interested in either of us—they didn't ask us anything beyond what we did and what school we went to, and even that seemed forced.

The one from Switzerland thought American culture was sorely lacking, particularly in cocoa and computers. Her Swiss-made computer, she claimed, ran cooler and faster than all other known computers made in the world. She had a bourgeoisie quality about her that wasn't so different from the average Georgetown student, sent there in the first place to build connections for a successful high-profile career in law, finance, or politics. Her other friend was a cute Russian girl whose sweet and kind boyfriend stuck on her like an amoeba digesting a meal.

The night went on and it became clear what would happen with a quick look at the couch. Bobby and Claire's heads were just inches apart. I distracted the Swiss girl before she could intrude (or cockblock, as we learned to call it).

Dating is different in college. Things are more about hanging out around campus in large groups than scheduling a two hour block of deep conversation at a local bar or expensive restaurant. Bobby couldn't do it alone—he needed a wingman. For the next month I would go with him to Georgetown as he tried to get in Claire's pants, but after our fifth red cup college party featuring Milwaukee Best beer, I noticed the relationship between them barely progressed beyond light petting. Bobby had some doubts about her.

"I like her, but she's too much of a nice girl. I feel like she's the younger sister I never had," he said on a car ride home.

"Yeah, the younger sister you kiss and grope!" I said.

"Shutup. We haven't had sex. It won't happen. I need to let her down easy because I don't want to hurt her."

But how can you not hurt someone who is falling for you?

Claire knew something was wrong and asked me if Bobby said anything about her. I could only speak in vague generalities like a palm reader. As much as I sympathized with her, I did not want to betray a friend. I hinted that Bobby is a player and it'd be best if she forgot about him. In fact he already moved on, falling deeply in love with a girl he met at work. I rarely saw Bobby after that and it gave me a glimpse of how most of my adult friendships would come to an anticlimatic end.

No one was surprised when Claire and I became good friends. She invited me to parties and there I pursued her space cadet roommates, until a year later when she graduated and moved back home to New York. She was my Georgetown connection and the sole surviving link to a youthful scene that I didn't get to experience much of myself.

My college days, which I hope to soon forget just like my high school days, were mostly spent memorizing facts and playing video games and poker. I like to tell people that I didn't party much in college because I was too busy studying, but the truth is I was an introverted

WASHINGTON D.C.

mess with no self-esteem. I couldn't say hello to a cute girl to save my life and the few friends I had were either just like me or bringers of horrible dating advice.

"If you want to have sex with a girl, you have to be best friends with her first," my buddy Prad would say. I tried that with a girl I met in my organic chemistry class, but after several months of friendship all that happened was she let me give her shoulder rubs. She never returned the favor. Every month there was a new guy she was fucking and I got to hear all about it in painful detail.

My dad never taught me anything about girls so my mom stepped up to the plate, telling me to "Be a gentleman" and "Never let a woman pay." I tried that with an Albanian girl I met in genetics class. We'd hang out and whether for snacks, coffee breaks, or fast-food meals I would pay. She invited me back to her place once, but told me I couldn't stay long because her boyfriend was on the way.

There was Kate, a cute girl in my advanced Biology class. I combined techniques from Prad and my mom by being both a friend and a gentlemen, but in the end I was deemed so harmless by her boyfriend that he actually encouraged her to hang out with me more often. It seemed like everyone in college was getting laid except me, and I didn't know what to do about it.

After college I had had enough and began learning the art of seduction ("game") from an internet website that I discovered by chance. My sole goal was sexual thrills to make up for lost time.

All my newfound science knowledge would come in handy. I methodically broke down every reaction and every result. I tested dozens of opening lines to see which ones hooked a girl's attention the most, even getting into seemingly inconsequential details like if "Hey" or "Hi" is a better way to start an opening line (I can confidently say that "Hey" is better). To quickly show girls I was a cool guy, I practiced short anecdotes called routines, like an interesting opinion on nightlife culture or a funny story about when I attempted to sail on the Potomac River. Since girls didn't do much talking until they feel comfortable with a guy, I learned to ramble on and on in the early stages of a conversation to avoid awkward pauses that would surely kill the interaction. I developed physical moves for getting to intimacy much faster, such as walking arm-in-arm with a girl on the street or putting my hand on her waist while she spoke. If I tried something five or six times and it didn't appear to help me in the overall goal of getting her in bed, I tossed it out and tried something new.

My new strategy was the opposite of what I used to do, and after two years and a couple hundred approaches, I was getting laid. I no longer saw meeting a girl as this magical, chance-driven act. Instead it was a mechanical process that could be explained on the molecular level. I know I overcompensated, but I didn't mind because I was finally getting what I wanted.

II

I did not declare a major when I started college at the University of Maryland because I had no idea what I wanted to be, unlike everyone else I knew who seemed to have their minds made up.

"I want to be an electrical engineer."

"I want to be a journalist."

"I want to be an ear, nose, and throat surgeon."

I took a test to match my personality to a career. Because I liked working with my hands and things instead of people, I scored high in manual labor. The test destined me to a future in carpentry, but in high school woodshop class I was incompetent at the most basic tasks of measuring and cutting pieces of wood. For a year-end assignment the class had to mass produce a single high-quality item and I picked a stool—two pieces of wood as support and one piece on top. My teacher would shake his head in disgust every time I asked him to cut rectangles of wood on the table saw.

It took me a year to settle on a major. Art History interested me the most, but I didn't know how I could make money from that. I disliked reading, couldn't write or draw, and wasn't a fan of problem solving. But my memory was good and in the life sciences all you have to do is memorize. As a kid I bought a science kit from Sears and I remember it entertaining me until the chemicals corroded through the box and my mom threw it in the trash. I knew I would only eke out an unglamorous life doing generic lab work, but it was better than the prospect of being an incompetent carpenter.

After college my first job was at a company that helped sequence the human genome. For the first two years I was a mindless lab monkey pipetting DNA solutions for several hours a day into little test tubes and welled plates. But I was never embarrassed about my job. Whenever a girl asked me what I did I could state with confidence that I was a *microbiologist* at a biotech firm. That suggested I was an intelligent person.

I wound up in the Process Development department where I became a specialist in fermentation. I grew yeast and *E. coli* bacteria in huge tanks, causing the lab to either smell like bread or shit, respectively. When we "harvested" a tank we trashed the cells and kept the antibody they produced, one that we genetically engineered into them.

I had to do endless series of experiments to determine the optimal temperature, pH, mixing speed, feeding schedule, mineral content, and so on to get these cells to produce the highest concentration of antibody. The cells were fickle and experiments often failed, so it was common for me to repeat weeks of work. Even if they didn't fail, the new experiments were barely different from the ones that preceded it. I could imagine curing a major disease (technically I could say I was curing cancer and AIDS), but I was such a minor cog in the machine and so easily replaceable that I never saw my work as important. Another tank to clean, another spreadsheet to plug and chug numbers into, another meeting to present data to. The ideas came from above and I just followed orders. It wasn't much different than listening to my mom tell me to clean my room as a kid.

My social life was lively and fun while I was still in the middle of mastering my game. I was so distracted by the girls I was chasing that I never stopped to think that I was spending eight hours a day, a third of my waking life, in a job that I did not care about.

III

I received a mass email from Claire one year after she graduated from college. I was in my fourth year at work. She wrote it in the third person to be funny.

Subject: TOP SECRET MEMORANDUM

Claire began interning at the U.S. Embassy to the Holy See three weeks ago. She lives in an apartment by herself located in Trastevere. There are two beds; she welcomes visitors…

I jumped at the chance. The only time I had been out of the country was when I was eight years old and my mom took me to her childhood home in Turkey to spend a two month summer vacation with her family. All I remember from that trip is setting off all sorts of fireworks that were illegal back home and taking showers in bathrooms that had small drains on the floor instead of bathtubs. I was unable to communicate with anyone besides my mom because I didn't speak Turkish, but vaguely remember having a nice time nonetheless.

Another travel opportunity came up at about the same time. My college buddy Prad, who was now getting an Indian restaurant off the ground, tried to convince me to come with him to Venezuela for two weeks. I drank at his bar after closing one night as he sold me the idea.

"I know a girl there who always used to come into the restaurant," he said. "She told me about Venezuelan women and we just have to go. I'll be able to get off around Christmas so start researching ticket prices."

"What are we going to do there? Does she have friends?"

"Of course she has friends. We'll visit them in the city, party, smoke some ganja, and see some nature."

"Isn't South America dangerous?" I asked, concerned.

"No more dangerous than Baltimore or the shady parts of D.C. But yeah, Venezuela is not the safest country in the world."

Prad had changed over the years. He went from twice monthly visits to the barber for buzz cuts in Hugo Boss sweaters to becoming a long-haired, bearded businessman eager to talk about art and the absurdity of life. He no longer believed in the "friends first" strategy with girls and after a few drinks we'd laugh about how little we knew in college. If only we were sent back there with what we know now.

Two weeks later he continued his pitch, saying Venezuela is an exotic, semi-tropical land that was rarely visited by Americans because of political "instability." Their loud-mouthed leader Hugo Chavez gave a lot of travelers pause before stepping foot into the country.

"If we go we'll do what most others will never do," Prad said.

"We'll almost be like pioneers," I joked.

"And you know how beautiful the women are down there. Per capita they have the most beauty queens out of anywhere in the world."

He was telling the truth. I was easily sold on traveling with a best friend who shared the same carnal interests as I did, and besides, I had a large pile of money sitting around from not having taken a single serious vacation in my adult life. I told him I'd go. But soon he began to stall when it came time to setting the date. I had bought a ticket to see Claire in Italy for one week in November and was hoping a trip to Venezuela would end the year on a high note.

Eventually I confronted Prad about his stalling and he backed out completely, saying he couldn't get off work. He didn't trust any of his staff to run the restaurant while he was gone. I was disappointed. I debated going alone, without the benefit of knowing a Venezuelan woman who lived in the capital city. I still had to take off another week of vacation from work or I'd lose it, and I didn't want to do what I did the year before when I took off days just to stay at home and watch movies.

Except for the safety issue, I couldn't come up with a reason not to go to Venezuela. I booked the round-trip ticket to Caracas, departing only four weeks after I was to return from Rome. My international travel experience was lacking and I wanted to "catch up."

IV

I was 13 years old the last time I was on an airplane for longer than three hours. I've grown over a foot since then and my 6'2" frame complained during the overnight flight to Italy in steerage class. I took out all the magazines and safety cards in the front pocket and placed them on the floor for two heavenly extra inches of legroom.

I only stayed with Claire in Rome for two nights because each day was a race to see as many cities as possible. I quickly traveled through Rome, Venice, Sienna, Florence, Naples, and Bologna. I saw the best of what these cities had to offer, their most magnificent monuments and sights, taking hundreds of photos in the process. I completed a sort of short attention span travelling theater where each sight had to be high-impact and only briefly experienced. I treated each city like an amusement park and returned home with only basic observations about the culture and people: cafes everywhere sell smooth espresso; girls are beautiful but snobby; Italian history is very rich; cars are small and fuel-efficient; drivers are insane and will kill you if you don't pay attention, etc.

The American travel strategy must be flawed because it felt shallow to pack each day's schedule full of activities in an attempt to see everything important in the shortest amount of time. I focused too heavily on historical sites and museums and staying busy rather than on soaking up the day-to-day life of the people, the culture. Yet it wasn't all bad. I was fascinated how the simplest tasks back at home like catching a bus or ordering food was a full-on struggle when you don't speak the language. I was amused at feeling like an illiterate when I had to carefully look at the pictures on bathroom doors instead of the words. How long would it take living in Italy until I felt comfortable with the new language and culture? Many months, most likely years, but definitely not seven days.

If Rome is like adult Disneyland, Caracas is like an abandoned warehouse with busted windows. The first thing I saw when I left the airport terminal was a shanty town just a couple hundred meters away, composed of little shacks that were constructed of red-brown mud bricks and metal sheeting. Like all the other shanty towns in Caracas, I saw clothes hanging out to dry from the distance but never any real people. Only when it was night and the hills lit up like Christmas trees was I sure that human beings actually lived there. The shacks are packed in so tightly that there is no public space besides narrow dirt alleys wide enough only for motorcycles and small carts.

During the day most of the shantytown inhabitants came down from the hills to loiter or sell imported Chinese merchandise on makeshift stands at subway station exits. Where pools of fetid black water collected on the street there was the faint smell of raw sewage. Mountains flanking both sides of the city acted as river banks to trap in exhaust put out by vintage American automobiles kept on life support by necessity. It didn't help matters that rush hour lasted half the day thanks to 10-cents a gallon gas subsidized by the government. (The concept of fuel efficiency doesn't exist in Venezuela because of their abundant oil reserves.) Roads had craters the size of men and even sidewalks had their own holes large enough to swallow little kids.

The first time I took out my camera in the city center a handful of men in ragged clothing eyed me up and down, looking for an opportunity to relieve me of my property. I quickly learned that I was no longer in Rome taking pictures of the Pantheon. Caracas was a rough introduction to South America and I cursed Prad under my breath whenever I strayed from the beaten path and found myself being watched carefully by groups of idle young men sitting on milk crates. I thanked my Middle Eastern heritage for giving me a darker skin tone that fit in with the Venezuelan appearance. I don't think I was suspected as a gringo, but I still did my best to put on a confident walk, a don't-fuck-with-me swagger that would make anyone else but me a more appealing target.

Most taxis were unmarked and unlicensed. They looked like any other car except they had a tiny eight-inch long plastic sign with neon TAXI lettering taped on the front windshield. I saw these exact same signs on sale at a handful of street markets. You could wait at an intersection all day and night before an official cab came by. I calculated that my odds of survival were higher taking a chance with the fake cabs than walking, even though I knew the driver could take me wherever he wanted and do as he pleased, alone or with his waiting gang. And I know what they think when they rob or steal: "You're a rich tourist, you can afford to lose a couple hundred dollars." Though it doesn't make theft right, it's true for the most part. All I could do to stop it was hold my head high, speak like I was sure, and pretend I wasn't afraid. You can't get by in a foreign country without trusting some people some of the time.

I compared the amount of mental energy I was putting in Caracas trying to stay safe to sitting in my office cubicle reading emails and making line graphs. I was not used to planning secure routes and exit strategies, observing crowds, watching my back, and protecting my pockets. Never before did I wonder why a particular car made a U-turn or how much blood I would lose if stabbed in an extremity after fighting off an armed attacker. It was nerve-racking and stimulating at the same time, and I was working my brain in ways it wasn't used to. I was being challenged. Being reminded of my survival told me things could be much different than what I'm used to. They didn't have to be so comfortable and seemingly pre-programmed.

I had a feeling of withdrawal after coming home from Italy. I missed their espresso and nightlife and wished I had more time to be able to bang my first Italian girl. They were tough, those girls. But I didn't miss Venezuela. There were plenty of good moments, like making new friends in my Caracas hotel and lounging on a small white beach in Margarita Island, but the shock to my system was too strong. There was no urge to return anytime soon.

V

I started developing doubts about my specialty in fermentation. My job was only being done within a few areas of the United States: Raleigh, San Francisco, San Diego, Newark, Boston, and Montgomery County, Maryland. If I wanted to move to a place like Miami or New York, I would have to get used to pipetting again for basic lab jobs that could be found anywhere. I thought things should be the other way around, that developing a valuable skill should give me more options to live the life I wanted instead of less. Maybe I should have gone into business or marketing instead. Even carpentry could be practiced anywhere.

At the same time I became increasingly annoyed at the petty politics that were married to large corporations. In the lunch room there were posted signs ordering me to clean up after myself and not to eat someone's apple. There were more signs in the lab ordering me to wash my hands and wipe my feet. It reminded me of my passive aggressive former roommate who would leave Post It notes everywhere ("Please don't leave the cabinets open!! Thanks!!!").

Human resources would nag me in weekly emails about new regulations that must be followed: no short shorts, halter tops, unnecessary color photocopying, or sexual harassment. There were the mandatory one hour seminars that taught us to say "red light" if someone was inappropriately flirting with us. There was the eight hour safety course on radiation even though I didn't work with radiation. There was the series of "training modules" with Standard Operating Protocols that read like manuals for television sets. And of course there were the irritating phrases that everyone copied from management, like "going forward" and "due diligence."

Last minute decisions frequently meant my dough-faced colleagues and I would end up staying late or coming in on weekends. Management could stay home. (Having a family and children was a more worthy excuse than having a happy hour to go to.) I had the privilege of training new employees with fancy degrees who earned much more than I did. I was nominated for a working group on how to fix the company's cafeteria lunch program. We met every week in catered two-hour meetings for two months. By the end, none of our suggestions were implemented.

Every month management held a huge cheerleader meeting with Krispy Kreme donuts. They told us that the company was about to turn the corner any month now and pull in massive profits, but failed to include useful information about how the company was actually performing. I stayed away from the employee stock purchase plan because I had less information about my own company than day traders who gathered on internet message boards.

Management required all peons to itemize the monthly work they did. After submitting my four or five sentence summaries, I spied on coworker reports averaging 2,000 words and chock full of colorful graphs, tables and fonts, with consistent abuse of bold typeface. The reports took them a full day to create while mine took ten minutes. I figured I was doing the company a favor for not wasting so much time on something so meaningless, but eventually I was pulled aside and told to put more work into them because it looked "kind of bad."

My coworkers competed with each other by announcing every little trivial task they did in meetings or emails that were carbon copied to everyone. They would perk up whenever management was around and follow them to lunch, including to restaurants they told me they hated. I remember the brown-noser who organized the lab supply stockroom in alphabetical order and then was praised by the big boss for her "initiative." She set a "good example for others to follow," though her example wasn't making the company money. I refused to play that game because I believed that my work in the lab should speak for itself, but even then it barely mattered. Every year like clockwork Human Resources would say times were tough and raises would be lower than usual, though still "above the national average," whatever that was. I calculated that doing only what was assigned and not organizing stockrooms or posting signs in the lab was costing me at most $60 a month. I believed I was a competent worker, but eventually my motivation and drive was being discussed behind management doors.

The way I was rated was through a bell curve. Management would always drive home that we were all working for the greater goal in making money for the company, but once a year I was ranked against my co-workers, including those on my team, to determine who received the highest raise and bonus. My boss was pleased with my work but his boss perceived me as an underachiever who needed a fire lit under his ass. I was put on the bottom of the curve and didn't get a raise for the first time in my five years at the company. My boss implied that if there was another round of layoffs, a very real possibility with the company hemorrhaging hundreds of millions of dollars a year, I would be one of the first to go. By then I was coming to work in my favorite pair of jeans that had holes in the knees.

WASHINGTON D.C.

Secretly I hoped to be fired. I wanted to be put into such a tough situation that I would be forced to use everything I had to work my way out. I wanted to see what I was made of. But when I finally received the company letterhead that had the big fat zero where my raise was supposed to be, I panicked. If I was fired then I would have to dip into my savings to pay rent. A smaller savings meant smaller vacations. I couldn't let that money stop coming in.

Living in a capitalist country taught me to have the mindset of a free agent. I'm only as loyal as my options. I fixed up my resume and sent it to a recruiter who was extra motivated to help because she'd get a large percentage of my first year's salary. Within only a month she landed me an interview at the only company in the United States licensed to make the anthrax vaccine for the military. One week after the interview, they offered me $10,000 a year more than what I was already making. The company was smaller, older and more conservative, but I immediately took the offer.

I couldn't hide the smirk on my face when I quit. They thought they could change or mold me? Fuck them! I'll go work somewhere else! My company was like a girlfriend setting the stage to dump me but I beat her to the punch by finding a hotter girl at the club. Unfortunately I didn't bother to notice how low the lights were. When I got her out during the day I noticed she was far uglier.

VI

Job interviews are bizarre. It's impossible for a company to find out if you're fit and qualified for a position based on 30-minute blocks of structured chat that always includes the question of where you see yourself in five years. It's even harder for an applicant to see if they'd get along with their future company and boss. I mean it's not like I could ask my future boss if he's an asshole or sadist, if his jokes are lame but he expects me to laugh anyway, if he's a micromanager whose forearm will be halfway up my ass during work hours, or if his English is so poor that I won't be able to understand his reports. Because if I could I would, but that's not how job interviews work.

I didn't get along with Dr. Wang, a 66 year old scientist from Taiwan whose dark hair was so thick I convinced myself it was a wig. The problem was that he passed by my cubicle at least ten times a day to give me comments and assignments in drip-drop fashion. Instead of one daily meeting like I was used to, it was several small meetings in the lab, in his office, in my office, in the lunch room, during lunch, during breaks, and after regular meetings with his boss. Sometimes he came by to inform me he just sent me an email and would like a reply soon. My title was Associate Scientist but I felt like Associate Child.

The sourness from my first job only got worse. Dr. Wang wasn't going to turn anything around. It bothered me that a large part of getting a good boss is based on luck of the draw. With bad luck you are stuck eight hours a day in a place that makes you unhappy, forcing you to search again for another job, but not too soon or else jumping around quickly would look bad on your resume. And what a shame it would be if you threw away a good job to go somewhere else that was much worse! Too late to change your mind now.

I didn't like the idea that I could do everything right, researching companies and asking respectful questions, but still end up unhappy through no obvious fault of my own. The problem must be with the system. The problem is having to depend on someone else for a paycheck. The problem is spending a third of my waking life in the company of a man like Dr. Wang. I purchased a book about taking a gap year, but before I could open it I was in Spain for a two week vacation

In Spain I got sucked into the nonstop drinking party with a constantly rotating cast of international travelers. I forgot about getting to know the locals or experiencing the culture like I had planned. Drinking espresso in cafes or visiting museums couldn't compare with chasing girls with sexy accents while under the influence of sangria or overpriced cocktails. The hacking cough I developed halfway through the trip barely slowed me down. Even the messy *La Tomatina* tomato festival, attended by more Australians than Spaniards, was just filler before the night's partying. There were no long, deep conversations in Spanish with a local who told me his concerns of the world. There was

WASHINGTON D.C.

no love affair with a beautiful Spanish girl who took me to her family's house and fed me seafood paella. I learned less about Spain than Italy or Venezuela even though I stayed there longest, but I didn't care because I was having the time of my life. I could hop on a bus or train to any city and spend time with beautiful girls from countries I may never see before I die. I was completely free from responsibility and being tied to the same place. The only decisions that affected me were my own, not someone else sitting in an office one floor above me. This was how I'd rather live my life.

I couldn't focus on work when I got back. Dr. Wang's requests went in one ear and out the other until the matter became urgent. I did the bare minimum of work like at my previous job, but I played along and made it seem like I wanted to stay with the company until I turned gray. Dr. Wang, surprisingly pleased with the work I did do, was looking for me to step up.

"Have you considered going to graduate school," he asked me one day. "Johns Hopkins has a master's program in biotechnology with night classes." I never got used to his thick accent and had to pay extra attention to understand what he was saying because when he talked it sounded like he had marbles in his mouth.

"I know several coworkers at my old company that completed the program. They had very good things to say about it," I replied.

"You need to start thinking long-term with the company. You're doing a decent job but to advance they would like to see more education."

The all-knowing, all-seeing *they*, pushing and controlling me through a proxy in the form of a Taiwanese scientist with a thick accent and lush black hair. The only way the tone would be more ominous is if he substituted "He" instead of "they."

"No, I understand. I'm not sure why I've hesitated so far, but this fall I'm going to register."

I lied through my teeth. I told Dr. Wang whatever he wanted to hear so the paychecks could keep coming and my upcoming bonus was at fat as it could be. I was already calculating how much more money I needed to take at least a year off. I wanted to travel for a long time, abuse my liver, and meet exotic women. Then after I tire of boozing I wanted to find some answers to what I should do for the rest of my life. Time off would help put me on a fulfilling path, because the answer obviously wasn't working as a microbiologist. Only a long trip could lead to my eventual happiness.

While Dr. Wang was urging me to attend graduate school, I went into poverty mode and put myself on a tight budget. I was six years into my professional career, a scientist with his own extra glossy business cards, but I was ready to put it on hold.

On hold. Like pausing a movie. You grab a soda and continue right where you left off without missing anything. If only that's how life worked. Too many things change, and by the time you come back you'll wonder why you picked this sorry movie in the first place.

I'd be lying if I said that it wasn't hard to quit my job, to "throw it all away" like my mom put it, but it was just one step out of many. It got lost in everything else like selling my car, buying travel gear, straightening out paperwork, getting vaccination shots, researching travel sites, purchasing travel insurance, setting up credit card PIN numbers, moving into my dad's house, buying the airline ticket, deciding on a route, and so on. Each step insulated me from what I was really doing, which, definitely, was throwing it all away. That way of life, anyway.

Once the unlikely choice to leave is made, the only thing more unlikely is returning to the same thing. Otherwise it would mean everything I felt before the moment I quit was a fraud, that the unhappiness and the misery were make-believe, just a brief glitch in the concentrations of neurotransmitters in my brain. Or maybe a boredom spell from not having enough hobbies to take my mind off work. I refused to accept those possibilities. The third of my waking life was real. And it was suffering. The job was destroying my mind and soul. It was suffocating me and if I didn't get out I'd be permanently damaged.

VII

I had trouble deciding when to quit because each month I stayed would add at least an extra thousand dollars to my savings account. I kept thinking of how much more I would have if I could hang in just a bit longer, but rolling out of bed was becoming impossible and I loathed Dr. Wang and his shit-smelling bacterial cells with a passion. Plus the lab was much less enjoyable to work in than the one at my old company. It had ancient equipment that was like a museum for fermentation. I imagined doing a tour of my lab for young scientists: "In the 1970's, before fermentation's golden age and the introduction of automation, you had to adjust everything manually, like the old car radios that had jumpy dials instead of digital read-outs. Imagine that!"

The best thing I have done in life is save money. While my peers were buying new clothes, bottle service at the club, and luxury automobiles, I was frugal and kept a monthly budget to watch every single dollar that left my pocket. If they spent $100 at a bar, I spent $30. If their rent was $800 a month, mine was $500. I owned my Honda Civic and had no intention of ever upgrading unless the wheels fell off. I left my first company with $15,000 earning 3.5% interest and saved $13,000 more after only nine months working for Dr. Wang. A pile of cash is a pile of freedom. If I moved into my dad's basement it would last me half a decade, and if I traveled to somewhere inexpensive maybe two or three. I decided to only work long enough to achieve a randomly selected goal of $35,000 that would be crossed when I sold my car.

The closer I got to giving Dr. Wang my two weeks notice, the more insolent I became. I started coming in extra late to minimize the time I would see him. I went home for lunches so he couldn't find me. I took walks to the convenience store nearby instead of hanging out in the break room. Just a bit longer, my wall calendar told me, and I could go, until finally the day arrived.

I asked Dr. Wang if he could talk for a minute. He knew something was wrong because I never asked him for a private conversation.

I just came out with it.

"Dr. Wang I'd like to put in my two weeks notice."

"Whaaaaaaaat?"

"Yeah, umm, it's just time for me to move on. I want to take some time off."

"But I thought you were so happy here. You were going to start working on getting your masters degree. Why would you want to leave?"

"I just want to take a long vacation I guess. I'm not sure, but I want to take a break."

"If there is a problem, we can fix it. Is it your pay? Tell me."

I wanted to tell him all the reasons I hated him and the work. I wanted to tell him why working for a corporation is a one way path to a stale, monotonous life where the only thing to look forward to are increasingly dull weekends. But what would be the point? I would just waste my energy on a man who believed in the system. There was nothing he could do to change my mind. I already told my roommate I'd be moving out. I believed in this decision too much to be convinced otherwise, and if my mom couldn't talk me out of it then definitely not him.

Now Dr. Wang had to do all the lab work himself because I was the only person on his team who was trained on the equipment. A part of me felt bad for the old man. I should thank him, really, for putting me on this path. Without him who knows how many more years I would have waited. I would have hesitated to leave the comfortable middle-class lifestyle. The Taiwanese scientist with a thick accent and lush black hair gave me unhappiness. He gave me the motivation to make a big change.

VIII

I moved into my dad's basement. I played with my little brothers during the day and ate my stepmother's delicious Persian food every night—her *kookoo* potato patties, her *abgoosht* lamb stews, and my favorite, her *ghormeh sabzi* meat dish full of fresh garden herbs. In between I'd have deep conversations with my dad about life, business, and politics. Later in the evening I'd go out, either on dates or to prospect for future dates.

At first I was worried that moving in with my dad would cut off the

WASHINGTON D.C.

flow of girls, that they wouldn't respect a 28-year-old man who lived in his father's basement, but I got more dates than I ever had before, all because I now had unlimited time to get them. I was enjoying my life, working on pet projects here and there at my leisure, waking up at noon every day with no pressure to do anything. I was living the dream and having such a good time that after three months I had to remind myself why I moved in with my dad in the first place: to prepare for travel to faraway lands and have my doubts and concerns about my place in the world answered, all while having sex with women who had accents. I had almost forgotten.

But where would I travel to? Since I was on a budget there were three regions on the table: Eastern Europe, Southeast Asia, and South America. Eastern Europe was a little expensive considering the strengthening Euro, and for some reason I had no interest in traveling to Asia. That left South America, a place I was already familiar with. It's cheap, the girls are pretty, and only two languages are needed to get around. Plus I had heard amazing things about the sensual girls of Brazil, the nightlife of Argentina, and the rich archeological sites of Peru. It was an easy decision.

I looked over South American travel guides in the bookstore to construct a list of countries I should visit. They were of little help, offering only names of lodging and eating establishments instead of pointed descriptions of what a man at my stage of life would like. It'd be quite the adventure if I visited all the countries and found out for myself. It's not like I didn't have the time, and judging by maps the continent was not much bigger than the United States. I looked at Chile, a tiny sliver of a country, and Paraguay and Uruguay, each the size of small U.S. states. It was decided then. I'd visit every country in South America, partying and chasing the local girls along the way just like I did in Spain, but also absorbing the culture, making deep observations, and learning Spanish. I couldn't stop thinking about how I'd visit thirteen new countries, bringing my total up from four to seventeen. What a cultured and experienced man of the world I'd become! Maybe I could even write a guidebook after the trip is done: *Roosh's South America Travel Guides For Men*. I could share advice on where to find the prettiest and nicest girls (without having to pay).

Not only did I conveniently forget about my rough experience in Venezuela, but I developed the expectation that traveling through South America would be like Spain and my dad's basement rolled up into one exotic party train. I ignored people who questioned my decision by mentioning how dangerous and poor South America was. I figured they have just been overly influenced by the news.

I decided to start the trip in Ecuador. I knew little about it besides the fact that there was a group of islands off the coast that helped Darwin construct his theory of evolution. I figured that as the trip went on and I made my way down south and east towards Argentina and Brazil, the dial would turn from possibly dull and sketchy to spicy and hedonistic. After Brazil I would travel back up north through the three small countries that no one visits, then Venezuela, then finally end it all in Colombia. It should be safe from tourist kidnappings by then. I estimated it would take 6-12 months.

I patted myself on the back for developing a great plan, one that could only be hatched by someone who thought things through carefully and deliberately. But no matter how careful and deliberate I was, I could not make up for the fact that I had only a tiny amount of international travel experience under my belt. I vastly underestimated the amount of energy and health it would take to get through third world countries.

Two weeks before my plane left for Ecuador, my friends threw me a nice little goodbye party at a bar. They must have seen how excited and eager I was, but on the inside I was nervous. I think my brain was trying to tell me both my expectations and plan were no good.

IX

My sister was born seven years after me and one year before my parents split up. By the time I was in the eighth grade I had to pick her up every day from the bus stop and watch her for three hours until my mom came home from her seamstress job. There was no way she could afford a babysitter. I resented my sister because my friends could go out and play whenever they wanted while I had to either stay in or, when she got a little older, check on her every thirty minutes. Eventually we worked out a system where every so often she would come out on the balcony and yell to show me she was still alive, but I still hated the responsibility and would rip the heads off her Barbie dolls anyway. (Putting the heads back on gave them an unnatural fat-face appearance.) I'd make her give me weeks of "beverage service" at a time, treating her like my own personal servant. There was also the night that I gave her a piggyback ride from hell and smashed her completely through the hallway drywall. I covered it with a red plaid blanket, thinking my mom would appreciate my creativity and never notice the two by three foot hole left by my sister's torso, but she eventually found out and beat me with a broom.

In spite of the beverage service and doll mutilation, we were very close. We developed identical senses of humor, insulting but self-deprecating, in a format we mimicked from watching *The Simpsons* and *Seinfeld*. We'd often think of the same joke at the same time and get mad that we couldn't say ours fast enough. We farted on each other's faces. We put dirty socks in each other's mouths. When she wasn't paying attention I rubbed her face in the "pizza," a small circular rug that our cat Furball loved to throw up on. Months or even years after a joke was said we'd remix it into new forms to keep the laughs going. Our whole relationship is based upon layers of recalled humor that means nothing to the average person.

To this day if you put us in the same room the back-and-forth is relentless. Anyone else in our company fades into the background as we regress back to our childhood, on our own in that apartment when our mother did her best to keep a roof over our heads. Like most people I like to think that I grew up fast because of a tough childhood, but I think in the end my sister grew up faster than I did.

I said goodbye to my mom first. My flight was leaving in only a few hours but she still tried to talk me out of the trip. "Are you sure you want to do this? You can always cancel it," she said.

"Mom I'm not going to cancel it."

"I just don't agree with what you're doing. I don't believe you quit your job. I didn't come to this country and work so hard raising you so you could do something like this. Where's your brain?"

"Mom, please," I pleaded. "I'll only be gone for a couple months and then I'll come back and get another car and go back to work. Just think of it as a long vacation. I need to see what else is out there." I hated lying to my mom about how long I'd be gone but she'd just feel worse if I told her the truth.

"I want you to call me every week and don't get with any bad people." I assumed that by bad people she meant drug users.

Back at my dad's I gave a hug to my little brothers before they went to bed, the smallest one at only four years old not understanding that I'd be away for a while. My dad put his arm on my shoulder and said to be careful. My stepmom lit a special candle and recited a Muslim prayer in Farsi under her breathe. They slept while I finished packing.

My sister drove me to the airport at four in the morning. Up to then she kept everything breezy, telling me to "wrap it up" and not bring back any diseases. When she pulled into the arrival gate I gave her $20 for gas and she reluctantly accepted. I got out of the car and struggled to pull my 50-pound backpack out of the trunk. I set it on the ground and looked at her. She was already crying.

It's always been that if one of us cries the other will cry too. This is true even if we're on the phone. I fought back tears while giving her a big hug goodbye. She told me to be careful and watch my back. I promised her I'd be safe and send her a postcard from every country I visited. She got in her car and drove off.

ECUADOR

I

Quito's international airport was modern. A carpeted skywalk led to immigration where a dour woman fed my passport through a printer. Excited people beyond the gate craned their necks searching for loved ones. I made my way through the crowd and stepped outside to look for a taxi. The air smelled like an old car repair shop. I looked around at the dilapidated buildings plastered with huge advertisements and old 80s era cars and for a second I thought I was in Caracas again.

I slipped into an official-looking taxi. At the first red light a young woman approached my window hawking packets of gum and newspapers. I shook my head sideways and she turned around to reveal an expressionless little girl strapped tightly to her back with cloth. (Later I was lucky to catch the sight of an indigenous woman methodically wrapping her child into a blanket for backpacking. It was like watching a department store clerk expertly wrap a holiday gift.) The cab made its way to Old Town, passing avenues named after important dates in Ecuadorian history. My mind filled with morbid thoughts. I figured my chance of dying for the next several months would go up at least a hundred times. Lounging in my dad's basement the chance was almost zero, even accounting for the possibility of death by bathtub. If I didn't get done in by disease or bus accident it would be through random violent crime. Nothing on the drive to my hostel screamed danger, but the "Danger & Annoyances" section of my Lonely Planet guidebook made it seem like it was a guarantee I'd get robbed.

Already I had doubts. Why did the Euro have to be so strong? For a second I wished I put up with Dr. Wang a couple more months so I could've gone somewhere a little more pleasant. I tried to focus on the scenery of gridlocked traffic and mom and pop shops lining the street, where every other store advertised *jugo* with colorful pictures of fruits. America has coffee shops, Ecuador has juice bars.

I checked into my hostel and went for a walk around Old Town, a mash-up of old concrete structures plopped down on hilly terrain. There were dozens of soccer jersey shops. I wanted to assume that every large South American city was a bazaar for jerseys, but it would only be Quito that I could grab any team's uniform that my heart desired for only $6. The material is thin spongy foam instead of cloth.

Locals sat and people watched alongside the occasional white-skinned gringo in the main square, Plaza Grande. The first thing I noticed were the shoeshine boys—little boys as young as six years old wearing tattered clothing coated with layers of brown, black, and red shoe polish. Their stained and leathery hands made it seem like they'd been working in a factory all their life. They carried their tools, chemicals, and rags in a wooden carrying case and kept their eye on the ground for potential customers—men and women walking in leather shoes. They didn't hesitate for a second to solicit business. With so many of them and so few pairs of shoes that needed cleaning I was surprised to see that they worked together and respected each other's territory with nods of recognition. When there was no business they played ball and jack games. They were children, after all.

The shoeshine boys shined shoes while women sold lottery tickets, gum, and cigarettes with the little ones strapped on their backs. Older, less mobile women sold strawberries, raspberries and other fruit, their bare hands colored from what they were offering. A boy not older than three years old approached me while I sat on a concrete ledge, one hand filled with packets of gum, the other empty and outstretched waiting for money. I looked around for a parent that was keeping an eye out for him but didn't see one, and he disappeared in the crowd, into Quito's foggy, Spring air. My four-year-old brother was at home at that moment, probably watching *Thomas The Train Engine* DVDs or playing PBS Kids games on the family computer. My instinct was to get mad at the parents for sending such young children out on the street, but for them every dollar matters. When the occasional sympathetic gringo gives a five dollar bill the whole family eats for a day.

The average high temperature is constant year-round in the low 70s because of the city's proximity to the equator, but the indigenous women—whose prominent mouths, noses and jet black hair reminded me of pictures of Native Americans I'd seen in history books—wore multiple layers of handmade clothing as if preparing for an upcoming frost. My teeth chattered when I learned what Quito's 9,350 foot altitude does to nighttime temperatures.

I settled into my private room for the first night after sitting alone in the common area watching *The Simpsons* in Spanish. My chest ached in different spots and I was nauseous with a pounding headache. With the short stair climb up to my room I could feel each heart beat shake my body. I figured it was the stress of starting the trip, but most likely it was altitude sickness since similar symptoms would reappear in other Andean towns. I sat on my bed going through my pack for whatever I'd need the next day when I noticed something gooey all over my clothes.

I thought it'd be a good idea to pack some protection for what I assumed to be numerous sexual adventures with the locals. I ordered one hundred of my favorite condoms from the internet to take with me, but due to space limitations I was only able to pack about sixty. I also packed a small bottle of Astroglide for both sexual and personal use. Unfortunately altitude changes caused the lubricant to explode in my Ziploc freezer bag of condoms and leak out onto my clothes. My first night in South America was spent washing and hanging dozens of condoms in the bathroom and blotting out goo from my t-shirts.

I laid in bed that first night unable to sleep. The excitement of leaving popped like a balloon. I enjoyed the journey it took to start the journey because it made me feel like a radical. It made me feel like a risk-taker who had the guts to make a move. But there was no one around to pat me on the back or encourage me. There was no friend to tell me he wishes he was me. There was no first night thrill with an 18-year-old Belgian girl to ease my doubts like in Spain. The reality of travel and not just vacationing hit me. I have never separated from my family before and I wondered if by taking this long trip I somehow damaged our closeness. They'd get used to not seeing me. It'd be even worse with my friends. If I stay away for too long would everyone simply move on? What would I come back to?

The condoms, puffed up from the altitude but still sealed in their wrappers, were dry by the time I woke up. I trashed what was left of the Astroglide.

II

For as impoverished as Quito is, it sure kept me busy with interesting sights. There was the cable car ride up to the top of Cruz Loma mountain at 13,500 feet, where I was greeted by freezing air, patches of slushy snow, and groups of plucky hikers well-prepared with heavy jackets, bottles of water, and high carb snacks. Then there was the Basilica del Voto Nacional, a European-style gothic cathedral with twin towers and turtle gargoyles poking out of the facade. Except for a small school group, I was the only gringo climbing to the top. The graffiti led the way until I reached a metal ladder for the final twenty foot climb to a flimsy wire mesh platform. The South American environment encourages development of common sense and street smarts starting at a young age. There would be no one to blame and no lawyer lining up to take my case if I hurt myself. With the large sinkholes, cracks, and random piles of dog shit outside on public sidewalks, short strolls were gladiator challenges.

The most popular sight was Mitad Del Mundo, the "middle of the world." It's located over a point where the equator passes through Ecuador (the country's name literally translates to "equator"). The admission fee was two American dollars. Ecuador's official currency is the U.S. dollar but since they don't have a printing press the decades-old dollars are soggy little rags that feel like used toilet paper.

Inside the complex I browsed through a few geographical exhibits, ate overpriced *empanadas*, and took my picture at the official sign that would announce to all that I stood at Earth's widest point. I didn't meet a gringo who passed through here without getting the equator picture taken with one foot on the north side and one on the south.

The nearby Museo Solar claimed to be over the "real" equator as determined by GPS positioning. English-speaking guides walked me through semi-bullshit tales about eggs balancing on their ends only over the equator (not true), guinea pig meat being savored by locals (true), the ancient practice of shrinking real human heads into smaller heads (true), and Incans stuffed into gigantic clay pot coffins upon death (undetermined).

I eventually returned back to Old Town and sat down in Plaza del Teatro with an afternoon snack from KFC. The sky was cloudy, like usual, and the gray of the concrete buildings and ground was broken only by the colorful hats and clothing of the indigenous locals. A magician with a small cart and karaoke microphone machine performed basic magic tricks for voluntary donations below the steps in front of me. I heard a whistle come from the right. A man my age with a shoe shine box got the attention of a younger man with brown leather shoes. A price was settled and the young man sat next to me. The shoe shine man got to work, sprinkling different brown powders on a clean palette in his toolbox to match the brown he was about to clean. It turned into a wax that he buffed into the shoe for several minutes, giving the shoe such a shine that I could see a faint hint of my reflection. After the customer left the shoe shine man continued whistling and making eye contact with the bodies of people attached to leather shoes.

His pants and hands were coated in dark shoe polish, just like the shoe shine boys I saw a couple days back. He approached a dozen more people but no one bit. He sat next to me to take a break and in his face there was no joy but no pain either, just a deep stare in the direction of the magician. I thought of how when I was a productive member of society I made more in one day than what he pulls in a month, to no obvious fault of his own. It was his luck that he happened to be born in Ecuador, and mine that I was born in a middle-class family near one of the richest cities in the world. I pitied him. It was unfair that he had to shine shoes while I could take months off work to travel for pleasure, but then I got up and walked off the square, eager for the next experience.

That night I returned to Plaza Grande to celebrate Quito's independence day. Hundreds of plastic lawn chairs were set in front of a small stage illuminated by mobile spotlights, roped off for VIPs. Standing in front of the stage were thousands of people waiting for what would turn out to be a series of patriotic speeches. Vendors were out in full force selling beverages and snacks to the crowd, and I noticed how much taller I was compared to the average Ecuadorian. With the typical male height barely five-and-a-half feet, I was taller than all of them, past, present, and probably future as well.

I set my up camera and mini-tripod on a building ledge to take pictures of the event. Being only my third day in South America I was in the stage where I wanted to capture every small moment to email friends and family back home.

After an hour of speeches, I decided to head back to the hostel. The crowds were thick and unruly where the sidewalks and roads intersected, like a slow-moving herd of cattle getting choked off on their way back into the pen. I tried to cross the main street but was immediately jammed up against other bodies because of young teenagers to my left laughing, pushing and shoving for no reason. I thought of how this pit would be a perfect environment for a pick pocket, and how smart I was to put my wallet in my front right jean pocket.

I couldn't find my wallet when I got back to the hostel. I frantically searched everywhere: my backpack, on the bed, under the bed, behind the small nightstand, the old file cabinet in the corner of the room, my jean pockets for the fifth time, and even the communal bathroom, a place it couldn't have possibly been. It was gone. The damage was $80. And a bruised ego. The teenagers set up a giggly distraction on one side and went in for the kill on the other. It didn't matter that I was mindful about the possibility of a pick pocket at the time. They're like mosquitoes, and it's their business for you not to feel them.

III

The only other person at the table for breakfast the next morning was a Belgian man with frizzy hair and a patchy beard. I asked him how long he'd been traveling and he told me a year, on an around-the-world ticket that was very common with other travelers. These tickets are package deals for several one-way flights that allow you to see many continents on one trip, but time is often short since you're always on a deadline for the next departing flight. I told him my pickpocket story.

"That stinks," he said. "On a bus in Bolivia I put my day bag in between my legs. I was asleep for no more than thirty minutes but when I got up it was gone. I didn't think we stopped so the bag still had to be on the bus. I got up and walked around and saw it on the top rack all the way in back."

"Do you know who took it?"

"There was a guy there who wore his hat low, like he wanted to cover his face. It was probably him but I couldn't just go accusing him. I took my bag and from then on left it on my lap with my hands over it. But even that isn't safe."

"Wouldn't I feel it if someone tried to snatch my bag from my lap?" These words came from someone who just got pick pocketed.

"Even if you're in a deep sleep? Some of these bus rides are long—twelve hours or more. I heard a story about a guy who strapped his bag to himself and kept it on his lap, but someone with a knife cut the straps and slipped it off him."

"Jesus."

"That's rare though," he assured me. "If you keep it on your lap and fold your arms on top you should be okay."

"Is my bag safe in the luggage hold?"

"Yeah, much safer than in the cabin."

With so many traveler stories told secondhand it was hard to tell between truth and urban myth, like the story I heard about a Lonely Planet travel writer who wrote the Colombia guide without actually going there. "He just called a bunch of places up," someone told me.

"How do you know?"

"Everyone who's been to Colombia knows about it." Apparently it was common knowledge.

Six months later, it was on CNN that a Lonely Planet writer plagiarized parts of the guide. Sure enough it was the Colombia author. He used the internet and his Colombian girlfriend to write it. He was also listed as an author of my Lonely Planet guidebook which was a three pound behemoth for the entire continent. In the end he was rewarded with a book deal.

The Belgian knew I was green and noticed how closely I was paying attention to him.

"Look, just never put your bag on the carry-on rack. It's the number one way travelers get robbed. You fall asleep and they put their hands in the bag and grab what they can, or just grab the bag outright and get off at the next stop." He looked at the hostel cook. "*¿Hay más mantequilla?*"

"Where are you going next?" he asked.

"Peru. I'm traveling south."

"Okay there's three border crossings in Ecuador. One is extremely dangerous, one is sort of dangerous, and one is safe. The safe one is through Loja. Whatever you do, don't go through Huaquillas. It's almost a guarantee you'll get robbed."

The cook brought out a small plate of butter.

"In Huaquillas, there are a couple miles of no man's land that is too long to walk. So you have to grab a taxi at the border, but the taxis are in with the thieves and so are the police, who look the other way to get a cut. The taxi gets stopped along the way to immigrations and then large men ask you to come out of the taxi. A guy I know was forced to the ATM and they made him take out the maximum withdrawal limit. But they let him keep his bag. He was lucky because that was during the day. At night it's worse. They take everything."

I'm definitely getting robbed again.

I got out a pen and wrote down the name of the border crossing I was supposed to use. I haven't even been in South America for a week and I was already scared for my life. If I hadn't talked to the Belgian I would have taken the bad border crossing since the guidebook didn't say it was especially dangerous.

At home I take for granted that I can go out with a wallet full of money and credit cards and an expensive digital camera and not get robbed. In most of South America you have to devote a good amount of mental energy to protecting your belongings, not only from the locals but your fellow traveler as well. Now I had all these new rules to follow. Always take a taxi at night, but never share one. Never display valuables. On the bus keep your bag on your lap. Only walk around with a small amount of cash. Don't carry an ATM card unless you're going directly to the machine. Act confident even if you're lost. Beware of fake cops. Don't walk into large crowds. The balance between common sense and paranoia is achieved only by those long-term travelers carrying few possessions, not the inexperienced vacationer with booze and sex on his mind. I remember the forehead-slapping story of an American gringo who put hundreds of dollars in his jacket pocket along with his passport and every single one of his credit cards. He took off the jacket during a soccer game and never saw it again. It was common to hear stories that make you wonder how some travelers survive in their home countries. I didn't want to be in that category.

The cook took away our dirty plates and refilled our teas. The conversation lightened and he gave me some recommendations in Peru. "Try the alpaca meat. I'm not sure what it is but it's very good."

A few days later I moved out of my hostel in Old Town for one in New Town, where there are bars and nightclubs that stay open past ten at night. I also found hundreds of gringos in a repeating backdrop of cheap internet cafes, laundromats, and restaurants with names like Red Hot Chili Peppers and Adam's Rib. In a city of one and a half million people we packed ourselves into a six square block area to have immediate access to mango smoothies and chocolate chip pancakes.

The sight of all these gringos bothered me. It took me years to get to the point where I could break the mold and go on a unique adventure, yet everyone else was doing the exact same thing I was. And by the looks of it most of them were barely in their twenties, either recent college graduates or still in college, traveling just to kill time. Their presence trivialized the amount of work I took to get here. They didn't have to sell most of their material possessions, quit their career, and take hours of grief from their mothers. My castle in the sky was their afterthought.

After a week in Quito I developed a routine. I'd wake up around 9am or whenever the hammer made its introduction. Every South American city has armies of hammer-wielding men banging away early in the morning. You would never see a man with a hammer—you'd only hear him. If it wasn't the hammer man then it was the gringo who packed everything in plastic bags and had to rustle around for twenty minutes until a pack of gum was located.

For breakfast I'd eat what the hostel provided, tea and bread with jelly, then I'd make a short plan of what new sight to visit from gringo recommendations or my guidebook. I'd follow that with time in a coffee shop, reading or studying Spanish with some of the several hundred notecards I packed from home. My favorite Quito café in Old Town served large cappuccinos in ceramic cups for only $1.75. The beans were ground one espresso shot at a time, and with my first sips I thought of Juan Valdez and his timid donkey. After coffee I'd go to an internet café for an hour to catch up on things not worth catching up on. In one not far from my hostel, complete with typical sticky keyboard and impossible mouse, I heard a young boy yell, "*¡Compra mi papel!*" I had a couple months of Spanish study under my belt and knew he said "Buy my paper!" I turned around and there was a short boy no older than nine years old with dirty jeans and a bright red shirt holding packages of Scott's toilet paper. After that I kept noticing young men walking door to door with packages of toilet paper, and wondered how often are they going to catch someone at that exact moment they're ready to stock up.

After internet time I'd head back to the hostel where I'd briefly chat with my fellow travelers to get the latest scoop on places to eat or cities to visit. If you're the patient type you'd wait until everyone could agree on a restaurant and then head out in packs at night to places where similar groups from other hostels were doing the same thing. Then a drink or two at a nearby bar and back to the hostel to sleep on paper-thin foam mattresses. To me it seemed forced to hang out with people not because you get along with them but simply because they share your living space. I spent most of my time alone.

ECUADOR

IV

The first South American I met was Hector, a stocky Colombian man I sat next to in a New Town sports bar. Televisions were tuned to what seemed to be a 24-hour soccer channel. I started to feel more comfortable with my Spanish and slowly got out of the bad habit of speaking in English by default.

I don't remember how we started our conversation, but at the bar he told me about Colombian culture and how neighbors hang out with each other after work. They spend time together like family. "Socializing is very important in Colombia," he said.

I was a poor ambassador for the United States. "It's not like that in America. Everyone is about having their own things and their own space. In the morning when everyone goes to work, the roads are packed with people in their own big cars." I straightened my back and mimed driving a big steering wheel. "In America it's called individualism." It seemed like he understood what I was talking about. His bad English and my bad Spanish complemented each other.

"For two years I lived in a house and I never spoke to my neighbors besides a couple hellos," I continued. "We never had a conversation like I'm having with you."

"Oh no, in Colombia you know your neighbors. They come and you eat and drink with them. You share what you have. It makes us happy to share."

"That doesn't happen in America. Even with friends you may not share like that." I'm sure I went overboard, but even simple things like a meal with friends had to be a grand "dinner party" worthy of electronic invitations and serious planning.

Hector told me he was only in Ecuador for the experience, working as a line cook to make ends meet. "I'm young," he said, "so why not?" I couldn't argue with that. We talked about travel and next thing I knew he went on about an erotic threesome he experienced in Brazil that would make a doctor cringe.

"Wow that didn't sound hard to do," I said.

"It was easy. You look good—you will have that too if you go there."

The conversation died out and I stared at the television screen as if I was interested in the soccer highlights. He's not the first guy to tell me about Brazilian women, but there were six other countries to visit before I'd step foot there. He smoked cigarettes and stared at the curvy bartender, nudging me with his elbow so I'd look at her and give my approval. I did. After my second beer I shook his hand and started on the short walk back to my hostel.

Two prostitutes greeted me in thickly accented English. Then a junkie crossed the street and tugged at my arm, obviously high on something. I yanked back my arm from his grip and he put his hands together as if pleading for a donation, but I kept going. My heart raced while I waited to be buzzed into the hostel.

V

There was an American girl staying in the dorm room next to me. She was a grad student from New York and the type of traveler that soaked in the culture as she went. Her backpack was covered with patches of countries she's been to and her clothing was a blend of Abercrombie & Fitch sweatshirts and multicolored scarves she bought in South American markets. I told myself before leaving that I wouldn't try to get with any Western girl in South America because it was time for something new. Up to this point I only knew the same type of girl: educated, English-speaking, ambitious, and overly concerned about the environment.

I was dating two girls at home before I left. The first girl was Sarah, a tall girl whose height made her the awkward, shy girl in grade school. She would fit well on those "Geek To Hot: Look At Me Now" talk shows. We were physically compatible but dated on and off because the emotional connection wasn't really there. Or that's what I think the reason was, but I still did like her. She always volunteered to cook for me and insisted on paying for dates, a nice change from the other girls I usually dated. She had no problem showing she cared. By the time I left we were on again and while the goodbye wasn't full of tears, it wasn't easy either.

Things were more breezy with Stacy, an ex-sorority girl. She was the sarcastic, biting type that hid her feelings deep inside and kept things superficial. My old cat Furball could express himself better then she could. That's not what I wanted in a girl so our relationship was based entirely on the physical, and both of us knew it. There were moments—usually after several drinks—that encouraged me to stick around, where she became a little more vulnerable and would look at me or hold me in a deeper way. With time I felt I could crack open her shell and pull out the emotional creature lurking inside, but it never happened. Our goodbye was her kicking me out of her house the Sunday morning before I left. She wanted to go to the gym before it got too late.

For two days and nights I had breakfast, lunch, and dinner with the girl from New York. Conversations consisted of her chatting and me nodding my head. She wasn't so much concerned with my thoughts or opinions but getting across hers, though she did ask me fluffy questions from time to time (probably just to see if I was paying attention). If I told her a story she would scan her brain for something similar she experienced and then tell it to me without acknowledging what I said. I defaulted to sarcastic comments to keep myself amused, and even though she spoke fluent English I can't say our communication was any better than between Hector and I.

It had only been less than two weeks since I last slept with a girl but on the way back to the hostel I found myself trying to get close to her, touching her hand and the small of her back. What a faker I was to come to South America to hook up with a girl just like the ones I meet at home! I couldn't even remember her name and by now I was too embarrassed to ask. I backed down once we got inside the hostel and retreated to my room. Two French guys were already asleep, snoring.

VI

Long blocks of boredom set in by week three after I knocked out all of Quito's major sights and coffee shops. There wasn't much to do besides learn Spanish, surf the internet, and lounge around with other travelers. One reason for the boredom is that unlike Europe, South American cities don't have as many historical sites. In terms of history South America is barely a teenager while Europe is walking around with a cane. In another 2,000 years when the Coliseum in Rome crumbles to the ground, tourists may arrive in Rio de Janeiro to see the Maracanã soccer stadium instead, the largest in the world. I was so bored I started noticing things like the candle flames, this natural element that brings heat and cooked food. Ah yes this is what travel is for—to notice things I didn't appreciate at home like fire and maybe air and water!

I'd flip through my guidebook fantasizing about all the future cities I was going to visit. I'd remind myself how the adventure has only just begun, hints of it shown on the weathered faces of travelers who have been on the road longer than I have. We're all after that true authentic experience where we take photos with actual locals, accept hand-made bracelets given by wise elders, and hold and burp indigenous babies. With the baby pictures safely stored in our Canon digital cameras we can then look down on the "tourists" with their khaki shorts, neck passport holder, and huge camera with the fuck-off lens. Their experience is less real then ours, we concurred, as we smoked weed in the back of a $7 a night hostel after checking our email for the fifth time in a day.

There was a late arrival the night before I left Quito, a girl with long hair and a round ass. She wore leather boots up to her knees, a rare sight among hostel girls. It turned out she was from Oregon. She lived in Brazil for three years and apparently has assimilated the look and vibe of a Brazilian woman. While most female travelers have sweatpants and old t-shirts, this girl had make-up, costume jewelry, perfume, and clubbing gear. I asked her about Brazil and the crime problem came up.

"In Brazil robberies are more direct than in other countries—they just put a knife or gun on you to take your stuff." She argued that this is better because "at least you know what's happening." I disagreed on the inside. I rather some teenager with sticky fingers swipe my wallet than have to stare down the barrel of a loaded gun held by a trigger-happy thug. I rather be surprised when I get back to my hostel, not when I'm walking at night on a quiet street. I used to believe that it's okay to accept being robbed in South America because it's so poor that people don't have a choice, but then I got robbed myself.

VII

The Quito bus station is a damp cavern of busted lights and makeshift stands. The same characters selling toilet paper and gum on the street make their appearances both inside and outside the station. Ticket booths were flanked by little restaurants with bathrooms so filthy that I watered a skinny tree beyond the sidewalk instead.

The bus system is how intercity travel is done in South America because rail is essentially nonexistent, car ownership is low, and air travel is too expensive. Several dozen bus companies exist in Ecuador, a country about the same size as Nevada, whereas at home I can only name two bus companies (Greyhound and the Chinatown bus to New York).

It was impossible to casually browse departure times written on blackboard or pieces of paper without being approached by a ticket agent begging to know where I was going. I picked the bus with the next destination to Tena, with no information on the bus company besides the company name. There are no reviews and no safety records I could browse before purchasing my ticket. The system was pick and pray.

There are three main characters on any South American bus route. First you have the fare catcher, whose job is to yell out destinations either at the station or while hanging halfway out the bus as it passes crowds of people standing at the side of the road. They're mostly thin, scraggly looking men with a jeans and t-shirt uniform. I've never seen a female fare catcher. They create catchy ways of yelling cities in loops of three's or four's with a sing-song intonation: *"Ten-a, Ten-a, Ten-aaaaaaahhhhhhhhh."*

Next you have the bus driver, a more rotund and older fellow who I've never heard speak. He just nods. If he was born in the United States he would probably be a skydiver or adventurer of some sort judging by his desire to make bus travel more exciting than it should be. The bus driver is also always male.

Then there is the ticket agent, a shady person who will say anything to get you to buy the fare. It matters little if he doesn't understand what you're saying. Since prices are not displayed he will size you up and give you the gringo fare, which is a dollar or two more than what the locals are paying. This is where women have broken through the sex barrier to find employment in the bus industry. These three individuals combine to create a surprisingly efficient form of travel.

The bus ride to Tena, the "whitewater capital of South America," started before the bus even moved. A handful of vendors boarded and tried to sell me reggaeton CDs, cloudy white liquid packaged in plastic bags, teen magazines, fake gold watches, potato chips, peanuts, bottles of water, and sympathy. A mute gave me his pitch on a copied piece of paper, an old man complained about the cancer eating away his insides, and a young father in a matching sweatsuit held a four-year-old girl and explained he was hard on his luck and needed money for food. Some vendors got on the bus as it was moving without having to pay a fare, suggesting that the bus driver and fare catcher have an unspoken agreement. There are even stand-up comedians who stay on for ten minutes or more to tell stories or jokes, asking for donations before getting off the bus miles away. I'm guessing they then hopped on another bus headed towards town and did the same thing, back and forth for the entire day. Even though most of the people on the bus were poor themselves, it was surprising how many gave money.

When you ask the fare catcher how long it takes to get to the next city, the time he gives you is based on maniacal driving. Regular driving takes twice as long to arrive and just isn't as fun for the adrenaline junkies that compose the bus driver corps. It didn't matter than the road to Tena was this gravel and dirt thing that days of rain had turned into thick mud. I could feel the back of the bus sliding as the driver hurried anyway like he was rushing the President of France to an important diplomatic meeting. The only assuring thing about the memorial crosses on the side of the road was that they came in singles and doubles, not the dozens that would suggest a large bus crash.

What if my driver was inexperienced? What if he had a chip on his shoulder because he hated his job and really wanted to be an airplane pilot? It's highly unlikely that he took a training course on mud road driving. I don't think I was the only one worried judging by everyone's stone-faced stare into the back of the seat in front of them. They were quiet because they were praying. I leaned back in my chair and closed my eyes, feeling somewhat assured that all the trees growing from the side of the mountain would break our fall and provide a soft landing.

VIII

Tena is a jungle town east of Quito that has a lazy feel common with small towns. People strolled around late at night licking ice cream bought at the lone coffee shop run by two women from Switzerland, or sat down by the main drag eating barbecue meat sticks sold off the street. Gringos preferred to drink cheap bottles of beer and shoot the shit at one of the two pizzerias stationed next to the brown river that halved the town.

I arrived on a Friday during culture month, which meant a free concert in the square. This square was unlike the ones I've seen in Europe—there were no carefully planned gardening and landscape plots, no striking sculpture or fountain, and definitely no pretty little shops that sold things such as flowers and artisan chocolates. The square in Tena was a grey mass of concrete the size of four basketball courts. It had bleachers on one side, an abandoned building on the other, a road on the third, and two restaurants on the fourth. The stage was set up in the far end of square in front of the restaurants, leaving an uncomfortable expanse of concrete between itself and the spectators. It was filled only by two police officers twirling batons. It must have taken half a second for the sound from the stage to hit the two hundred people watching the show. Local talent gave it their all, singing and dancing in the sticky jungle air, but the crowd was stingy with applause.

I stayed at a mom and pop hostel near the pizzerias. The owner of the hostel greeted me every day in his bath robe, then later his wife gave me advice on places to check out and areas to avoid. I lounged around for a couple days until I signed up for a whitewater rafting tour. I should've been planning a deep jungle hike to spend weeks with an indigenous tribe without electricity or toilet like so many other gringos, but instead I was content to stir alone for most of my time. When I wanted to feel better about my lethargy I thought of all my former coworkers: compared to them I was Magellan.

A day before my rafting trip I sat down on a park bench and studied my guidebook to plan out the next couple weeks. I was spending at least an hour a day reading the guidebook and it was shaping my trip more than anything else. I didn't bother to ask travel advice from locals like I imagined I would.

Two girls sat down next to me within sight of three empty benches. One stared at me while the other kept brushing her leg against mine. It was the afternoon but both wore short skirts, bedazzled cut-off shirts, and a thick coating of make-up. It looked like they were about to go to a cheesy club. They talked to each other and sighed deeply, an invitation for me to say something, but I didn't bite because I knew they were working. At least they were obvious about it.

Two years prior I was partying in a beachside nightclub on Venezuela's popular Margarita Island. With me were two waitresses I met at a restaurant who were pleased to be talking to the rare American who made his way down to Venezuela. I thought I was going to get with one of the waitresses, but when the restaurant owner showed up to shove his tongue down her throat I realized I was on my own.

I made half-hearted attempts to dance to salsa music with the native girls but didn't get very far, and went out through the back of the club onto the beach to get some air. I dodged drunk couples making out to sit on a sand ledge facing the ocean. The wind quickly cooled me down and I leaned back and placed my hands on the sand behind me. I thought of how this type of moment is best experienced with another person. Not two minutes later my wish was granted and a girl I didn't notice in the club sat right next to me.

She wasn't the cutest girl in the club but she wasn't ugly either. She wore slutty black boots and a skimpy outfit that revealed her large breasts. In bad English she asked me where I was from.

"United States. And you?"

"Brazil," she said slowly, glancing at my lips. She moved her head towards mine until it was just a few inches away. I've already heard how sexual Brazilian girls are so I wasn't too surprised when we were kissing within seconds. Eventually we made our way back inside and I bought a round of beers. She danced and I sat back to watch, as if she was putting on a show for me.

"Where are you staying?" she asked.

"I have an apartment two blocks away." It had its own bedroom and kitchen, luxurious by the hostel standards I was currently experiencing in Ecuador.

"Why don't we go back there?"

Now I've had American girls move fast on me before, but this was ridiculous. I only knew her for five minutes. I assured myself that this was the nature of Brazilian culture, but to be sure I wanted to see if she didn't mind hanging out a little bit longer in the club. If she was a prostitute then she would quickly get discouraged and move on to easier fish.

I grabbed a second beer and we kissed and danced for more than half an hour. By then I was convinced she definitely wasn't a prostitute. She was already headed for the door when I suggested she have a drink with me in my apartment.

I gave her a brief tour that ended in my bedroom. I left her there and said I was going to the kitchen to get some water. I put cash and credit cards from my jean pocket into the refrigerator's butter compartment, just in case she thought of robbing me after I went to sleep. (I've always had paranoia problems.) I went back to the room and we got down to business. Within five minutes we were naked. Not used to girls with enormous breasts I couldn't stop squeezing hers, as if I was at the grocery store picking out tomatoes. She laid on her back, begging for more, and I was not about to let her down.

My condom use at the time could best be described as a smidge short of 100% compliance, but on this random girl there was no way

I'd let my dick touch any part of her without protection. I leaned over the bed and fumbled with my bag for twenty seconds until I found a condom. I ripped the package open and pulled the condom out. It was on within ten seconds, perfected with years of practice as a virgin. I was right about to put it in and notch my belt, when she spoke.

"Pay me."

"What?"

"Pay me!"

She was a prostitute all along.

It's one thing to be deceived, but it's another thing to be completely naked when the deception happens. I felt humiliated. I rolled off her onto the other side of the bed.

"You did not tell me that. I don't pay for sex." I barely got the words out.

"Uhh, it's okay," she said, and snuggled up next to me. Did she want to have sex with me anyway? Didn't matter—I was no longer in the mood.

I stared at the ceiling trying to process what happened, the condom still choking my softening manhood. I was so stupid for thinking a girl would have sex with me in under an hour because she wanted me so bad. I imagined she was thinking about all the money she lost wasting her time on me, a gringo who believed that all Brazilian girls were super easy.

She got up from the bed and put on her clothes. I took off the condom and put on my boxers. I followed her out to make sure she didn't go for a late night snack and find my stash in the refrigerator. No more words were exchanged and after she left I went to the bathroom to clean my mouth from the hundreds of other dicks I kissed by association.

The two girls on the park bench wouldn't stop trying to get my attention. A suspicious man in a red soccer jersey came by every few minutes to check on them, talking too fast for me to understand. Was he their friend or pimp? He didn't seem flashy enough to be their pimp, not by American standards, anyway. He was missing nice clothes, gold jewelry, crocodile-skinned shoes and most importantly, a pimp cane. After about ten minutes, the girls gave up and walked off.

It was remotely possible they weren't prostitutes and I missed out on my chance for a flag, a concept that I was introduced to by an Australian guy I met in Spain. It goes like this: if you have sex with a girl that was born in a different country, you accumulate that country's flag. It's a more worldly way to brag about your conquests instead of the more bland method of stating how many girls you've slept with. Before my plane touched down, I dreamed of all the flags I would score in South America. In the poorest countries—Ecuador, Bolivia, and Peru—the girls would find out I'm American, from the richest country in the world, and throw themselves on me. I would start off strong in Ecuador and then ride the wave to Brazil, where I'd satisfy every sexual dream I had, including the threesome that Hector said would be cake to achieve. While I'm at it I might as well go for a foursome.

Instead I was off to a rough start. I couldn't find girls. The bars and clubs I stepped foot into were usually empty and had more gringos than natives, and during the day I'd only see school girls or young mothers towing little kids. I could not find the ambitious career woman out for a hot night on the town looking to hook up. There was no obvious pick-up spot where I could find a bountiful supply of cute girls open to getting laid on the same night. My most intimate encounter so far was in the coffee shop owned by the two Swiss ladies. Every day the waitress would lock eye contact me and wouldn't let go, capping off each stare with a slight smile. If only I was attracted to her. She was short and stumpy with no curves and greasy black hair. She would do during desperate times but it was still too early.

IX

A large group of English teenagers checked into the hostel. They were loud, obnoxious, dreadlocked, and smelly. I'm sure it was one of them that turned the number nine on my door to a six. When my door knocked I thought it was them playing another prank, but it was the wife of the owner. Behind her was a man trying to catch a peek inside. She asked me if he could take the second bed in my room. I didn't know I had a choice. In walked a clean-shaven man with hiking pants named Henri. He was from Paris and a self-proclaimed bourgeoisie, which according to my studies from high school history class meant he'd be decapitated if there happened to be another French revolution.

After we exchanged basic information like where we were from and how long we were traveling for, he asked me about the whitewater rafting. I told him that the next day I was signed up for Class IV rapids, just one grade short of the most violent rapids possible. I gave him directions to the rafting company and he left to sign up.

We had dinner afterwards at a restaurant whose specialty was a monster cheeseburger topped with a fried egg. It was served alongside a heaping mound of french fries. The burger was surprisingly good and all that was left on my plate was a shallow pool of oil and egg yolk. The only way it could have been less healthy is if they just deep fried the whole thing.

I was still full when I woke up the next day, my body begging for water to dilute the salty fat sludge circulating through my bloodstream. Henri and I walked together to the rafting company office and met the other people in our group: two goofy German guys, an American couple with their two young boys, one Australian girl traveling solo, and an Irish guy with a Canadian girl. On the Land Rover ride to the river, the Canadian girl asked me what I do.

"Right now? Just traveling," I said.

"Yeah, but what were you doing before?"

"I was a microbiologist."

"Oh cool. How did you get time off?"

The last thing I wanted to talk about was my job. Didn't she understand that that's the reason I'm here? Why couldn't she just ask me what everyone else asked, like what countries I've visited and where I'm going next? We were tightly packed into the Land Rover and our knees banged against each other over bumps on the road. There was no escape.

"I just quit my job. Not doing anything now. What do you do?"

"I work for a small magazine. I took a two month sabbatical from work on an around-the-world ticket and that's where I met him." She smiled and looked at the Irish guy. "I only have two more weeks left and I wish I could stay a little longer but I really miss home."

"That's cool." I gave a pursed lip smile. She was an around-the-worlder, a traveler on speed. With only one night in Tena she wasn't going to experience the awkward culture concert, the friendly Swiss ladies, and the egg burger with enough fat and cholesterol to instantly kill old men.

When the Rover drove past a village outside town, a handful of kids yelled and ran to catch up with us. I thought they were excited to see foreigners but instead they were excited to work. The tour agency hires them to carry and set up the equipment on the river a half-mile away from where the dirt road ends. I've never seen a teenage girl so happy to carry a fifty pound deflated raft on her back through deep mud and rock before. The only thing that the gringos had to carry were plastic paddles.

"She wants to prove to her family that she is capable of doing hard work. Otherwise they won't let her work in the future," one of the guides said. "Her and her friends want more work than we have."

Everything was set up by the time we made it to the river, swollen from a storm up mountain. The rafts were inflated and positioned alongside two kayaks to be steered by spotters, whose job was to keep an eye on the gringos and mark upcoming dangers. Coolers full of drinks and food were fastened tightly to the back of the rafts.

Locals watched from a shaky footbridge that connected to the next village while the guides instructed us on how to pull someone back in the boat if they fell overboard (grab the shoulder part of their life jackets and drag them in). The river moved surprisingly fast. The white peaks formed miniature waves and made the Canadian girl nervous. She had to be assured by a guide that everything was safe.

The guides were the same type of junkie as the bus drivers and didn't seem like they'd want to miss out an opportunity for tougher rapids. I can only speak for myself, but I'm pretty sure no one was assured when a guide said, "Don't worry, we've never lost anyone on this river." Henri and the American family went on one boat while everyone else and I went on the other.

It was surprising how the power of five people paddling could overcome the strongest of rapids, as long as everyone paddled in unison. Our raft leader yelled instructions for each stroke, "Hard front, front, front, HARD front, right front, right front," and since I sat in the rear I had to watch the person in front of me to make sure our strokes were synchronized. Each rapid would provide a big splash and hoots and hollers from us all, followed by quiet rest for a couple minutes. Then the sound of the next rapid bouncing off the trees became louder and we tightened our grips on the paddles.

I thought we'd surely be doomed in the "waffle maker" rapid with its huge one meter drop, but it was just a thin wall of cool water, light brown from the rain's mud runoff. It drained immediately from the holes in the bottom of the boat. Only for three seconds on each rapid would we be completely helpless, our paddles useless against the drops, but then very quickly the water would clear from our faces and the guide's barks would become audible once again. Paddles struck the water at the same time and in an instant the boat was back in our control.

We kept crossing under footbridges, increasingly rickety in construction. I whined and begged to cross one, like the characters in my favorite childhood movie *The Goonies*. We parked next to a dangerous looking bridge after lunch. It was constructed with two cable steel wires wrapped around two sad trees on the banks. Shorter cables came down from the main ones every couple of meters to allow for a shaky platform of loose pieces of rotting logs. (Missing was a sign that told you the "Maximum Load" with the imprint of the engineering company that commissioned the bridge.) It was impossible to walk on the bridge without holding the thick wires for balance. In this case that was only half the point since we jumped down into the river. There is nothing like some bite-sized adventure on a safe and planned tour to make you feel good for traveling. We all celebrated with bottles of beer at the end.

That night Henri and I walked next door to the pizzeria. We nodded to our guides who ate just two tables over from our spot on the sidewalk. I remembered seeing them my first night.

"I know I've only been here a couple weeks but the rafting was the best experience of my trip so far," I said, taking a chug of cheap beer.

"Isn't there a lot of rafting in America?"

"Yeah, in West Virginia, which is just one state over from where I live, actually. One of the guides told me West Virginia has Class V rapids and every year someone dies or almost dies. I've never done rafting at home though."

The cheese of the pizza tasted differently than the Papa John's or Dominos I'm used to—sharper, with more bite. We easily finished a large but my arm and back muscles were hungry for more and I briefly considered eating the cold pizza left by the family next to us. The next day my body would feel like it had been tenderized. I couldn't lift my arms over my shoulders.

"What do you think of 9/11?" Henri asked in a vague way that made it hard to pin down his intentions.

"I think it has given my government a good excuse to grab more power."

"No I mean the official story, the way it happened."

"With the hijackers and the planes? I haven't really thought about it."

"Do you think a plane crashed into the Pentagon?"

"Yes.".

"Don't you think it's weird that the same size plane brought down the buildings in New York but only damaged a very small section of the Pentagon?"

He continued before I could think of an answer.

"Have you seen the surveillance footage of the impact of the Pentagon—the grainy still photos that show an explosion but no plane?"

"Yes."

"The Pentagon is the most important building in the United States besides the White House. It has thousands of cameras. Isn't it weird that they only have a few grainy pictures of the impact?"

"Yes I did think of that."

"There's a fighter jet base just next to Washington that can respond within minutes. They couldn't track down a hijacked jumbo jet making its way from New York? The whole thing is a lie."

The phrase "conspiracy theory" popped in my head. If you don't believe the government's official account of events then you are a conspiracy theorist and halfway in the crazy house. "You think the U.S.

government was behind it?" I asked.

"I don't know. Look, governments have done worse. If the government tells you one thing, there's a good chance the opposite is true."

We jumped from topic to topic, 9/11 to the French government, to French food, French women, American women. He told me how he met his last girlfriend when she rear-ended him in a car accident. They broke up almost a year ago and he had been single since.

"Do you approach women?" I asked.

"What do you mean?"

"Do you see a girl you like and then walk up to her and start a conversation?"

"No. I've never done that. It happens naturally more or less, like when a girl looks at me first or gives me some sort of sign."

His method was common among guys I've known besides the close friends who were just like me. I don't blame them: there is nothing natural about walking up to a girl you don't know and start talking in a way that shows your most positive traits in a short amount of time. Approaching girls is like door-to-door sales, but you're selling yourself instead of insurance or knives that cut through empty aluminum cans.

"Well I have an example for you," I started. "Two years ago I was in a huge club with a couple of friends. I saw a group of four extremely tall women. They didn't look like they wanted to talk to anyone, but one of the girls in the group was very cute and I definitely wanted to have sex with her. I walked up to all of them and said, 'Hey guys I need some advice. I'm throwing a house party soon with my roommate and I'm not sure which party theme to have. Should it be a teacher and school girls theme or pimps and ho's?' It wasn't a very good line but it broke the ice and they offered me a couple suggestions. I kept the conversation going, making my girl laugh and telling her short stories that highlighted the cool things I've done. I got her phone number after about an hour. We kissed on the first date and on the second date she invited herself to my bedroom. If I didn't approach her, I would never have banged her. She didn't even know I existed before I opened my mouth."

He raised his eyebrows. I felt compelled to give him a disclaimer.

"But that's not how it always is. For every one of her there are more than ten failures where the girl doesn't like me. Still though, I think it's worth trying if you see a girl you like."

He looked off to the side and rubbed his facial stubble with his hand.

"Okay say I see a girl in line at a café and I want to talk to her. What do I say?"

"You can say, 'You look like you're having the most fun here out of anyone.' It's generic enough that you can use in most places, but it doesn't come across as a line. It'll break the ice and then you have a conversation with her. Make observations about the café you're in for example, or ask open ended questions. It's better to say anything than nothing."

"Say the line again," he asked.

"You look like you're having the most fun here out of anyone."

"Not bad."

If you give a man the tools or knowledge to meet more women he will devour it and want more. While most guys use the strategy of impressing women with nice possessions in an attempt to show their financial success, I believe in talking to a girl in the way she wants to be talked to. Teasing a girl and making her laugh goes farther than giving her a ride in a nice car.

"Oh, the reason why she and her friends were so tall was because they were college volleyball players." I grinned and finished what was left of my third beer. The pizzeria was closing and we decided to go back to our room instead of hit another bar. We were exhausted from our day.

In the room I turned on my laptop and put on some Ministry Of Sound house music. I showed him pictures of girls I dated, not to brag but to prove that a man of average looks like myself can get more and better simply by putting himself out there. He complimented the pictures and confirmed what my opening line was once more, taking out a pen and writing it down. I also showed him pictures of girls that rejected me: the Russian girl who was in town for a weekend and got with another guy instead of me, the Persian girl who preferred an all-American white guy, the law school student who stood me up on the second date, and the young Portuguese girl who I could never get alone. The nature of the game is you win some and you lose some, but in the end it's worth it because you eventually get what you want. There's just one problem: once you're deep in the game it's hard to quit even if you do meet the right girl. Things become more about conquest instead of finding a happy relationship. Settling down becomes an unnatural concept.

Henri took out a water bottle half full of whisky and we each took a capful. I exaggerated its burn. The next afternoon I said goodbye to him at the bus station. He went to Quito for his return flight to Paris and I to Baños, a resort town in the middle of Ecuador, famous for its steaming hot mineral baths. Henri was my first travel buddy.

X

All that talk with Henri about hitting on girls got me so charged I was ready to approach impenetrable groups of girls. On my first night in Baños I pulled out my two young dorm mates and we prowled around the deserted city center. All we found were four girls in a club encircled by seventeen horny guys. It doesn't matter how excited you are—if you can't find girls then you get nothing.

The guidebook, which other travelers called "the bible," led me to a café owned by a round American man who would quietly read in the back corner. My favorite item on the menu was the lemon rum cake that leaked just a bit of sugary juice when pressed with a fork. I'd order it with the smooth cappuccino. It was hard to let go of a comfortable place to read and study that reminded me of home, so I stayed two extra days than I had planned.

Activities like hiking and mountain biking are good time killers, especially in Baños with its prime position between two rows of mountains, but they cost money and assume you like the outdoors, which I don't. Everyone but me had hiking pants with specially designed fibers and sweat holes for long, strenuous climbs. I had a pair of dark jeans, and felt no need to add to that.

In my hostel's computer room I met Karl the Dutchman when he asked me if the internet was down. A sling holding his right arm was inside his shirt and made it look like he was masturbating. He went on one of those activities, mountain biking, and broke his collar bone when he lost control of his bicycle. The sling was to stay on his arm for three weeks while his trip had four months to go.

That night we went to a bar downtown where he recognized an American girl who sat with him on a bus ride from another city. He pawned her off on me and she seemed interested, asking a mountain of questions about myself in a short amount of time, which made sense later when she mentioned her ex-boyfriend was Arab (Persians aren't Arab but it's close enough). She told me about her experience living in Peru and how she's been away for a year. When I asked her if she missed anyone from home she said, "Not really."

"I've been thinking about home and family," I said to her.

"I think that's the first time anyone has told me that down here."

I did find it weird that no one talks about their family while traveling, and it made me wonder if daily thoughts about home made me weak in some way.

A teenage English girl threw herself into our conversation, asking me how much I was enjoying the trip thus far. I was honest with her and said it was just okay. I could see in her face that she was slighted. "How do you not enjoy the beauty here? The people and the views. It's amazing. Maybe you are not experiencing enough."

"He misses his family," the American girl said. I groaned on the inside.

"Oh really are you serious? They'll be there when you get back. I don't even think about my family that much now," the English girl said.

Was she practical or just cold? I couldn't tell, but I found her hard to take seriously. She was a little kid being funded by her parents to travel with a best friend who couldn't stop singing the praises of cocaine. She was the type of gringo that pulls out her digital camera to show me self-portraits of her eating *cuy* (guinea pig), a local delicacy that is supposedly an aphrodisiac. Up to that point I hadn't met a gringo who ate guinea pig and didn't take pictures of it, usually a shot with a wide-open mouth and guinea pig meat only two inches away.

I looked at the English girl and said, "Well you still have a lot to learn." It was a cheap statement, but then again I was just matching her tone. She turned her back to me.

After another beer I walked with the American girl to a quieter bar. It was my chance to make a move. I touched her in a flirty way here and there, but I felt nothing. She had several extra pounds and the same short haircut that many girls get before they travel to the third world. I beat myself up for even thinking about hooking up with a girl that I never would go after back at home. It was almost a replay of what happened with the girl from New York in Quito.

If I wasn't going to try to get her in bed I might as well pick her brain. She was an experienced long-term traveler and could help me better understand the lows of travel, the boredom and homesickness.

"So as the trip goes on I'm thinking of home more, not less," I said.

"That's normal, but when you go back home you'll be bored again after a week."

"What do you mean?"

"Nothing will change. You'll have all these experiences and have seen all these cities, but everyone at home hasn't. They will be the same. The bars that you spent time in with friends or the things you did with them will feel different than before you left."

I didn't want to know more. I didn't want to worry that by taking this trip I may have ruined all my relationships back home. I steered the conversation to the favorite places she's been to.

XI

The next night Karl and I met up at a bar with two English girls from the hostel. One of the girls was named Zoë. I've always been fascinated with that name and find that if you name a girl Zoë it's a guarantee she'll be artsy and a pensive thinker. This Zoë was actually a museum curator who was careful with her words, but she had a lot of colorful accessories so I like to think my theory holds. She looked like the cute girl next door that guys would throw themselves on (just a little bit hotter and they'd think she's out of their league).

After talking to Zoë for a while, I checked in on Karl, who was flirting with a random Dutch girl. In my ear he told me that Zoë was "boring." It's true she was boring, but it never crossed my mind that that's a quality I should judge a girl on before I had sex with her. If she was cute it was full steam ahead until she rejected me or I got what I wanted.

We all walked to another bar guarded by a bouncer wearing a bulletproof vest. That would draw away most rational people but instead the bar attracted quite a crowd, including me and my Western-educated friends. Once inside I asked the Dutch girl to take a picture of me and Karl. I turned on my camera and passed it to her, but the strap got caught up on my wrist and she moved her hands away before firmly grabbing it. I helplessly watched the camera crash on the concrete floor. The lens became loose and crooked, and just like that my camera was gone.

If a gringo goes to a country and doesn't take a picture, did he really go there?

All my gringo friends left including Karl. I didn't follow them, and remained at the bar alone, moping. Travel didn't feel right unless I had a camera. Distorted salsa music blasting from the under-powered speakers didn't motivate me to get up, and there was no fewer than three guys for every girl. Where are the girls, anyway?

Out of the blue, an animated, short Ecuadorian guy I'd never met brought me a beer. I thanked him and watched his crew of equally short guys work on the gringas in the crowd. One thing white girls love about South American guys is that they can dance, and they'll rarely turn down an average looking native when he offers his hand. With no prior experience the girls will look like princesses of the ball while the guys spin and flip them around.

I watched my new short friends have a group of four American girls putty in their hands, but the girls suddenly left after they had their fix of dancing. Only cheek kisses were exchanged. I would watch many of these groups of native men work the girls in Baños and be surprised at their pitiful success rate. Turns out you need a bit more than just amazing dancing skills to get with a gringa.

The guys dragged me to Leprechaun Bar across the street, a happening place where all the gringos seemed to know each other. The deck upstairs provided a nice view of fistfights on the street below while hostel cliques danced in large circles. My friends wouldn't stop pointing out men they thought were gay.

"So do you guys like to have sex with men?" I asked.

"*¡No, nunca! ¡Solo mujeres!*" one yelled.

"Yes yes he likes a man!" another said, laughing. "Me, no."

I said, "Maybe you like men sometimes, just to hug or kiss. Not all the time..."

"*¡No no no no no no! ¡Soy hombre!*"

Another flexed his bicep, suggesting that his large muscles made it impossible for him to be gay. One pounded his chest like a gorilla and another demonstrated how rough he gives sex to girls with simulated hip thrusts and ass slapping. The denials and counter-accusations continued for ten minutes. Then they asked me if I was gay.

"Sometimes." I tilted my hand back and forth like Mr. Roper from the show *Three's Company*. Their eyes opened wide and they took a step back.

"*¡Estoy jodiendo!*" I said. They were relieved, and gave a look like I just told them I disarmed a nuclear bomb and they weren't going to die after all.

During this time I noticed a girl dancing with a young man. She was the most beautiful girl in the bar, which in these parts of the woods didn't say too much. I blatantly stared at her long hair and curvy body, enchanted, watching her dance with a guy who had to be her friend—they weren't even touching. His presence still scared all the other guys from making a move. I didn't think that approaching her while dancing would work (she'd turn me down with a smile, I imagined), so I had to use something in the environment to insert myself. I thought about it while my homophobic friends unsuccessfully approached chubby gringas. They resorted to dancing wildly by themselves, hoping girls would notice their practiced moves.

The girl's male companion took out his camera and snapped a picture of her. He extended his arm to take a self-portrait with her, but before he pushed the shutter I made eye contact and gave the universal

"I can take a picture" sign with my hand. I took the picture and then handed them the camera.

"Where are you two from?" I asked in English.

"From Guayaquil." The largest city in Ecuador.

"I made some friends here that are teaching me Ecuadorian culture." I pointed to the gringa lovers dancing alone. She laughed.

"Are they teaching you to dance?"

"I'm more of a talker than a dancer. Once you get older that's what happens. Plus I don't want to embarrass everyone with my amazing dance moves."

"Very funny. How old are you?"

"I'm 28. And you?"

"I'm 23."

She was asking questions. At least she was curious. I sat down on a stool nearby so our heights were the same and I wouldn't have to lean in.

"The crowd here is very mixed," I said. "Lots of gringos and locals."

"Not many people live here, they just come for vacation. I'm with my cousin and his family. It's his birthday today." She smiled and introduced the young man who kept so many other guys at bay. I've never been so happy to meet someone else's cousin before.

When I desire a girl, the best of me comes out. Of course I think about ways to get her into bed, but I enjoy the process, the conversation, the flirting, and I don't see things as just a means to an end. I put in an honest effort on this Ecuadorian girl, unlike those American girls I half-assed it on only to wuss out on in the end. I told her about my background and the trip so far and I asked questions about her and her country. The chemistry wasn't too strong but it had to be a positive sign that I was the only guy she was talking to. When she said it was getting late and it was time for her and the birthday boy to leave, I offered to walk her out. Outside there were two parked police cruisers trying to keep the peace after the fights from earlier.

"How long are you here for?" I asked.

"Three more days."

"Do you want to get coffee tomorrow? I know a good café."

"What's the name?"

"Casa Hood. It's near the central park."

"I don't know. Maybe!"

Maybe? What was I going to do with a maybe? I didn't have a cell phone and there was no way to get in touch with her besides email. I can't assume she checked it daily like I did.

"How about this… tomorrow I will be there around 2pm. Why don't you stop by then?"

"Okay, I'll try."

I shook her cousin's hand goodbye and gave her a hug. I held on for one extra second longer to keep her body against mine. The date wasn't solid but I couldn't think of a reason why she wouldn't show up. It was just coffee. I went back in the bar and high-fived my friends, who by now were so drunk they could no longer dance.

I woke up the next day at noon, hungover. I changed, ate breakfast, brushed my teeth, and walked to Casa Hood. The American owner was reading a book thicker than a large-print bible while his niece and nephew used candles to light pieces of paper on fire. I took out my Spanish notecards and textbook so it wouldn't seem like I was idly waiting once she walked through the door.

I made it through about a dozen notecards before my mind started to wander. I fantasized about how the date would go. After she ordered a cappuccino and piece of lemon rum cake I'd show her my Spanish textbook. She'd flip through it and pause on certain pages that caught her interest. Our hands would accidentally touch on the table. I'd make a few jokes. I'd tell her how I was ready to be a salsa champion with her mentorship. After an hour or two we'd part ways and agree to meet later at a bar. We'd dance and get closer. I'd pull back when she was ready to be kissed just to build more tension, until it finally happened. The only question that would remain is where to take her once the bars closed.

The fantasy was very reasonable, I thought. Assuming she showed up. She never did.

ECUADOR

XII

I tagged along with Karl the Dutchman to see the semi-active Tungurahua volcano. Rides were offered by *chivas*, small buses with additional chairs bolted to the roof. In the process of looking for one we ran into one of the natives I partied with the night before. He led us to a reasonably priced bus and talked his way into a free ride since he brought two paying gringos along.

At the volcano lookout point we were greeted by more than a dozen empty buses that had already unloaded their gringo cargo. We met up with the herd in a clearing where fire entertainers had just started their act. People were so into them that they missed the tiny splashes of red-orange lava jumping from the top of the volcano. Baños has volcano shelters spread throughout town for the next time it erupts, but no one knew exactly where they were. "They're spread around," I was told.

Karl wasn't a fan of my native friend, who blatantly pointed out girls (especially gringas), mimed ass slaps on them, and kept trying to push our crotches onto their rears. On the way back, for which he avoided paying again, we sat on the roof and had to duck every time a power line or tree branch approached. One particular gringo wasn't fast enough and a branch cut his head open. Lawsuits waiting to happen in the United States, good ol' fun in Ecuador.

Back in town Karl went back to the hostel because his collarbone was hurting. I returned to Leprechaun Bar with my new wingman, who approached girls no older than sixteen along the way. He had zero fear and was willing to talk to any girl, a quality I hadn't seen in travelers I met so far. His only weakness was that he couldn't keep his hands off girls before establishing at least a drop of rapport. At the bar I'd be flirting with a girl and he'd go octopus on her friend and that was that. I partly hoped to run into the girl that stood me up at the coffee shop. Maybe she went to the wrong café and was looking for me?

A random guy from St. Louis asked me to take a swig of his beer in what seemed like an American male bonding exercise. I put my lips on his half full bottle of beer and drank without thinking about it.

On the deck I stared at the drunken guys stumbling from bar to bar below. I gave a simple hello to two Ecuadorian girls nearby. One was thin but not very pretty. Up to that point everyone kept telling me I'd have a much better South American experience if I knew the language, and while that may be true, when it comes to hitting on girls simply knowing a few hundred words will only have a small benefit. Talking to girls involves a lot of humor, sarcasm, and word play, something that my Spanglish helped very little with. It wasn't a problem with this new girl since she spoke English, but it was with many others. I felt like I was going backwards in my ability to build the right chemistry within the first few minutes of meeting a girl.

I kissed the girl from Ecuador and danced with her until the bar kicked us out. We tagged along with her friends to sit on a nearby bench. She was the first woman I touched in three weeks, but I wasn't all that pumped to get her in bed. She wasn't my first choice. Besides, the logistics weren't in my favor. I stayed in a hostel that had a watchman and she slept in a hotel room with three of her friends. I didn't try to find an open hotel, assuming she would be up for it in the first place.

We walked one of her friends to the bus station, who wanted to go back to his home three hours away. We waited for the bus and they asked me questions about how Americans view Ecuador. Besides the Galapagos Islands I told them the truth: Americans don't know anything about Ecuador. For a second they were worried Ecuador was viewed in a negative light, but I assured them that a lot of other countries are viewed much worse. After the bus picked up the friend I dropped off my girl at her hotel. I kissed her goodbye and gave her my email address but never heard from her again. My wingman had walked home alone many hours ago.

XIII

I took a cab to the bus station, picked a random bus company, arrived many hours later, and took another cab to my new hostel, which was very similar to the old hostel. I lounged around and walked and drank for a few days while taking pictures. Rinse and repeat. The backpacking lifestyle is unglamorous and surprisingly tiring, but it's the cheapest way to see so many cities and places. It's true I see much more than the tourist who flies off to a resort to sit on the beach drinking piña coladas with umbrellas, but at least they get to sleep on real mattresses. Maybe they're smarter for that.

Next up was Riobamba, a city with a party name. It was completely deserted when I arrived on a Sunday—only convenience stores and internet cafes were open for business. I was the lone guest at the 20-bed hostel, disappointed to find a hyper pug in the courtyard instead of the advertised llama I saw on the hostel brochure in Baños. I'd see enough llamas to last me a lifetime soon enough.

My private room had cable TV and I watched *The Two Towers* and *Point Break*. The only reason I came here was to chop up a long bus ride further south, and with nothing to do besides climbing a nearby volcano, I left after just one night. It wasn't a total bust: at last I was alone with my laptop full of porn. The next day I was the most relaxed I'd been on the trip thus far.

XIV

It's dangerous to drink any water before a long bus ride. There are usually no bathrooms and no planned rest stops. If I needed to use the bathroom I'd ask nicely, but there was always the fear the bus will leave my big bag behind. I'm sure it has happened before. If the bus is crowded with people standing in the aisles carrying bags of produce or bundles of children, there is a good chance I'll have to argue for my seat back when I return. If the seat thief is older then I say nothing and stand.

The bus stops for anyone sticking out their hand. Anyone can get off anywhere they please, and that's a reason why I rarely saw taxis outside the cities. The fare catcher would put people in the baggage hold if he could because the more fares he gets the more money he makes. When you combine these hundreds of short stops with the poor roads, you cover 25 miles an hour if you're lucky. A couple hours on a bus doesn't sound like a big deal except when the native highlander sitting next to you hasn't showered in days and her baby is puking his brains out in a small plastic bag because the 30-year-old bus rocks worse than a dinghy.

I felt a rush of relief and excitement whenever I arrived at a new city, which I verified with people sitting next to me by saying the name with a confused look on my face. The excitement faded during the cab ride by downtrodden neighborhoods and finally busted at the dirty hostel that was highly recommended by travelers before me because of its "party atmosphere." It's a dump like the others. The room smells like mold and there are stains on the sheets. The sink doesn't drain.

XV

Colorful colonial buildings were dotted around the main square. Young adults walked around in sharp professional outfits and teenagers caroused in Catholic school uniforms. Mostly absent were the shady characters and dense pollution common in Quito. I arrived in Cuenca.

On my first night I was searching for a restaurant not more than two blocks from my hostel when I saw a blonde girl walking very slowly towards me. I couldn't place her until she called out my name in an English account. It was Zoë, the "boring" girl from Baños. Not only did she just check in to the same hostel as me but she was also in the same dorm room. What a coincidence!

Or maybe not.

This type of thing happened more often than chance would predict. When everyone is using the same Lonely Planet guidebook, a huge continent becomes transformed into a small town, and it was uncomfortably common to run into the same people many countries away.

After she watched me eat tacos we returned to the hostel to have a drink at the bar. I put in that half-assed effort that guaranteed I wasn't going to get anywhere. Like an automaton I just went through the motions, saying stories and jokes that had zero effect without the right energy behind them. I couldn't even make eye contact with her half the time.

When I ordered a second caipirinha, Zoë got water. I don't think it has ever happened in the history of hooking up that the guy kept drinking but the girl abstained. I backed off, giving a green light to other guys in our dorm to put in their attempt later. Before we retreated to our room, a friend of the bartender drew a skillful portrait of us on a napkin with deadly accurate detail of my thick arm hair. His ploy to gain her favor might have worked if he spoke English.

XVI

Café Eucalyptus throws a ladies-drink-free night every Wednesday. I didn't hear a lot of buzz about it so I was concerned it was a scam. Sure enough everyone had to pay a cover and ladies drink for "free" up to four drinks. By 11pm the ratio of guys to girl was even, less favorable than one would expect, and most of the girls were sitting down in tables instead of mingling and flirting. I could finally put to rest the fact that "ladies night" is nothing more than a promotions ploy to get more men into a bar or club.

The girls inside looked much different than ones I'd see on the street. They had fair skin and were decked out in nice clothing with reasonable amounts of make-up that didn't remind me of the '80s. Their hair was soft instead of greasy. Even the guys were noticeably more well off: I saw my first South American Blackberry resting on a table next to a guy's martini. They made it. In Ecuador if you were to guess a person's income based exclusively on their skin color, you wouldn't be far off. This would hold true for the entire continent.

I met up with Zoë and two other guys sharing our dorm, one from Chicago and the other from Germany. Both of them had an obvious crush on Zoë but only the German would make a move before the night was over. I didn't fit into their conversation of Southeast Asia and favorite kinds of rice so I headed downstairs to check out the scene on the dance floor. The women dancing were definitely the prettiest I've seen in Ecuador. I could call upon my six hours of salsa lessons I took before I left, but all the guys on the dance floor were so good that it discouraged me. My feet remained planted.

The hostel crew joined me at the bar and the German made his first move on Zoë. He danced for a minute to the live salsa music and then grabbed her hand. Zoë politely said no. But he persisted.

"Oh come on let's dance," he pleaded.

She stood still with her arms crossed. He then danced alone next to her for the next twenty minutes, pretending like he had a partner with his right arm curled around an imaginary body. It was hard to watch. He tried once more five minutes later, grabbing her hand.

"I just want to try something," he begged.

She shook her head no.

"Oh come on!"

Zoë stood her ground. I felt the pain visible on the German's face because I've been there. Granted I'd get the hint after the first refusal, but he deserves credit for trying. Karl was right about Zoë.

The Richard Feynmann rule states that if you wait long enough in a bar, something will happen. The only downside of the rule is that it may take several hours of wall staring and doodling on napkins until that something happens. At 1am, three hours after I first arrived, I said a few words to a cute girl next to me at the bar. It was my first good opportunity of the night.

She spoke back in English, her eyes lighting up with enthusiasm at this gringo struggling to speak in her language, and she led me to the dance floor. Salsa was still playing and I tried my best to keep the rhythm. She spun me around a couple times even though I think that was my job, but I didn't care as long as we were making progress.

Earlier in the night I had watched as guys who were experts at salsa danced with girls who bowed out after only a couple songs. The problem with salsa is you train so long and hard to make a girl feel good for a few minutes until she pats you on the back and moves on to the next expert. It didn't build attraction as much as I thought it would, so I tried to talk to this girl more than dance.

The guy from Chicago ended up herking and jerking to the salsa music with my girl's friend, his muddy hiking boots shedding chunks of earth onto the dance floor. The beret and cargo pants didn't help his cause or mine. My girl asked if I was his friend with such a tone that she might as well have asked why I was hanging out with him. I threw him under the bus and said I just met him an hour ago at the hostel. I insinuated that he was following me around like a lost puppy dog.

My girl suggested we all go to La Mesa nearby. She told me to wait by the door while she says goodbye to one of her other friends inside. Over five minutes pass and I was still waiting on the sidewalk like an idiot with the guy who I'm sure is the reason why she's taking so long. We left before we looked too desperate. That was the first and last time I danced to salsa music in South America.

Friday arrived. There had to be something going on. After a day of avoiding the guy from Chicago, I overshot my 9pm nap and woke up at midnight, groggy and not in any mood to find girls. Zoë and the other gringos in my room were asleep. I put on my shoes anyway and walked two blocks away to a bar that had nine guys and one girl. I went deeper into town back to La Mesa, which my guidebook described as the "hottest" club in town. It was completely empty. "Come back on Wednesday," the doorman said. He pointed me to another bar down the street that supposedly had girls. Off I went, determined, wondering if I should have made better use of the cute girls I saw during the day.

I found the bar because of the drunk patrons spilling out onto the street. There was no sign and nothing to tell me this was a drinking establishment and not just someone's ramshackle house. Inside was a small, dark room of rough-looking men groping large women. There were pieces of glass and puddles of beer on the floor with broken stools shoved off to the side. It smelled like vomit.

No one paid attention to me. They were too busy drinking, spilling and groping. I couldn't believe this was the best I could find on a Friday night, but at least there were people. I ordered a beer and sat on a working stool next to a man in a black trench coat. He kept spilling beer on a husky girl who either didn't notice or didn't mind. I withdrew my suede Adidas to my stool's foot rest a foot off the ground. I liked that there were no gringos, but the vibe was very odd. In the movies it seemed like the place where the hero's best friend goes in for a drink but then blacks out and wakes up on a torture table or in a bathtub of ice with one of his kidneys gone.

There were other rooms. I walked to the back and found couples staking out corners in various stages of foreplay. One man had his hand inside a girl's skirt and was fingering her with a rapid speed that didn't seem at all pleasurable. I watched for a few seconds. People were hooking up in the main room as well—it seemed like everyone was getting it on except me.

I noticed a thin girl who couldn't have been older than 18 years old. She was probably much younger (there was a bouncer at the door but he wasn't checking identification). She had a tiny top that was nothing more than a triangular piece of cloth and a shiny silver miniskirt that would catch the light at certain angles. I couldn't see her face because it was too dim.

She talked to a clean-shaven man wearing a sport jacket that was way too classy for the bar. Without any warning she flashed him her titties and put his hand on one. She then pulled him away and they vanished to the back room. I quickly chugged what was left of my beer and left, wondering what the going cost of a girl was. Not like I would ever pay for sex, I think, but it would be good to know. I knew my friends from home would ask.

I refused to give up. I hailed a cab and told the driver to take me to a club with girls. I nodded yes when he told me something in Spanish while pointing in a direction due west. We're driving, and driving... and driving, and I notice we're leaving the city proper and entering a suburb. I wondered if it was a trap.

In Tena, I told Henri my biggest fear was getting beaten and robbed from a taxi ride gone bad. His advice was to look at the driver's face before getting in. He argued that you can tell when someone is honest by looking at their face, and while that may be true, it doesn't give you much assurance when you're alone in the middle of the night, watching the city's main cathedral get smaller and smaller until it finally disappears. He told me a story about a near miss in Rio.

"I picked up a cab on the street to go to the bus station. But the driver took me by the same point twice. At first I thought he was trying to scam me for a higher fare, but then we went into a bad part of town I've never seen before. I got right behind his seat and asked where he was taking me."

"You asked him in Portuguese?" I asked.

"No, in French. He kept saying 'bus station' but I knew we weren't going to the bus station. I yelled at him to take me there."

"What did he do?"

"He got nervous and told me to calm down, but I started going crazy. I grabbed the sides of his seat with my hands. I kept saying 'bus station, bus station' while shaking his chair. Eventually I made it to the bus station."

"Could you tell from his face that he was a bad taxi driver?"

"Looking back, yes. He was anxious. I didn't trust my instinct. You can tell."

I have noticed that when someone is trying to scam me there is a tension in their face that comes from a desire to complete the interaction as quickly as possible. This was apparent in the two instances a street vendor sold me a bottle of water that was already opened. I felt something was off when I handed them my money because of their shifty body language and lack of eye contact, but at the time I couldn't consciously explain what was wrong. Very few conmen are good enough to reprogram their body language, and even though studying faces is wholly unscientific, it was worth a shot.

I imagined shaking the chair of the cab driver as we got farther out of the city, but I was reassured by the young man's face and the color photograph of the Virgin Mary. I deemed him honest. I relaxed when I saw signs of family or religion, as if thieves are universally single and atheist. I had him make a U-turn about fifteen minutes into the ride. I gave up. The entire night cost me $11.

Overall, I didn't have a particularly bad time in Cuenca. In the middle of town I found a nice Austrian café that played classical music. I went to a fancy restaurant and ate a steak dinner alone. I bought contact solution from a vision store. I walked around and got lost on cobblestone streets. I ate tasty local food at street stands. I sat inside the colonial churches and watched other people pray. I went to the biggest museum that had a real collection of the infamous shrunken heads, composed of a ancient person's bone, skin, and hair. But none of this inspired me. I imagined the trip would be about something more than doing basic activities, but what that "more" was I could not explain.

The small romantic in me wanted to fall in love in South America. Not necessarily with a specific girl but with a country, city, or way of life that would make me look forward to rolling out of bed and give me that meaning where I can say, "This is it—this is the main reason I'm motivated and pushing through life with all I got." I was losing faith that the answer was in sight-seeing, drinking, or girls. Instead, I felt isolated and uncomfortable, never relating to my surroundings and the young gringos who were in a different place in life than I was. Whatever problem I had at home I brought it here, with the addition of being alone. In the internet café I researched room rentals in Washington D.C., also calculating if I could swing for a used car. It hadn't quite been a month since I left home.

PERU

I

It was a twenty-eight hour bus journey to Trujillo, Peru's most important northern city founded by legendary explorer Francisco Pizarro. He defeated the Incans with a couple dozen soldiers, give or take a few. On the way there I befriended an American couple and a German girl who made the same bus connections I did. While in a nameless northern Peruvian town waiting for a bus to take us further south, the German girl told how she put her bag up on the bus carry-on rack and fell asleep for several hours. I already knew how the story ended. Needless to say her bag was picked of all her cash and credit cards. South America is unforgiving to those who make mistakes.

Another story out of that ride was an Israeli girl whose zipper fleece pocket was picked while she was asleep wearing it. I was thinking what an amateur the German girl was, not keeping the bag on her lap, when minutes later I used an ATM at the bus station and walked away without grabbing my card from the slot. I'm sure the machine ate it back up but it was still a mad rush to find the number of my credit card company and then put a stop on the card.

From the bus station of Trujillo I shared a cab ride with the two Americans to the nearby beach suburb of Huanchaco, a gringo haven with ocean waves that surfers ride for literally minutes. It wasn't all that different from an American beach town with the tourists, souvenir shops selling shell necklaces, hippie surfers, and ice cream parlors. For only 50 cents I took a walk on the pier and sat for an hour watching the sun set below the Pacific Ocean. I took pictures with my new disposable camera.

The Americans went to a campground and I settled for another dorm. A girl from Holland checked in after me and in the typical introductory traveler conversation, I found out it was only her third day in South America.

"Is there anything else to do? I feel guilty for saying this but I'm already bored," she said.

"Welcome to South America!" I said.

She noted how much time at home we spend bullshitting by hanging out with friends, watching TV, messing around the house, or surfing the internet. There are sixteen waking hours in a day and it's a challenge to fill them all with interesting activities when a third of it is not already gobbled up by a job. Like the wise old veteran passing on knowledge to a younger generation, I told her the highlights of Ecuador if she ever decided to travel up north. I don't think she went in that direction because two months later I ran into her on the streets of Córdoba, Argentina, in front of a bar that was recommended in Lonely Planet.

II

Making do without a car had never been easier. The *combis, collectivos*, or *chivas*, depending on what's available and what term locals prefer using, came every five minutes or less to take me from Huanchaco to Trujillo and back again. I flagged them down with my arm and they dropped me off directly in front of my destination as long as it wasn't too far from the main route.

The typical Peruvian transport wasn't much larger than a mini-van. It's the price of a bus, the service of a cab, and the comfort of a go-cart, especially if you sit over what's left of the rear axle. But the system works and is more flexible than bus transport in a Western country. Why send out these huge buses every thirty minutes when you can send out six small vans every five? There was no need to ever know a bus schedule in South America. It can be chaotic to a new rider since you can't just pull up routes on the internet, but as long as you know the name of your location the fare catchers will help get you there.

There wasn't much to do in Huanchaco's off season besides hang out at cafes, which I was becoming an expert at. I could take an afternoon of nothingness and eat up four hours with my little journal and Spanish notecards. After a day sightseeing, where I found portions of the wall Pizarro built to keep out the Incan barbarians, I decided it was time to visit Huaraz, a mountain town due south known for the best hiking in South America. Even though I was experiencing random stomach cramps a few hours before the ten hour bus ride, for lunch I ate spaghetti with tomato sauce and a tall glass of hot drinking chocolate. The pain grew sharper and it didn't help matters that before boarding the bus I grabbed a cold *empanada* with loose ground beef, fried onion, and soft-boiled egg.

Super paranoid now of theft, I stared at people's faces as the bus loaded. I wanted to see if I could spot out potential thieves. It must be the guy I least expect, which ruled out the creepy looking dude with the backwards baseball cap who made direct eye contact with me. It had to be the quiet guy looking out the window. It's obvious he didn't want me to catch a good look. He doesn't want me to see his criminal face.

I thought about what I would do if I saw a theft in progress. Maybe I'd yell the Spanish word for thief at the top of my lungs—*ladron*, or stand up and deeply stare at the thief to intimidate him with my increasing rugged appearance—my long, tangled hair and scruffy beard that hid half my face. I figured I was bound to catch a thief in the act since theft on buses is so common, but turns out it's like trying to catch two endangered pandas mating.

I developed a fascination with the buses and started keeping track of how many hours I spent on them. My interest may be well warranted: 7% of my time in South America was spent riding on a bus. They were my third home away from home.

As the bus made its way through the Andes mountains, my stomach made noises like a hungry grizzly bear coming out of hibernation, and I couldn't stop burping the acidic taste of meals past. I was handling myself pretty well until the third hour of the ride when I felt a sudden urge to evacuate the contents of my bowels. Only six more hours to go.

I wondered if everything would come out of my mouth or anus.

I couldn't use the bathroom on the bus since it was for urine only. I was sure it'd be just liquid ejecting from my body, but the bathroom was filthy with no toilet paper, running water, or soap. It would be impossible to clean myself after. I meditated. I controlled my breathing and thought of all the beautiful Brazilian girls I was going to have sex with. I faded in and out of sleep, clenching my ass cheeks every twenty minutes as waves of contractions swept through my gut. Other people around me slept like babies and had no idea that there was someone on the bus who was in desperate life or death need for a clean toilet. My shirt was soaked in sweat from the straining and I clenched my jaw every time my stomach announced its intentions to get rid of the poison it was swimming in. Stabbing pains ripped through my torso but there was nothing I could do but hold out. I did not want to shit myself.

I don't know how my pants weren't soiled by the time the bus pulled into the terminal early in the morning. Perhaps I underestimate my strength. Still breathing carefully, I grabbed my bag and dodged a dozen people trying to steer me into their guesthouse. I ran into the American couple who rode in on a different bus line but could only give off a terse hello. I hailed a cab for the biggest hostel in town and once I dropped my bag in my new room I ran to the bathroom and pulled my pants down. Before my skin touched the toilet seat my ass erupted like the Tungurahua volcano. For twenty continuous seconds I spewed a violent stream of partially digested tomato sauce, chocolate, ground beef, and egg. The matter splashed everywhere, coating the toilet bowl and my butt cheeks with a thick, drippy paste.

I sat there and grinned for five minutes, crouched on the toilet seat with my head resting on my lap. I have never been so relieved in my life. Everything was okay. The relief quickly turned to pity for the cleaning lady that had to deal with my shit. I had to take a shower to properly clean myself of the mess. Thankfully it was still early so no one else knew it was me that ruined the bathroom.

III

I'm not sure why I went to Huaraz when I don't hike. Everyone else had hiking boots, revolutionary hiking pants, North Face coats, synthetic gloves and hats, and ice picks I've only seen in Mount Everest documentaries. The most hardcore of hikers came to South America specifically for the mountains around Huaraz and would climb as many peaks as the weather and their bodies would allow. At the bare minimum, travelers would take a three or four day guided hike that would send them over worn paths passing pristine streams and fresh snow. You'd almost be considered a moron if you came to Huaraz without experiencing one of these hikes, but I did have a good excuse: I was sick. I spent my first day in bed with a fever and body aches. My only meal was two bananas and stale sweet bread I bought from a bodega two blocks away.

In my dorm was a good-looking English guy named George who I met in Quito. He had a baby spare tire he'd smack and bounce when changing. Unless you get sick and shit your guts out over an extended period of time, a scenario I was playing out, the calories lost from carrying 40-pound backpacks is compensated by local cuisine dripping with vegetable oil. The concept of baking anything but breads and cakes hasn't fully made its way down to South America yet.

George recognized me while I laid under the sheets. He sat down in the bed opposite mine to see how my trip was going. Our routes were almost identical so it was a surprise it took us so long to run into each other again. I wanted to see how our experiences compared when it came to girls.

"Did you get lucky so far?" I asked.

"No not yet. A couple times I was close but no full shag."

"Yeah me neither." I was pleased at his answer.

"Last week there was a group of school girls that kept staring at me on a bus ride to a smaller town. One of them grabbed my hand once we got off and led me to some woods. She had a small bottle of alcohol and we made out but she seemed too young so I couldn't go through with it."

"That sort of thing never happens to me. I got with just one Ecuadorian girl so far but had no place to take her. The girls in Ecuador were hit or miss."

"Yeah their faces are rough, but there's always the Australian girls in the hostels! South America is not a good place to come if you want to get laid."

"Why not?"

"The girls come here to see nature or volunteer to help the poor. They don't come to party on beaches every night. For that you need to go to Southeast Asia. Every girl goes there to hook up. I shagged so many girls there." His eyes rolled up, reliving at least one of the encounters. "There's a lot of hot Swedish girls who go there."

"I see. I feel like there is a pressure to get my first lay out of the way. It's been about a month."

"Yeah me too. It's not a big deal though."

In George I saw a potential wingman and wondered if traveling alone became unnecessary after a while. Is there a point of diminishing returns in "finding yourself" through travel where it's then better to hang it up and have some laughs with a buddy instead? I felt better after taking a couple Advil and played a game of Risk with George and a guy from Wales. George acted like he didn't know the rules but killed us both and conquered the world.

The next day started well. My stomach pains, fever, and body aches were gone. I eased myself into normal food by eating a tuna and avocado sandwich for lunch at a café run by an American who married a Peruvian woman. Later I went to dinner with George and a new guy named Keane, a lanky Irishman with graying hair and a beard that had white leopard spots. His gray said 30s but he was actually younger than me. He came from the opposite direction so George and I listened to him closely as he described all the other countries we were headed to, with a focus on the girls. He said Buenos Aires in Argentina had the best looking girls but Cuzco in Peru had the easiest.

"The girls of Cuzco love gringos. If you're white then you're getting laid," he said. "All you have to do is go to this club called Mama Africa's and wait by the bar until a girl approaches you. You'll be making out within a few minutes. It's as simple as that."

"Where is Mama Africa's?" I asked, ready to take notes. I always carried pen and paper with me.

"It's off the main square, but everyone knows where it is." Our pasta dishes came. I got the pasta with green pesto sauce and a side order of french fries. "There's a lot of hotels where you can take the girls. Both of you will get laid there. Everyone does."

Everyone? How could he make that assertion without even knowing us? It seemed too good to be true. Keane didn't have model looks so his success in Cuzco couldn't be explained by his appearance. He spoke less Spanish than I did so language couldn't have been a factor either. And I'd soon find it wasn't his dancing. He didn't seem like an exaggerator though—he didn't even brag about his Paraguayan, Argentine, and Chilean flags that I had to squeeze out of him. Therefore it was safe to accept his conclusions about Cuzco as fact. I was going to get laid in Cuzco.

After George ditched early to prepare for a four-day trek through the mountains, Keane and I went to El Tambu, a club whose cavernous space was filled with only two dozen people. Large, fake trees rose from the floors to the ceiling and made the space feel like a Japanese guest house. I didn't mind the club at all because I was used to thin nightlife crowds in Ecuador, but for Keane it was shit because he started his trip in Buenos Aires, which arguably has the best nightlife on the continent. Every time he looked at the empty dance floor he just shook his head. We ignored a group of four Peruvian women who were staring and moving closer to us. They were too old.

In the middle of our pitcher of sangria, Keane spotted a smart-looking native having drinks ten feet away with another man. I pointed out that she was looking in our direction and Keane agreed. He gave her a goofy wave and a come-hither with his right index finger. I've never tried that before but with my massive pick-up experience I knew that it wasn't going to work. It worked.

Right away the two joined our table and we all exchanged introductions. The ensuring conversation of bad English and bad Spanish was difficult due to the salsa and reggaeton music blasting through the speakers. I was reluctant when the girl, who was from Lima, pulled me to the dance floor while Keane was talking to the guy friend. This was Keane's girl and I didn't want him to think I was trying to steal her away. It wasn't so much that I felt loyalty for Keane, who I only knew for three hours, but a respect for a guy who put in the hardest part of getting with a girl—the approach. If a guy does the approach, he should get unlimited, uninterrupted time with the girl of his choice in that group. It's only fair.

I danced with her for a couple songs, making sure to keep my hands off her slim body, then sat back down to talk to her friend. He was a tour guide and tried to sell me an excursion through the mountains. I told him I was a coffee shop guy and for him that was a suitable answer. Then I looked over and saw Keane making out with the Limeña. Not more than twenty minutes had passed since he waved her over, and she didn't speak a word of English. They communicated more by hand motions than anything else.

The rules of the game seemed different. From watching Keane and others in Ecuador and Peru, aggressiveness, light skin color, and height are valued far more than style, humor, wit, and dancing ability. Make-outs come lightning fast if the girl likes you and she may very well attack first if you wait too long. Sitting back and looking cool can sometimes work if you have the right gringo look, but with so many aggressive natives and drunk horny gringos floating around, if you snooze then you will most likely lose. Those who approach are rewarded more than those who don't. Back home you can stare at a girl for thirty minutes before you do anything and still get a favorable result. Here you have three minutes.

The pesto sauce and fries didn't agree with my stomach and I had to return to the hostel bathroom. I should have stayed on the bread and banana diet a little longer. Keane was all set with the Limeña so I bowed out and returned to the hostel a half-mile away. I don't know why I didn't grab a cab—there was no reason to take an unnecessary risk in a sketchy area when the ride costs only two dollars. At the hostel I made love with the toilet.

The next morning I emitted a constant flow of noxious gas so foul that the air trapped under my blanket was more offensive than a Port-O-Potty on the Fourth of July. I dirtied the bowl once more after waking up to the worst dream I've ever had in my life.

I was walking through a neighborhood that looked very similar to my father's. The rows of townhouses were laid on the land in the exact same manner and even the speed bumps were placed in identical spots. Because I believed the dream was taking place in the present, while still traveling through South America, I concluded that it couldn't have possibly been my dad's neighborhood. It felt different, quieter.

I took out my camera to snap a few photos so I could show my dad when I returned home. He'd be interested to see the South American version of his neighborhood. I walked in the direction of where his house would be and when it was within sight I dropped a bottle of water. It rolled against gravity up the hill towards the house, as if someone was pulling it on a string. But it looked more and more like his house as I got closer. On the steps there were even the potted plants he'd set aside during the warmer months.

The bottle stopped in a neighbor's yard. When I reached the bottle and bent over to pick it up, I heard my mom's voice calling my name. At that instant I realized that I was in the future and not in South America after all. This really was my dad's neighborhood.

It was strange my mom was there since they divorced when I was very young. I thought about hiding because I didn't want her to see the past me and disturb some space-time continuum (I've seen *Back To The Future* too many times as a kid), but it was too late—she was only a couple feet away. Her hair was shorter and entirely silver, no longer dark brown like mine. I walked up to her and she said, "I really missed you." The only reason she would miss me is if she hadn't seen me in a while.

"Mom, did I die?" I asked. She looked in my eyes and started crying without saying a word. We hugged and I put my head down on her shoulder. I woke up with tears streaming down my face and for a while I just stared at the bottom of the mattress above me.

The dream shook me. This was my brain's way of punishing me for not taking the cab. For the duration of the trip whenever I was about to take an unnecessary risk the dream would pop in my head. It reminded me that my mortality, as fragile as it may be, was mostly in my hands.

My mom is the superstitious type who can read fortunes on the random patterns left by a finished cup of Turkish coffee. She also had a dream analysis reference guide that was known in the house as the

"Dream Book." It was older than me and in such a state of decay that she preserved it in a plastic bag in the fruit compartment of the refrigerator. If I told her I dreamed of my death she would demand I come home immediately. I'm pretty sure she'd even offer to buy the plane ticket.

IV

I ran into Keane inside the common area where George defeated me at Risk a couple nights before. "So how did the night end up?" I asked.

"It was just so weird."

"Why?"

"You know the guy she was with?"

"Yeah the tour guide."

"Well he treated her like a prostitute."

"She's a prostitute?!" To make him feel better I was getting ready to tell him the story of the Brazilian on Margarita Island.

"No no! She was getting horny after you left, so I asked her where she was staying. It was with her guy friend. I couldn't bring her back to the dorm obviously, but the guy said I can go back with them at his place and hang out. We left the club and he's telling her things in Spanish that didn't sound quite right. Then I realized we're walking back to the hostel. He said, 'You want to sleep with my friend? You and your friend go on trek with me.'"

"Whoa."

"Yeah, yeah, I was shocked. See, she doesn't understand a word of English and is asking what is going on because she can tell in my face I don't like what I'm hearing. He kept telling her '*Negociación negociación*,' to make it seem I was bargaining for a trek. I didn't know how to confront her in Spanish about what he was doing, so when we got to the hostel I just said goodbye to them."

"That's the worst cockblock story I've ever heard."

"Cock... block? What's that?"

"Oh, umm, it's when someone literally blocks your cock from a girl.

They interfere with your chances of getting with her. You don't have that word in Ireland?"

"I've never heard it before."

V

I went back to a bread, jelly, and bananas diet. My diarrhea and sulfur gas subsided enough to go out at night with Keane back to El Tambu. It was packed with ten times as many people. I decided not to drink in case it was the alcohol that was the cause of my most recent eruptions.

The cutest girl in the bar was dancing with a gringo wearing emo glasses while Keane and I hung out on the fringe of the dance floor saying hello to girls who walked by. I spotted what was arguably the second cutest girl in the club in a circle with her friends. Keane pushed me to go dance with her but before I could strategize a good approach (i.e. while I was hesitating), she walked up to me and grabbed my hand. I've had girls ask me the time or something simple, but never had one initiate physical contact with me first. I danced with her for a few songs, thinking I was guaranteed action since she made such a bold first move, but she never let me get too close, backing off every time I moved in just a little. I was confused by her intentions.

A different girl that Keane kissed in Huaraz before I arrived confronted him about making out with the Limeña the previous night. She called him a "ladies man." Apparently she watched him from the shadows of El Tambu's fake trees. Keane gave off an uncomfortable smile and changed the subject. Two hours later he took her to a hotel room and fucked her. I was already sleeping at the hostel when it happened.

Even on a plain bread diet, I couldn't stop the cramps, rumbling, gas, and hideous solids. But I kept going out, and I'm not sure why, especially since I wasn't crazy about the girls. The next night Keane and I wandered out and waved to three girls passing us on the street a block away from the hostel. To my surprise they stopped and engaged us in light conversation. It turns out one of them was the second cutest girl who approached me on the dance floor the night before. She was slightly insulted I didn't recognize her, but without makeup and clubbing clothes she looked like a different person. We convinced them to come out with us.

We went to the top floor of a bar that had a bachelorette party with gringos and natives alike getting trashed. The handful of gringos knew everyone including the bar staff, suggesting that they lived and worked in Huaraz, maybe as guides. Who eventually walked in but Keane's Limeña from two nights prior, alone, without her third-rate pimp. She joined us and very soon Keane was giving me a *what the fuck do I do* look. The Limeña was obviously into him but the friend of my dance partner was a little cuter and giving him plenty of attention. My girl was also giving me love, sitting next to me and rubbing my leg on an old but comfortable couch. She wasn't drinking because of a stomach problem, like most everyone else in Huaraz if the hostel's dirty toilet bowls were any sign.

I gradually moved in closer, setting things up for a kiss, but she kept withdrawing. I got the hint and slowly distanced myself from her. When I declined her invitation to salsa dance she interpreted my refusal as anger. For the next hour she hounded me about "What's wrong?" and what I was thinking about, until I finally got annoyed on the walk over to the next club.

"Can you shut up for just one minute?" I said.

She stopped walking. I turned around and she looked like she was about to cry. My cotton jumper was useless against the night cold and I didn't want to stop moving. It was mild during the day, but once the sun went down I jealousy stared at the heavy coats other gringos brought with them. When you live at sea level your entire life you don't think about the huge effect altitude has on temperature. She had to know I was freezing.

"If you don't tell me what you are thinking, I'm going to leave!" she said.

Without saying a word I raised my eyebrows and started walking again. Her friends had to console her, which made me look like the big jerk. Keane caught up to me.

"What happened?"

"Man she's just acting dumb. She doesn't want to hook up or whatever, that's fine, but she keeps hounding me like we're in a relationship. I'm cold and I want to go somewhere else."

"It's okay, you know how women are. Just relax."

"I am relaxed!"

I wasn't relaxed. I was ill, trying to mount a girl who was also ill. She obviously cared or else she wouldn't put so much emotional energy trying to solve whatever problem she perceived us as having. At any other time I might have indulged her games with a little more humor.

We all ended up in another bar but my stomach was in too much pain. I sat quietly on a couch. The girls left, leaving just me, Keane, and the Limeña, who he decided to go for after all. I took a taxi back to the hostel and Keane ended up visiting the same hotel for the second night in a row.

He returned at 11am the next day. We went to a café to talk about his newest conquest over cups of tea. It was our last day together so I let him know how much I enjoyed his company and watching him work in the nightclub. The guy pushing love triangles in Peru is one I would have never expected. He sort of tries but not really. He games but it's hard to notice. He smiles at girls he likes and dances like a happy elephant without a care in the world. He has a warm vibe with no seeming intent and girls just get drawn into it. If I was a girl, I'd pick Keane over myself.

We finally got around to talking about our jobs. Turns out we both studied science and worked with microbial cells. He had about as much enthusiasm for the little monsters as I had. Eventually, I asked him if he misses home.

"Not really, it's only been a month," he said. "Another month and I'll be back at work."

"That's how long it has been for me but I miss it. Maybe because I have so much more time to go?"

"Could be, or maybe you're just homesick. It will get easier as you go on."

"Maybe."

"I have a friend who traveled for years. He returned home and on the second night he confessed his depression to me. He said, 'I've been away for three years but nothing has changed. The same people go to the same pubs.'"

I took a sip of my coca leaf tea, which was supposed to settle my stomach. "True but I may be missing out on good times with those friends in those pubs."

Keane tilted his head and looked at me. I knew he was about to say something important. "Roosh, you know exactly what is happening there. You're not missing a thing."

It was true. I did know what was happening. I read the emails. My friends were going to the same bars and hitting on the same girls. Besides the random one-night stand, nights ended the same way, with a phone number that goes nowhere most of the time. The single friends were still single, the ones in relationships were still in their relationships. Maybe I missed the routine and the comfort more than I wanted to admit. Here my stomach was in shambles, I was having trouble with the girls, and I was dreaming of my death. And I had eleven more countries to go.

Later that night I said goodbye to Keane. I'm sure if we lived in the same town we'd become best friends and grow and learn from each other, but such is the nature of travel. The most interesting person I may meet is short on time and has other places to visit.

VI

With a population of nearly eight million, Lima is the largest city I've been to, one that continues to expand like a puddle in the rain. On the long bus ride from Huaraz it took almost an hour to get from the suburbs to the center without any traffic. The city's size would have been even more impressive had it not been for the fall fog that concealed the skyline—and the shantytowns.

The mood of the fog matched the people with the plain faces, a result of the hard lifestyle that has established itself in urban South America. The street children, the beggars, and the crumbling infrastructure are always the same. Only shapes and colors are different. Been to one large South American city, been to them all.

In the posh neighborhood of Miraflores I checked into my hostel and walked through the common area to find five guys watching rugby. I walked back downstairs and read the activity board that described Lima's best sights, like the cathedral that housed Pizarro's coffin. There I caught an olive-skinned girl glancing at me. I let out a closed-mouth smile that encouraged her to ask me where I was from.

"The States. You?"

"Brazil."

She and her friends were in the process of checking out but we chatted anyway. The tall one talked the most and seemed most sure of herself; the middle one, who was a little darker with short hair, chimed in every now and then with fast spoken sentences; and the short one, the whitest of the three, talked the least because she was still busy stuffing things into her bag. They could all be easily mistaken for being Middle Eastern, perhaps Israeli. We talked for no more than five minutes and at the end when they had to leave I suggested we exchange emails. They lived in Rio and I planned on getting there eventually.

I went back into my fourteen bed dorm feeling a little surge of confidence. In walked two girls, one morbidly obese but the other incredibly cute. I took a line from the Brazilian girl playbook and asked the cute girl where she was from. "Spain." It's funny, I told her, that while I was in Spain I met people from all over Europe except Spain. I had a light conversation with her as much as the distance between our top bunks would allow. Before I went to sleep I mentally prepared for the next day when I'd endure the surely cockblocking friend to seduce the cute Spaniard.

Sleeping in a room with up to a dozen other people is something you get used to but never enjoy. If you're a light sleeper you need earplugs to get more than a couple hours of continuous sleep due to the constant, noisy traffic of people coming and going throughout the night and early morning. If alcohol happened to be involved they'll stumble in the darkness and step on your pack or knock down your drying towel from its hook to soak up grime on the floor. In the morning they have nightlife recaps loud enough for the neighboring room. If I politely ask them to lower their voice it takes on average two minutes until they're louder than before. Oblivious or passive aggressive? I couldn't decide. If travelers are more independent than the average person then they must also be the least empathetic.

Many gringos preferred to walk barefoot inside the hostels. Their exposed black feet would be visible from the ends of the short beds while sleeping under winter blankets that never get washed. Bedbugs stay in business and see the world by traveling in rank backpacks. The moldy cheese funk coming out of hiking boots can be smelled from several feet away. Every night is an excuse to get drunk and act obnoxious. The scene gets old after a couple weeks and I craved privacy and isolation. The only time I would get it was around one o'clock in the afternoon when everyone was off sightseeing and the room was clean thanks to the maid service. I wanted to be alone in my home, but entertained with company outside it.

If I'm in a room with at least four other people, it's a guarantee there will be at least one person who talks in their sleep, usually unintelligible strings of five or six words including names like Margo and John. But every now and then someone has a painful dream and talks throughout, with no's and pleases and painful moans. And that person gets up and goes on about their day not knowing someone saw a secret side of them reserved for someone close. Sleep gives away some, displaying vulnerabilities they didn't know they had, no matter how tough their exterior may be. I wonder what I give away in my sleep.

When I woke up in the morning the Spanish girls were gone. They checked out. My disappointment quickly evaporated with the discovery of a Starbucks. Familiar and comfortable. It had a price menu that was strangely just as expensive as what I saw in America, but it was crowded anyway with the best and brightest of the Peruvian middle and upper class. A security guard was posted by the door at all times and assisted with cleaning up the tables and opening the door.

Four teenagers with metal braces sat next to me on my first visit. One of them blatantly stared at me, but not the type of stare where eye contact is broken after a second or two—she kept at it until I wimped out and looked away. They watched my laptop while I was in the bathroom and when I came back I asked them if they spoke English.

The one with the gigantic fake boobs spoke very good English and acted as a translator for the others. Before I left fifteen minutes later they invited me to the starer's birthday party, which I imagined would be packed with young girls getting drunk after the parents went to bed. But it wasn't for another two weeks, much too long to spend in Lima. I took a picture of them with my disposable camera for my friends.

My stomach calmed down and I was more determined than ever to find fruitful nightlife. I went out alone to the unfortunately named Bartini lounge. It had red walls, lights, and chairs, and reminded me of generic lounges back home that used plush seating and electronic music as an excuse to charge over $10 for cocktails. I stared at my beer bottle until I chatted up two Canadian guys, joking about the minor differences between Americans and Canadians.

My temporary wingmen got me into a talkative state that helped me approach two pretty girls next to us with a simple *hola*. They ignored me. Getting rejected by pretty girls in a foreign country felt the same as getting rejected by pretty girls in my own country—not exceptionally pleasant, but not a big deal either.

The Canadian guys left and I was back to beer bottle staring, adding a slight head bob to match the beat of the music. I was standing by the bar when I heard a *POP POP*. My body jumped and I looked towards the front door. It sounded like it came from outside. No one else seemed to care so I figured it was nothing, maybe firecrackers. Then I saw one of the bouncers brace himself against the door like someone was trying to come in. A slim man in a suit jacket right behind him reached towards his hip and pulled out a dull black object, yanking back on the top with his other hand. It was a gun.

For two seconds I stood there, dumbstruck, staring at the door and the man pointing the gun straight up in the air, leaning against the big bouncer, holding up the door. When it hit me that I was in danger I got down along with the crowd and shuffled to the back of the club. I was quickly surrounded by a ring of bodies. Selfishly, I felt assured that if there was a shootout I'd be protected. The music kept playing, probably because the DJ was high and didn't notice what was going on. I crouched in my protective ring for no more than a minute when people gradually stood up and began talking about what just happened.

The adrenaline was flowing and my hands were shaking. I was told that this type of thing is rare in Miraflores, but you couldn't tell it from the crowd, who so easily resumed smoking, drinking, flirting, and laughing. While they made jokes about it, I was worried the shooter would return to finish the job. No longer in the mood hit on girls or drink, I waited for the coast to clear before I grabbed a taxi back to the hostel.

VII

A thin, hyperactive Chilean guy checked into my dorm room. He was a photographer who came to Lima to record a music festival happening during the weekend. He had an interesting way of combining bad English with descriptive body language, like holding an imaginary spoon and making a shoveling motion towards his mouth when asking people to eat with him. If he wanted to go dancing he'd swing his arms back and forth as if he was taking a leisurely jog.

Within ten minutes of meeting he showed off his rather large bag of cocaine and offered me some. I declined, but the only other person in my room, a bearded Israeli guy who disappeared at night to gamble at nearby casinos, got out a crisp $100 bill, his most recent winnings. He rolled up the bill while bragging about how his supreme poker ability was funding his worldwide travels.

The Chilean locked the door and they both took turns doing bumps off a small abandoned book. I observed them to see if their behavior would change, but other than glassy eyes and a lot of sniffing, there wasn't much difference. Many gringos talked of using cocaine but this was the only time I witnessed its consumption.

Later that night I was about to go alone to El Dragon when I noticed a plump Australian guy in the room looking at me from his bed, obviously bored. I asked him if he wanted to come and he did. It was his first night in South America. My traveler duty was to warn him of the lurking dangers on the cab ride over to the club.

"First thing, don't ever walk into a crowd. That's pickpocket central. I got pickpocketed on my third day here."

"Well I keep my wallet in my front pocket," he said.

"Yeah well..." I paused for added effect. "I did too."

"Oh."

I already saved his ass.

"And on the bus never put your bag on the rack above you. It will definitely get stolen."

"Wouldn't I notice if someone grabbed it?"

"Not while you're sleeping. The bus rides are too long and dull—you'll fall asleep. On a bus I was on from Ecuador to Peru, one German girl got all her money stolen when she put her bag on the rack. And another girl got her jacket pockets picked *while* she was wearing it. Put your bag on your lap with your arms across it. I heard a story about a guy who strapped his bag to himself, but while he was asleep they cut the straps with knives and slid the bag off."

"That's crazy."

"I know. The baggage compartment underneath the bus is pretty safe though. I haven't heard anyone getting their big bag stolen there. Oh, with cabs always get the fare before you get in. If they have a meter and don't turn it on, point to it and say *"Metro, metro."* When a taxi driver tells you the inflated quote, divide it by two and offer that. Tell him that's how much you spent the night before, even if it's a lie. You'll get a price somewhere in between. There are so many cabs in cities like Lima that any price you counter with is believable. Cab drivers though are the one group that will always try to rip you off—always. If there's a meter you're automatically getting the scenic route. And then you try to pay with a big bill and he cries that he doesn't have change and tries to pocket the whole thing. Yet if you tell him you'll get change from a store nearby he suddenly has small bills."

I looked up and saw a gas station we already passed. Our cab driver was hopelessly lost. Since the fare was set I didn't think this was a scenic route scam, and his weathered, honest face didn't seem like one that would make a turn into a dark alley. Plus he had a picture of the Virgin Mary above the radio. Still, while I was telling this fresh Australian arrival how to stay safe here we were going in circles through questionable neighborhoods and stopping random people for directions.

It turned out the club was one of those that didn't have an obvious sign on its door. We passed it three times before we noticed a velvet rope and small crowd lingering outside.

Once inside, El Dragon reminded me of another house club with a dragon in its name: Dragonfly in Washington D.C. It shut down right before I left, eventually replaced by an "exclusive" club that filled with patrons eager to pay $350 for a bottle of liquor they could buy for $30 at the store. That was the trend, anyway. Both featured slightly yuppie crowds dancing underneath dim lighting to European house and popular American music. Bartenders were unusually attractive.

With the Australian I got in a nice little groove, flirting here and there with the girls, smiling and laughing with them, more relaxed and genuine. More Keane-like. Within half an hour a thick Peruvian girl stuck on me like glue and made it clear she wanted to take me home, but there was no point in that—the club was filling with beautiful girls who I hadn't talked to yet. Who knows what stunner I'll get now if I keep this up!

I danced with girls I couldn't understand and talked with girls I could, until the clock struck five and the bouncers kicked us out. We had no girls. I felt a tinge of regret that I passed on the sure thing, even though at the time it seemed like the right decision.

The next day the beast inside my stomach awoke and I had to be within ten feet of a toilet at all times. I went back to a bread and jelly diet. For three days the only other food I got calories from was beer. My stomach was putting out two types of noises: one a deep rumbling that coincided with bursts of pain and the other a high-pitched growl when it was emptied of bread and jelly sandwiches and wanted more. I could handle the pain, but the horrible, tiring trips to the bathroom and offensive gas wore me down. The gas would come no matter how empty I'd leave my stomach. I was a one man propane tank refilling center, open twenty-four hours a day. Conversations with people were stressful endeavors where I would hold the gas until the coast was clear. I'd excuse myself to the bathroom and lean my arm on the wall, wondering when it would stop.

VIII

I forced myself to go out alone on a Friday night to Gotica, a club the Israeli recommended from a previous stay, before he was addicted to gambling. He said, "The only problem with Gotica is you will get a girl and then wonder if you can do better." I concluded it'd be better if I went out. Otherwise I'd just feel sorry for myself in front of a computer looking at the latest batch of pictures from friends.

I got there at 11:30 and it was dead. It didn't have a goth theme like I expected. Instead it was a generic club I'd been to hundreds of times before. It had the VIP area a few steps above where the commoners party. It had the large island bar, stocked with beer bottles and cute female bartenders. It had the dance floor illuminated with programmable lights, surrounded by smaller bars dotted around the periphery. The only difference between Gotica and an American club was that the bouncers had guns instead of mini-flashlights.

I sat at the big bar. By my second beer, a girl to my right waved me over after her two friends got up to use the bathroom. She had a slim body and a look that suggested she was a quarter-Asian, a feature common with many Peruvians. Compliant, but with a three second delay so I didn't seem too eager, I moved a couple chairs over to sit next to her.

She was an educated Limeña, had a good 9-5 job, and spoke fluent English. We hit the dance floor after some basic chat. After a song she accused me of having practiced my moves alone at home. I didn't know if she said that because I was good or because it seemed like I was trying too hard. Nevertheless, we kissed not long after that and couldn't keep our hands off each other for the next three hours. I didn't notice when someone stole my disposable camera out of the jumper pocket I hung on a chair.

"Who steals a disposable camera?" I asked her.

"The guy probably didn't even look at it. He put his hand in your pocket, felt something big, then took it quickly and walked away."

Every twenty minutes, when I could no longer withstand the air pressure building inside my gut, I excused myself to the bathroom to release a cloud of gas and reset the clock. It was plausible enough that I had to urinate from the beer, so to her I was a completely healthy American man, not someone who was melting from the inside.

Other girls were gawking at me and I wondered if I could do better, just like the Israeli told me, but I was satisfied. I actually liked her and all my jokes made her laugh, even lame ones that were tired from overuse.

She kept asking me if I was having a good time. She offered to buy me drinks and would throw in little bits of advice on how to be safe in her country, as if she sincerely cared about my safety and well-being. And she felt familiar, a quality I began to see as a source of happiness while on the road. She looked and felt just like a girl I'd date back home. Well, almost—she'd sing along to most of the songs in Spanish and I couldn't understand what she was saying to her friends. Plus her kissing style was rougher. She'd grasp my lips with her teeth and not let go, like a lion clamping down on the neck of a zebra. The feeling of familiarity mixed with the raw, dangerous backdrop to made holding her incredibly surreal. The passion level so high that by the time the club closed I was about to burst. *That* was definitely still working.

I walked out with her, arm in arm, onto the street. There were only a few taxis on the road. She lived with her parents like 99% of all other single girls on the continent, and had to wake up in three hours for work. I didn't make a strong effort to continue the night because I didn't mind seeing her again to deepen what we had. It'd be worth it.

We agreed to meet at the Starbucks the following night at 8PM. Before I put her in a cab we embraced and she said, "I love you." Those were her exact words, and I couldn't recall the last time I heard them from someone besides my parents. I knew she was drunk and didn't really mean it, that she just got caught up a nice moment where saying it felt right, but it told me this had the potential to become something serious.

IX

It was 8:30PM and she hadn't shown up. Maybe she went to a

different Starbucks? Impossible. Lima has only one Starbucks. She never came.

It didn't make any sense. My head spun in circles trying to think of a reason why she would stand me up like that. But I would never know for certain. She was stupid for not showing up. She could get fucked for all I care. She's not even worth thinking about. I'll go back to the same club and get a better girl who won't waste my time. There were plenty of girls eyeing me while I was with her. Now it was their chance.

I returned to Gotica at midnight and it was absolutely mobbed—a total flip from the previous night. I started pounding beers and psyched myself up by visualizing the hotter girl I was going to get with. I forced myself to approach through curses and put-downs since being alone in a huge club is the antithesis to natural fun, but it wouldn't be my night. Girls averted eye contact with me. They spoke no English and didn't even try to humor me by speaking slowly. There was no shortage of stunning beauties, but they were hanging out in their big groups, rejecting guys left and right, me included. They brushed me off like I was nothing. I was so invisible that for a time I thought my blue t-shirt wasn't stylish enough.

After three hours, a ten minute conversation was my only success. Girls probably thought I was the creepy gringo in the club who didn't have any friends, stinking up the place with his atrocious stomach problem. I went back to the hostel and jerked off on the toilet bowl.

X

The Cruz del Sur bus line makes me never want to fly coach again. They play American movies, serve hot meals, lay out clean pillows, have seats that recline almost horizontal, and provide bingo games with chances to win free bus tickets. They also videotape you as you board with a Betamax camcorder, for what I'm guessing is identification purposes in case the bus gets attacked by kidnappers.

As comfortable as the bus was, it still wasn't easy to deal with twenty-two hours through sharp turns and steep drops that crisscrossed the Andes and tossed my stomach like a Caesar salad. While ill, every bus ride was becoming an unwelcome feat of bodily strength where I tested the limits of how much I could tense my body and hold in what wanted to come out. How many hours would I have to fight this time? Would I puke in a bag like the person sitting near me?

I balanced the ride to Cuzco with meditation, watching movies, and wondering what the poor sap next to me thought of the toxic brew entering his nose. Maybe he thought it was the person in front of us. I still rather be him, experiencing the goods instead of being the factory that produces them.

The elevation made for a sleepless night—temperatures plunged below freezing and frost coated the windows. I drew my name in it while cursing my lack of preparedness. Others brought blankets in addition to their coats, and looked so peaceful and comfortable as they slept. I finally snoozed when the sun returned and melted the frost.

The first thing I did when I checked in to my hostel was ask for a doctor. They sent for Zura, a woman in her early thirties with a long, black ponytail. She had a very slight Asian hint to her appearance like the girl who stood me up in Lima. She smiled while thinking and paused before each sentence, probably to translate words from Spanish to English. That was the slowest way to speak a language, I learned. The goal was to think in the new language instead of adding the arduous step of translation which slows everything down. Easier said than done.

I laid on my hostel bed examination table where she checked my pulse, blood pressure, and oxygen levels, noting that my 90% reading is excellent for this altitude (she was born in Cuzco and has 92%). She tapped my stomach and asked about my symptoms.

"Stomach pain, very bad gas, and loose, watery stools," I said. "Pretty much any food I eat makes it worse."

"How long have you had this?"

"About two weeks."

She came up with an instant diagnosis: giardia, a nasty parasite common in South America that infects the small intestine. The human body is capable of clearing out the infection on its own but sometimes not for months. "It was a smart decision you sought treatment," she said. The infection meant I ate a meal prepared after someone wiped his or her ass without washing up. Or I ate raw vegetables rinsed with water from the tap, maybe lettuce or tomato on a cheeseburger.

Zura gave me a three day course of anti-parasitic medicine and I became hopeful my stomach would return to normal. Afterwards I went to the post office to see if my new digital camera arrived. When I was in Cuenca I instructed my sister to ship it to Cuzco using the *poste restante* system. It was there. This would be a new beginning. The medicine would cure me and with the camera I could go back to capturing important moments. In the hostel I ran into Karl the Dutchman and he told me he got his first notch from a Canadian girl staying in his dorm. He said she just kissed him while they danced at a club. Good for him.

All my life I had taken my health for granted. With my stomach, things quickly changed. The illness brought out the worst in me, sapping my strength, my spunk. My motivation was drained. I looked around to other healthy gringos and wondered why I fell and they didn't. I would never wish my problems on anyone, but why me? Even though I was in Cuzco, an archaeological haven, I didn't care much for exploration. I just laid like a lump in my bed waiting for the medicine to kick in, eager to ditch the bread and jelly always present by my bedside. I couldn't wait to eat ice cream and hot meals with multiple side orders and spices and thick creamy sauces and hunks of meat once again.

Before coming to South America I questioned if I should visit Machu Picchu or not due to its hyper-touristic nature, but now I was prepared to skip it. The only reason I dragged myself to the train station to buy a ticket for Aguas Caliente, the town nearest Machu Picchu, was because the young people in my hostel said I'd be *stupid* to come to Cuzco and not see the greatest sight in the country—even the continent! They really did use that word. I concluded that they were correct.

I took a cab to the tourist train station and got a number and waited patiently to be called like I was at a Department of Motor Vehicles. There were tourists ranging from teenagers to the cane-wielding elderly. At least five continents of the world were represented. I felt as if I was getting ready to see a summer blockbuster that was targeted to anyone with a pulse.

I considered walking out because I knew Machu Picchu was going to be the worst that mainstream tourism had to offer, but when would I ever come back to Peru again? The fear of regret and loss motivated me to buy the ticket more than the desire to see it, two reasons that should never serve as motivation. My train was set to leave in four days.

I couldn't touch alcohol while on the medicine. Makings friends at a hostel is tough if you don't drink (or are not a cute girl), because it's during the nighttime boozing that the connections happen.

A pretty Swedish girl arrived the same day as me but was the most popular person in the hostel after only two days. All she had to do was smile and be friendly. She turned out to be an unstoppable force and a queue of guys formed to take her to bed. Besides her, no one else knew my name. Even though the attention she gave me was the same as her two dozen admirers, I did enjoy someone engaging me in conversation. Men need attention from time to time, too.

To kill some time until my magical Machu Picchu journey, I bought a tourist ticket that gave me access to the lesser but still important ruins around Cuzco, such as Tombamachay, an ancient stone bath featuring a slow stream of mountain spring water, and Saqsaywamán (pronounced like "sexy woman"), a fortress in the shape of a tiger's mouth that was built with colossal stones put together like Legos. As amazing as it was to see improbable constructions by ancient peoples, when all that's left are stones it's hard to put things into context and imagine how the people lived, interacted at markets and social functions, constructed crafts, made goat sacrifices, and had sexual relations. I needed education in archaeology or architecture to fully appreciate the structures because blindly visiting them is like putting the greatest works of 19th century literature in the hands of a plumber and wondering why a wet spot isn't developing in his pants.

I also visited Pisac, a mountain fortress two towns over. There is no train or cable car to the top so like everyone else I made the hike on crumbling rock pathways formed thousands of years ago, past steep stone shelves covered by wild grass. I walked by a group of three pale French girls who set up an impromptu picnic with wine and snacks. I briefly entertained the thought of inviting myself to the party, but after letting out a stiff greeting I continued up the mountain. I started late in the afternoon, after most other tourists had already come down. If I slipped and broke my leg it'd be possible I wouldn't be found for hours. That's the type of thing I thought about when I was alone: how I would be maimed and die.

The problem with Pisac was that it never ended. There was the apparent end of stone housings and ruins near what at first seemed to be the top, but the trail continued around another mountain. It was too late to find out where it led because the last thing I wanted to do was get caught on a mountain with only jeans and a t-shirt after the sun fell.

After taking a few pictures, I sat on an uncomfortable stone thinking about nothing in particular, within eyesight of three other Pisac conquerors: a happy couple further down the mountain on a clearing and a red-headed gringo higher up eating a brown bag lunch. The air was clean and crisp unlike the cities and I sat on the rock for fifteen minutes, the limit to how long I can reflect alone at the top of a mountain until I get the urge to move on. Down below was a small town that not long ago was just a tiny village. I felt slightly nauseous but wrote it off as altitude sickness.

Once down the mountain, I filled my stomach with an alpaca burger before hailing a bus back to Cuzco. I thought alpaca was lamb, but after finishing the delicious half-chicken, half-beef tasting meat, I suspected it was actually llama. That's the only animal I've seen in Peru's countryside. The meat was so tender and lean I wouldn't be surprised if it was baby llama. If that's the case I could no longer get a pet llama when I returned home as planned—it would know I ate its kind and gnaw at my face with its gummy jaw while I slept.

It turns out alpaca is… alpaca, a llama-like animal that is smaller in size but cuter, if that's possible. With uncut hair it looks like a sheepdog. The medicine was working and I was able to enjoy my burger with little fear of an ass attack later. My gas had subsided.

The nausea got worse on the bus ride to Cuzco. I became cold and weak, and could barely stand up on the crowded bus. With one hand I held on for dear life to a metal bar and with the other I guarded my pockets. My head rested on someone's luggage in the overhead compartment.

I stumbled into my dorm and found two girls sitting on my bed, talking to a third in a strange language full of nasal sounds. Before I could claim my territory I looked at their familiar faces and realized they were the Brazilian girls I talked to when I arrived in Lima. They recognized me and there was a nice reunion complete with hugs. I mixed their names up and had them remind me once more. Joana was the tall one, Paula the middle one, and Benita the short one, who laid in bed ill with stomach problems of her own.

"Did you guys already see Machu Picchu," I asked.

"Yeah the other day," Joana said.

"Well, how was it?" There was an uncomfortable pause.

"Terrible!" Paula said, shaking her head. "It rained and we couldn't see anything. Our tour guide was explaining a mountain, but we couldn't even see it because it was covered with clouds."

"But in the afternoon it cleared up a little," Joana added. "It was okay. When do you go?"

"In two days. I'm taking the train."

They talked about which place to drink at later, but I interrupted to ask if they were cold. They weren't. I knew that chills were definitely not a symptom of altitude sickness.

I went underneath the covers and in just two hours my body was so cold I couldn't stop trembling. I was fully clothed with winter blankets stuffed around me but I might as well have been atop Pisac with the moon. And this was the day I finished my medicine!

Benita managed to get out of bed to enjoy the night's festivities in the hostel bar. She came in and out of the dorm to check on me along with the other two. They all gently placed their hand on my forehead and expressed their sympathies. There was nothing more they could do.

Soon my breathing became labored and my pulse shot up. My heart felt like it was going to jump out of my throat, and every thirty minutes sharp cramps stabbed my stomach like knives. All I could do was curl into a fetal position. Six hours ago I was climbing a mountain at a brisk pace and now I couldn't even gather the strength to lift a bottle of water off the floor two feet beside my bed. The only movement came from my heartbeat—I could see my hair move with each thump. I'd never been so cold and weak.

I tried to sleep, but would wake up after vivid, incomplete dreams that blended elements from home with South America. At first I thought it was the flu but the stomach pain ruled that out. Then my mind moved to malaria. I did spend one day in the jungle rafting with Henri and remembered getting a handful of mosquito bites on my legs. What else could it be?

The Brazilian girls were asleep in the morning, except for Paula. Her bed was empty. Maybe if I wasn't sick something would have happened between us, but an Irish gringo got his claw into her first, and that was that.

It took the strength of Zeus to lift myself out of bed and make it to the front desk. They made the call to Zura. She came in twenty minutes and unpacked her equipment, taking the same measurements as before.

"You have an infection, but there is no way to tell what it is unless we do lab tests."

"Could it be malaria?" I asked.

"It could be anything." She paused to prepare the translation. "I recommend you come to the private hospital to get tests, for your security." I knew she meant "for your safety" because the Spanish equivalent of "safe" was "secure." My Spanish was getting better.

I balked. On one hand I did feel a little better. Maybe I should wait it out and see what happened. But then again look how far that got me with the giardia.

I took out a three-month travel health insurance plan before I left. I picked a deductible of $500 instead of $100 which would've cost me only $30 more. How much I regretted that decision while Zura stood over me waiting for an answer. If only she hadn't kept repeating "for your security." It burned into my brain. Was she trying to get me admitted for a fat payday? She said I may have to stay at the private hospital overnight. Even in Peru that wasn't going to cost less than hundreds of dollars. There was silence while I stared at the ground. South America is not kind to even the mildest of hypochondriacs, which I had to accept I was. In the past I easily diagnosed a slight rash as scabies and odd headaches as brain tumors. When I got tested for HIV I'd browse through AIDS forums on the internet and calculate the odds I actually did have HIV before the results came in. A little twitch in the leg and I might as well be in the advanced stages of multiple sclerosis, a pain in the chest and it was a serious heart problem. Those events were spaced far enough that I never thought much of my sick mind, but in South America health conditions wouldn't stop popping up. Now it was malaria. Soon it would be worse.

I needed to know if I had malaria or not. I accepted her recommendation and admitted myself to a private hospital.

The hospital felt like an old psychiatric ward. It was musty and dark with no signs of life besides the occasional nurse. There were no flower pots or generic paintings on the wall. I imagined gringos in the rooms laying on their beds, healing from stomach infections or broken bones caused by adventure sports like ATV trail riding and paragliding.

I was deposited in a wheelchair and sent off to my own room where the nurse drew my blood into a test tube. She placed it in an old metal carrying bin, uncapped and unlabeled. Next they hooked me up to my first ever IV line. There is something very uncomfortable about having a needle permanently stuck in your arm, especially in a hospital that requires you to bring your own soap and towel (I determined it would be more sanitary if I didn't wash my hands after urinating). There were no alcohol sanitizers in the hallways either, and I never saw anyone wear gloves. It was a mistake to come. My mind was torturing me now. There was no way I'd make it out in one piece. There was nothing to distract it, nothing to trick it into focusing on something else. God knows what new infection I'd leave this place with!

I had to take the IV bag and tall metal stand with me every time I wanted to change the channel on the television or use the bathroom. Quickly I learned that if I put my arm above the bag the flow reverses and blood snakes out from my arm. I remembered reading that you could die if too much air gets into your blood stream—embolism I think it's called. I tried to tap out the bubbles in the tubing.

Zura came back midday with a clipboard of my blood test results. I had salmonella poisoning. She said it with a slight smile, as if she was pleased that the mystery had been solved. "The giardia infection probably made it easier to happen," she said. She asked me about my future travel plans and warned me about Bolivia, where even she got sick. If that's the case then I had no chance. I questioned my strategy of visiting the lesser countries to build up for the better ones. What a failure if I couldn't even make it to Argentina and Brazil—amazing Brazil, where everyone was outgoing and sensual. Thousands of years ago the Europeans came to South America and wiped out the indigenous populations mostly through disease, and here I was the Western man coming to South America and limping through because of theirs. Atahualpa and his people are getting revenge nearly 500 years after Pizarro routed them.

I was pumped full of antibiotics and my condition improved so that I was released after a twelve hour stay. The total bill was $530 and out of that Zura got $100, a fair price for thoughtful care which included a follow-up visit two days later. I didn't bother to file a claim with the health insurance company. "The $530 antibiotic prescription," I joked to my sister on the phone. We were talking regularly every week and she'd give me updates about her life, like the drama she was experiencing at work or the clubs she was going to at night.

"You've been there almost two months and you haven't told me anything good yet," she said.

"Yeah it's been a lot harder than I thought it would be."

"If you're not having a good time why don't you come home? I mean is this what you want?"

"No it's not, but I can't give up so early. I'm sure it will get better. It's impossible not to."

I called my parents less frequently, once every two weeks, and when I did I glossed over the bad because I didn't want to give them a chance to tell me "told you so," especially my mom. Instead I would tell them how inexpensive everything was and how I was subsisting mostly on *empanadas*, cheeseburgers, and *jugo*. They were still scared I'd be kidnapped, the one thing I actually wasn't worried about.

Back at the hostel the Brazilian girls showed genuine concern for me. They told me they wished they gave me one of their cell phone numbers so I could have kept them updated with my condition. It felt nice that someone cared.

I was supposed to see Machu Picchu a day after my hospital stay. The tickets were non-refundable, and since Zura cleared me to go I was going. Lucky to even wake up because of an AM/PM switch with my travel alarm, I made it to the station on time for the four hour ride. In the car I was surrounded by elderly gringos who all wore passport holders around their necks within easy snatching range. They were well-prepared: they offered me cookie snacks they brought along for the ride and their supplies and equipment were the best that money could buy. This was because of their greater wealth I'm sure but also for a desire to experience comfort instead of roughness. The young ones valued roughness as a correct means to travel because it was more "authentic."

The ride itself was uneventful, and I napped in and out of sleep as we passed through mountainous countryside. There were small villages here and there with waving and smiling children and the couple stops we made were greeted by big shouting women selling hot corn on the cob. Chomping down, the gringos explain how cheap the food was. Cheap until you get sick.

The train dropped us off at Aguas Caliente ("hot water"), a tourist town full of hotels and souvenir shops. It was even more touristy than Baños and served no function other than being the last stop to the ruins. I bought my entry ticket then got on a bus that took me through a dozen switchbacks up the mountain, until Machu Picchu was within sight.

XI

It's not Machu Picchu's fault that a couple years prior I saw Pompeii, the small, ancient city that was destroyed by the eruption of Mount Vesuvius. I toured it on foot with an audio guide that explained the bathhouses and the markets and the stadium where gladiator shows entertained the masses. I stared at plaster casts of people buried alive by hot ash and examined still colorful frescos hanging on building walls. Pompeii sees plenty of tourists, but I easily found quiet spots where I could sit and relax and enjoy the breeze blowing off the Tyrrhenian Sea.

Reflective moments were impossible in Machu Picchu—it was densely packed with as many gringos as the relatively small space could allow. Backpackers who hiked on the Inca Trail poured in alongside the train and bus crowd to admire typical Incan stone structures. They had names like Temple Of The Condor and Industrial Mortar Structure. The prime attraction that awed many was a lackluster archway that acted as a front door to the lost city.

The government of Peru took full advantage of Machu Picchu. There was a $40 admission charge, a luxury hotel built right outside the compound, and a monopoly on transportation to and from the ruins. It was their ATM cash machine, and while they had every right to profit from the ruins it was my right not to care for it. Unless you had a tour guide you were stuck staring at large rocks with no idea of what they meant and how they got there. And to my untrained eye they looked almost the same as the structures in Pisac.

I ran into the girl from Holland I met in Huanchaco, the one who told me she was bored after only a couple days in South America. She was exhausted and covered in streaks of dirt from a three day hike on the Inca Trail. Her face was cherry red from the sun. Along with her new friends, she was appalled that I didn't speak highly of the ruins.

"How can you not see that this is the most incredible thing?" her friend said, as if I was deficient in mental capacity. I might as well have been in an art gallery exclaiming "I don't get it" to an refined crowd nibbling on raw sheep milk cheese. Was I the problem, or did people build Machu Picchu so much in their heads that they couldn't bear to see it as anything less? Whatever the case, at least now I can say I saw it. I would be seen as well-traveled by others, though without the spiritual awakening.

After two hours I saw most of the ruins and was ready to lay down. I grabbed a bus back to town where I had my choice of two dozen restaurants serving pizza. I ate at the most crowded restaurant and then went back to the train station to wait patiently for my ride back.

XII

I got some of my mojo back thanks to a nighttime conversation I had with a Frenchman, a chatty Canadian, and the girl from Holland (she happened to check into my same hostel after her time on the trail). For the Canadian, this was his second trip to South America, his first ending abruptly right here in Cuzco because of a bad case of salmonella. We all joked and talked, them drinking while I abstained, the climax of it all being when the Frenchman unapologetically said, "Women have not been active in the history of the world."

The girl from Holland seemed less offended than when I told her I didn't care for Machu Picchu.

That night I came up with a plan. With my guidebook next to me and reports of other travelers simmering in my head, I wrote a list on a napkin of the next ten cities I should visit. Next to each city I put how long I was allowed to stay in each, plus or minus a couple days. It was time to introduce a little structure and discipline or I'd never finish the trip. Instead I'd just keep getting sick in cities I didn't care for and miss out on the ones I wanted to visit most (Rio, Buenos Aires). At the bottom of the napkin I wrote down two rules that became my new travel strategy: "Only go to a city if it has something you want to see and experience," and, "Only stay longer than planned if you are having the time of your life. No exceptions." I wanted these rules to last beyond the ten cities I listed, until the end of the trip.

There were two problems with my napkin that I didn't realize at the time. The first was that it conflicted with my existing goal of visiting every country in South America. There was nothing in countries like Paraguay, Suriname, Guyana, and French Guiana that I wanted to "see and experience." The second problem was that my napkin strategy was based on visiting places based on a generic guidebook and reports from people who were different than me. It turns out that if I wrote down the population numbers of the cities I did pick, I would've seen that they strongly correlated with the most populated cities in each country—ones that had the most pages dedicated to it in the guidebook, and therefore most visited by the gringos I was talking to.

After I gently folded the napkin and tucked it into the middle of my passport, I accepted that I had little clue what I was looking for. I was a bird without a compass, hoping he'd stumble on the right nesting ground thousands of miles away. The best that bird could hope for is a nice view during the flight. In other words, I was doomed. But the napkin did give me hope that the trip at least wouldn't end prematurely, and that maybe I'd still stumble on exotic women and meaning, in that order.

It was time for me to leave Cuzco after the follow-up visit to Zura's office. The medicines did their job and I was ready to put giardia and salmonella behind me. I promised the Brazilian girls I'd contact them when I make it to Rio. If I make it to Rio.

XIII

The only thing to do in Puno, a city on the Peruvian side of Lake Titicaca, was visit the floating islands of the Uros people.

Hundreds of years ago the peaceful Uros built their own islands with reeds growing near the shores of Lake Titicaca to get away from aggressive tribes. Those tribes are long gone but the Uros remain, living and breeding on reeds. Modern way-of-life has passed them by, so their existence continues to be centered on the reed, bundles of which need to be constantly thrown on top of their islands as old ones rot off from the bottom. Their houses and small, Viking-shaped boats are made of these reeds as well. It wouldn't be a stretch to label the Uros the South American Amish, who shun technology yet fascinate the moderners with their horse-drawn buggies on the highway, marked with the little triangle reflector sign.

The Uros used to be a self-sustaining people, but lower fish catch rates have forced them to rely on tourists such as myself to survive. With a steadily declining population, their future is dim, since young Uros head to the mainland in search of opportunity and a better life. I can't blame them. The islands themselves are small, spongy things, and living on them means you have a choice of only three possible careers: fishmonger, reed builder, and souvenir shop owner specializing in the sale of key chains and miniature reed boats and houses. From what I saw there wasn't much for the children to do except chase each other with reeds in their hands. Tourists were not allowed to wander off and take a look at the residential areas, but the poverty was evident with glimpses into the crowded living conditions and lack of refrigerators, dishwashers, televisions, and so on. There was no running electricity.

On the boat ride back we ran out of gas a mile from shore. The two life jackets were quickly put on by Peruvian men, leaving the three women on board with a nervous look on their faces. In Peru it's the women and children last. Another boat came out to tow us back, though I was confident the lake winds would have floated us to land eventually.

That night I sought out a nice meal in Puno's main pedestrian walkway of restaurants, hotels, and craft shops selling a wide assortment of fisherman hats. The restaurants all served the exact same food—pizza, *empanadas*, and local stew fare. The safest choice was the guidebook choice. The fate of your gringo restaurant rests almost entirely on a chance visit from a travel writer and his onetime perception of the service and food. Otherwise you are reduced to heckling at tourists from a bar stool out front, which I think does more to reduce business than drum it up. No tourist wants to dine in a restaurant with a desperate owner.

I left Puno for Copacabana, Bolivia. The ride was only three hours long and felt like a quick trip to the grocery store after the marathon, ass-clenching rides I'd been through. I determined that Bolivia, the third country of the thirteen I had planned to visit, would finally be the place of my fresh start.

BOLIVIA

I

The first thing I did when I arrived in Bolivia was buy a straw cowboy hat and knitted gloves and scarf for ten dollars. Up to that point I felt bad for haggling with vendors over a dollar or two, but I figured they wouldn't sell their wares to me if they weren't making a profit. I didn't see why I should pay more than other people for the exact same thing. The second thing I did was wet the bed.

I was on a pier next to the ocean, most likely the Pacific, about to go on a long boat ride with a group of gringos. I wanted to urinate before the boat set off. What better place to do that than off the pier with my back facing whomever might be watching. The urine flowed and I closed my eyes and let out a huge sigh. I could hear the sound of the waves slapping the pier's supporting wood columns. Then mid-stream my eyes opened and I could feel that it was not just a dream. I squeezed my pelvic muscles and immediately ran to the bathroom holding my dripping wet crotch. From what little was left for the toilet, I emptied almost a full bladder of urine on myself and the bed.

I took off my boxers and dried myself and stared at a wet spot the size of an exercise ball. I didn't know it was even possible for a 28-year-old to wet his bed. I've heard stories of people getting drunk and urinating on themselves, but I didn't have a single drink the night before. Maybe it was the stress of the trip and the medications? I flipped the mattress over and with a fresh pair of boxers on I tried to go back to sleep. For the next several weeks I compulsively grabbed my crotch whenever I'd get up to see if it was dry or not.

If I'm one to believe in dream analysis, a dream of urination signifies a need to "relieve" yourself of bad to begin a... fresh start! But there was nothing I could find that describes why my brain could not tell the difference between a dream piss with a real one. It was some sort of neural hiccup, or an alternate universe that I had unwittingly tapped into. I imagined how much more embarrassed I'd be if this was a dorm instead of my three dollar a night private hotel room. I would have to check out immediately and leave the city. I'd probably keep running into people that witnessed the soiling until I returned home.

The rest of my time in Copacabana wasn't too enjoyable because of the anxiety that came with trying to find clean food. In restaurants the dishware the Bolivian waiters brought out was not even washed, with pieces of food and hair still attached, greasy and streaky to the touch. The meals themselves had fine little hairs and I'd give up picking them all out. Asking for another plate was itself a risk because it could have more hairs. I was feasting on safe snacks every day like crackers and candy bars but my body craved real, hot food. I'd do anything not to go back to the bread and jelly diet. My hotel room, now filled with the sharp, sour smell of concentrated urine, didn't have a kitchen so with little choice and the knowledge that in all likelihood I would be poisoned, I chowed down.

II

I visited Isla del Sol, a small island first inhabited in the third millennium B.C.E., via a two-hour motorboat ride with a handful of other gringos. The little boat would fly off one peak and crash down to the next, creaking the chipped old wood that it was made of. The action spurred hoots and hollers from the more outgoing gringos and silence from the paranoid ones who noticed there were not enough life jackets on board. For the last half-hour of the ride we traveled parallel to the waves, which caused the boat to rock sideways like a child's seesaw. My head spun in circles. To prevent spewing I buried it in my lap like I was on a Huaraz toilet, until we finally made it on the north side of the island.

The idea of Isla del Sol is to view some ruins on the north side of the island and then take a few hours hike down the south side where the motorboat awaits to take you back to Copacabana. I paired up with a young American guy and we hit the main trail after staring at the ruins, which compared to Machu Picchu looked like the result of little kids playing with rocks. Of course there was no context as to what these structures meant.

Both of us were traveling alone and I asked him if this was getting to him. "You're only alone if you want to be," he said. "There are too many opportunities to find someone to hang out with." While he was right, it wasn't always with the people you wanted to be with.

We ran into two girls, one also American and the other English. The English girl was cute and made a comment about how she saw me on the boat looking ill. A girl noticing you and later mentioning she noticed you is a pretty big indicator of interest in my book. She complained her ankle was sore from a previous hike even after taking her medicine—cocaine. When I have body pain I take Advil. Most of her stories ended up with her getting drunk or high on coke, marijuana, or pills. We had nothing in common besides our present location and I couldn't even fake an interesting conversation like with most other traveler girls I'd met. I lost interest. I'm sure I seemed anti-social when I broke off from the pack to hike faster. After an hour I looked back and saw there was no one behind me.

I was atop an elevated slope and to either side of me was Lake Titicaca. The temperature was brisk but the hiking (more like fast walking) kept me warm. The landscape was barren besides some small bush and short grass. The only sign of civilization, besides the tiny village coming up on my right, was the stone trail I was using, the same trail made and used by 15th century Incans.

I stopped and stared at the lake for a few minutes. I took several deep breaths of South America's freshest air and paid close attention to how the wind shaped the chop, forming white streaks that danced across the top of the water. I was alone again. Like in the bars, doodling on napkins and staring at candle flames. Like on the kayak I rented the day before, paddling as far as I could from the shore until I wondered if I had enough energy to get back. And like at Pisac, spacing myself as far as possible from the couple other humans on the mountain with me.

III

The bus station in La Paz, Bolivia's capital, was surprisingly organized. You still had the vendors selling candy and junk with people shouting destinations to get business, but there were clocks, televisions, clear lighted signs, and a semblance of planning. Ticket counters even had baggage windows that would preload your luggage before boarding.

For lunch I went to the station's only restaurant. Other than the broken carnival rides off to the side, it seemed like a clean establishment. Condom optional. I got hamburger, fries, and a bottle of water, a safe meal I figured, but halfway through the burger I noticed the meat was red and undercooked. I stopped eating it. A couple hours later I was on a bus to Potosí, skipping La Paz because it wasn't on the napkin. During the ride, the beast awoke once again. The damage was done. I hate Bolivia.

With my strong love affair to the toilet now rekindled, I began to only see the bad. The food in Bolivia is horrible and will kill you if it could—if not the food then the water, full of parasites and bacteria. Cities are foul and wretched, unfit for human habitation, dumps even by South American standards. The landscape is beautiful but the people are short and smelly, with no concept of personal hygiene. At a restaurant I saw a woman cook chicken on the grill and turn it over with her hand after satisfying a belly scratch. Another woman used the bathroom and washed her hands in an open barrel of water that served as a home to flies and other insects. On buses many women had crumbs of food stuck in their clothing left over from many meals past. Bathrooms never had soap and even if they did it'd go untouched. Bolivia has no redeeming qualities beside what nature bestowed on it, not to the credit of the people or culture. I hate Bolivia. I was on the road to health but Bolivia destroyed it, and now I was sick again. I should have rode the bus right through the country.

IV

In my Potosí hostel I met two guys from Argentina who gave me the scoop on their city, Córdoba. They hyped the beautiful women, the pumping nightlife, the cheap prices, and the excellent, safe food. "You will love Córdoba," they repeated. I remember I was told similar things about Cuzco.

We went to the open air market to purchase ingredients for a basic pasta meal, all of us too scared to eat in a restaurant. Two other Argentines joined us for dinner, one of them female, and we had a simple but non-poisonous meal. I noticed the Argentines would directly place their bread on the table instead of on a plate.

"Is the Spanish in Argentina much different from the other countries?" I asked. "I heard the accent is different."

"It's similar enough that they will understand you if you speak normal Spanish," one of the guys said. The Argentines all spoke competent English.

"Yes but our Spanish is the more correct way of speaking. It's how they speak it in Spain," said the girl. "For example, if you want to ask for someone's name you pronounce it *Como se ya-ma*, but in Argentina it's pronounced *Como se ja-ma*."

"Also we use the *vos* form instead of *tu*. But use *tu* and you'll be fine."

I have to note that down on my notecards, I thought, which now numbered in the hundreds and took more than an hour to go through.

"Our nightlife is different too. We don't go out until 2am."

"Yeah someone else told me already. Why is that?" I asked.

"Well we don't eat until very late, after nine or so. We like to eat slow and then go to the bar for a while before the club."

"If you go to the club before two then nobody will be there. It probably won't even be open," the girl said.

I encouraged her to talk so I could keep looking at her. She was wearing a loose wool sweater and ugly hiking pants that kept her body a secret, but she had the cutest face I'd seen in South America. Her hair was long and dark and her skin had just a slight hint of brown. I tried not to make my interest obvious, but while we were talking the guy I thought was her friend came over and planted a fat, wet kiss on the side of her lips. He marked his territory, and just like that the fantasy was over.

We all watched *The Shawshank Redemption* on the hostel television after dinner, and he kept leaning over to kiss her during the movie while she sat unaffected. He seemed insecure of his ability to keep his girl, but it would make no difference for my cause. By the end of the movie all the Argentines were crying. I would have cried too if I hadn't already seen it a dozen times.

Later I looked in the mirror and noticed a large pimple on my chin. I popped it, but instead of white juice bursting out it was flesh and muscle, pouring from the hole until most of my face was in the sink. I looked in the mirror and I could only see two stunned eyes and empty space where my nose and mouth used to be. I woke up terrified, grabbing my crotch, but I realized it was just another bad dream. My face was still intact and my crotch dry.

This dream took me a little longer to figure out. Once the pimple exploded in guts and blood, I looked in the mirror and knew I would never be the same. The dream was a warning about my stomach. It was changing before my eyes, into something that would be a lot harder for me to live with.

V

You can't come to Potosí without doing a tour of the Cerro Rico mine, the economic engine feeding the town. Without it there would be no Potosí.

The minerals in Cerro Rico were first discovered by the Spaniards in the 1500s. Predictably, they enslaved the local population to extract silver for export back to Spain. So many locals died from the horrifying working conditions that the Spaniards had to bring in African slaves and subject them to a stint in the mine called *La Mitad*. The slaves lived and worked for six months stretches without seeing a beam of sunlight. Most did not make it out alive, and today scholars estimate eight million slaves and indigenous people died in the mines. That would be the population of modern day New York City.

The easy silver has already been mined and most of what they extract now is zinc, a necessary mineral in most modern electronics. Since the mines are a cooperative owned by the people of Bolivia, anyone can form a group and cheaply rent mine space from the government to make a go with axes and shovels. But accurate tunnel maps are impossible to come by and territorial fights between rival groups are not uncommon, with tossed dynamite sticks used as weapons.

The smaller groups use hand tools like in colonial times while the bigger groups use modern equipment. I wondered why anyone would sign up to work for a small group and their primitive tools, but turns out they have the remote chance of getting lucky and striking a large mineral vein. With less people to spread the wealth and practically no overhead, fortunes have been made based on chance discoveries by the man with the lowly pickaxe. A story goes that one man, working alone, found a vein so large that he might as well have won the lottery. Today he owns several local businesses, and hasn't stepped foot in the mine since.

I signed up for a tour of the mine. It started at the miners market, where we bought gifts for the miners and dynamite to set off for fun. A stick of dynamite costs only $1 and there were no restrictions on who could buy it. (Sometimes during protests, citizens light off sticks to give their demonstrations more oomph.) We also bought bandanas to wrap around our faces to filter out the dust. Proper masks made it too hard to breathe, we were told. Most of the miners don't even bother with bandanas.

There wasn't much activity at the large, lifeless brown mountain that contained the mine, nothing that showed how many people it killed during the past 500 years. Definitely no bodies strewn about on the ground. Our safety course consisted of one rule: move off the tracks when a cart was coming through. With that in mind and our miner jumpers, rubber boots, and hard hats already on, we entered the darkness.

Initially, walking through the mine wasn't difficult, with its spacious clearance and lighted pathways, but gradually the jagged roof lowered and the lights disappeared until we were in a permanent state of crouching and waddling in near darkness. The sound of tall gringos hitting their hard hats on the roof constantly echoed through the mine, along with the occasional "Ow, fuck!" Two thin pieces of metal on the floor served as tracks for carts that rolled by every few minutes, when we'd hug the side walls to prevent being struck by the three or four car mini-trains. Drivers of the trains kept their heads tilted to prevent hitting the ceiling rock at high speed.

All the miners had their cheeks stuffed with the precursor to cocaine: coca leaves, a plant that in its natural state is said to provide energy and stave off hunger. It made them look like hamsters storing peanuts. One large mass of coca would last for hours and provide a steady stream of coca-infused saliva ready for swallow, though it'd leave their lips and teeth green. With all the dust it's impossible to eat in the mine so men work their eight hour or more shifts on just coca and cheap sugary soda.

We looked at the division of labor in a medium sized cooperative. First, we met the miner whose job it was to receive large cauldron-shaped bags of rock, delivered through an electric-powered pulley from a lower floor. He unloaded the rock into a massive pile where another man would shovel it into a cart to be driven out of the mine. Then we slowly descended straight down through zig-zag paths with decades-old wooden ladders. One ladder was positioned in such a way that I had to brace myself against the side of the walls to lower myself until I could sense that my foot met the first rung. Two people from our group decided to pass and wait as they were.

We met the two men shoveling rock at rapid speed into the bags we saw above, and they let us have a go. Only me and one other could fill a bag without stopping. We had to remove our bandanas to breathe. I watched floating mineral particles get vacuumed into my nose but it was better than the feeling of suffocation. I did not volunteer to fill another bag.

Our tour guide said the mine was like a "second home" to these men. They memorized the labyrinth like they would their neighborhood streets. This offered me little assurance while navigating through the tunnels with dynamite sticks exploding nearby, shaking dust and small pebbles off the roof. There were no geologists or engineers to ensure the cave system would hold. Sometimes it doesn't.

Deeper in we met the source of the rock—two men armed with a steel wedge and sledgehammer pounding at the wall once every second, breaking pieces of earth from the mountain. This I also attempted. The violent shock of each impact sent a painful tremor through my arm and shoulder, and after only four hard whacks I sheepishly handed the tools back to the miner. Dynamite did only a small portion of the work.

For his labor, each man received a wage that was far more than he could get with any other unskilled job in the city. Along with it came life spans shortened by 20 or 30 years. The miners smiled when you asked them questions and gave gifts of dynamite and soda, but when you were on your way out and they thought you were no longer looking, they went back to hammering and shoveling with a solemn resignation impossible to find in any cubicle or laboratory I've worked in.

The only highlight of working as a Potosí miner are Friday afternoons when he treats himself to 96% alcohol (192 proof). The superstition goes that if you drink pure alcohol, the Spanish devil god will give pure mineral. Even if I was superstitious, I don't think it would be the devil I'd try to get on the good side of. My guide, who used to be a miner but jumped at the chance to take a pay cut to give gringos tours, gave us a small sample of the liquor. It tasted like molten fire death and can only be consumed in small capfuls by those not used to the potency. I was told that the difference between rubbing alcohol, which kills you, and the miners' alcohol is just one extra step of filtration. A small two dollar medicine-shaped bottle could throw a crazy party for ten people used to puny 80 proof vodkas and rums diluted with juice.

As much as my guide tried to say these men appreciated their jobs,

I'm sure they would do just about anything else if offered decent pay. It's true that they are not slaves forced to work in the mine, but with so little opportunity elsewhere I wonder how much choice was involved in their decisions. Until the output of the Potosí mines cease to be profitable—and it's a matter of when and not if—these men and future generations who follow will die miners, much younger than is fair.

I was only able to crawl through the mine for a couple hours before I was ready to collapse. My throat was burning and for one day I hacked a cloudy grey mucus. I felt small for complaining about my relatively easy job at home that paid me a salary the miners could only dream of. How did I come to the conclusion that a professional job with fair pay in a modern building was actually torture?

Outside the mine my guide went a few hundred feet down the mountain, lit a stick of dynamite, and then ran like hell. The gringos and I filmed the ground-shaking explosion with our cameras.

VI

My napkin said the last Bolivian stop was Tupiza, a launching point for the famous Bolivian Southwest. Rumor has it that this was where Butch Cassidy came out to live out his last days. Upon arrival, after a several hour bus ride, I witnessed with my own eyes a middle-aged man disembark from the luggage hold.

Tupiza was a dusty but smiley town full of teenagers, built around large mounds of red-brown dirt that managed to find its way everywhere. With no mall or movie megaplex to go to, the teens performed their mating dance in the public spaces. The boys would cock their heads a little sideways with a cheesy smirk on their faces to flirt with girls who would play coy to keep the attention train rolling.

The girls were more attractive here than in other parts of Bolivia, perhaps because Tupiza is in close proximity to Argentina, but even with the age of consent set at puberty I wasn't tempted or inspired. It'd been almost two months since I'd last had a woman. I didn't care much with my stomach in the shape that it was, but every now and then I'd see a gringo with a pretty girl on his arm and get jealous. I'd vow to work harder at getting a girl, but quickly the jealousy would fade and the paranoid thoughts about dying or bed wetting would return to take the spotlight.

The guidebook said travelers often stay in Tupiza for a week or more, entranced by its charms, but it was becoming clear the "bible" sugarcoated everything. Lonely Planet wouldn't sell a lot of copies if they criticized half of the places they wrote about. One day in Tupiza was more than enough.

I did some research on the internet while waiting a day for my tour to the Southwest to begin. (How I could make it four days without constant access to toilet I wasn't sure.) I learned that Bolivia is the poorest country in the continent by GDP per capita. If you include Central America, it's second behind only Haiti, a place so sad and impoverished that the worst off subsist on cookies made from mud.

I thought about all the countries I was now "qualified" to visit, places I would most likely survive with only somewhat serious intestinal problems. But it's doubtful I'd enjoy myself. Even Bolivia's rough, pink-colored toilet paper was getting to me. After a few days it began to feel like someone was trying to jam jagged rocks up my butt with every wipe, and after extended walks I began to notice an odd, unpleasant itch in sensitive areas too embarrassing to discuss with other gringos. How sorely I missed the luxurious softness of American toilet paper! It didn't help matters that the pink color made it hard to tell when I was done cleaning or not. I theorize that Bolivians have dirty asses because of this.

The transport for the tour was a spacious Toyota Land Cruiser that everyone referred to as "the Jeep." Besides the male driver and a female cook, there were three other gringos on the tour—one couple, an Australian guy and English girl, and an older Australian woman traveling alone.

The Aussie guy, Alex, let out a quip about me holding everyone up when I was ten minutes late for the start of the tour, but it was in such dry delivery I couldn't tell if he was being sarcastic or not. The English girl was friendly, with a homely, girl-next-door look. It was hard to pin down if her relationship with Alex was sexual or merely flirtatious. The older woman was approaching forty and had a habit of talking even when no one was listening. She imparted upon us her great wisdom from years of traveling (her passport with its rainbow of stamps made an early appearance).

All that studying with notecards paid off because my Spanish was the best among the gringos. I acted as translator between them and the crew, Mateo and Elena. "Americans are known for being arrogant and ignorant of other cultures, but they speak the best Spanish," said Mary, the English girl. It was unanimously agreed upon that Australians have the worst Spanish.

The entire first day was spent driving through desert canyons. We passed the occasional herd of llamas, their ears tagged to signify their owner, and every hour the Jeep stopped to take in the scenic view of red rock hills. The road itself was narrow and unpaved, and for every approaching car it was a game to see who would pull over to the side first to allow the other to pass.

After lunch we arrived at a village smack in the middle of the driest part of the desert. There were no jobs and no wealth in this part of Bolivia, nothing for dozens of miles except mud dwellings and dirt. The gang of little children who came out to greet us were coated in dirt head to toe. It even filled the dry cracks on their faces, formed from the dry air.

A group of three dirt children huddled around me and within a couple seconds one was examining my keys, another my pen, and a third my camera. They were very fascinated with gringos and the objects they brought with them, and did not hesitate to ask questions in Spanish, yet they never asked for money. When I watched them play there was no doubt how all that dirt got on them—they literally rolled in it. When I patted one on the back a cloud of brown dust released from his sweater. I looked closer at their rags, their lone rope toy, their extreme living environment, and realized these children were most likely the poorest in South America. They had nothing but each other, and dirt.

The accommodations on the first night were challenging. Our mattresses were made of cheap foam—the same type of material used in America as shipping box filler—laid atop concrete slabs covered with smelly sheets. I had borrowed a sleeping bag from the tour agency but I still pulled out my silk "Dreamsack" cocoon for the first time to shield me from previous gringos' stink. Alex told me to stop being a sissy when I complained about my bed's smell and lack of comfort.

The next morning I had to do my big business on our shack's lone abominable toilet. I prayed to the Spanish devil god that there'd be no splash-back onto my ass, considering there were stubborn shit stains coating the bowl. There was.

Back at home I can rough it out the most among my friends, and am least sissy-like, but not out in South America. The majority of gringos I was meeting in hostels were capable of putting up with incredibly bad conditions. I'm convinced some of them would sleep soundly on a soft bed of dead worms. There is a wide scale of what humans can withstand and as an American raised with creature comforts, I was ill-prepared to learn how to "tough it out," as Alex kept repeating.

The next two days I saw teal and red lagoons, mountains with orange-sulfur covered peaks, gurgling hot springs, stunning cliff formations, ten thousand llamas, and a rock that formed into the shape of a tree, with a narrow base and bulbous head. You'd be hard-pressed to find a traveler who doesn't gush about the Bolivian southwest, how beautiful it is and how it will sweep you away with the most breathtaking views imaginable, but regardless of how rich a tapestry the scenery paints, in the end it's just a visual image, another sight. It will fade and become blurry in just a couple months, only rekindled by the sight of photographs on a computer screen. Other memories lasted longer. I won't forget how I interacted with Mateo in Spanish and stayed up late at night laughing with my fellow travelers about bet wetting. I'll always remember Alex lap up cheap rum spilled on a dirty table. The major sights were affecting me less than the experiences before and after them.

By the third day of the tour I had become close to Mateo. He was a short but sturdy man with a floppy bowl haircut and steady smile that revealed one missing tooth from the top row. His wife and one-year-old son stayed at home most of the week while he drove gringos like me around for ten hours, only to tend to the Jeep for two more, always accommodating us with his goofy smile. Though he is not a rich man, I figure he lives a comfortable middle class lifestyle by Bolivian standards (the tips he earns alone are more than the average salary most Bolivians make). Like the miners of Potosí, he made me feel embarrassed for having complained about my job. I have a feeling Mateo would kill to be managed by Dr. Wang if it came with the income that I was making.

VII

For our last night we stayed at a salt hotel, so called because it was constructed from the salt found in the Uyuni Salt Flat, the final highlight of our tour. The floor, the walls, and even the dining room tables and chairs were made of lickable salt (the popular photo here being the gringo's tongue pressed against the wall). We bought several bottles of Chilean red wine from the convenience store nearby and shared them with other groups of gringos from different tour agencies. A beautiful blonde German girl with long bangs sat and drank next to me, her right wrist crowded with handicraft bracelets. Only a couple more months until I'd succumb and buy one for myself.

Like a light switch the beast came on—the good beast, the one who knows how to flirt, joke, and tell stories. I finished telling her about the tour of the Potosí mine, adding that I bought a dozen sticks of dynamite for "personal use" since I felt they'd "come in handy soon." She gave me a suspicious look, like she was trying to figure me out. She was curious. It was going well, I thought.

"How is your beefy gas doing?" Mary interrupted, loud enough for even the dirt children playing outside to hear.

The first night of our tour we had a fried beef meal. As a result, for the next day I continually passed gas that smelled like the beef. My nickname in the Jeep became "Beefy Gas." Mary decided this would be a great time to bring it up.

"Oh it's extra beefy now, thanks," I said. I wanted to jump across the salt table and strangle her, but I knew if I got defensive it would just confirm to everyone that I did in fact have beefy gas. I had to play cool.

It's possible the German girl did not get what Mary meant by beefy gas and I was safe, but a few minutes later the target of my attentions dropped a bomb: "It has been much harder to leave my boyfriend at home than I thought." Our conversation trailed off and I sat there twiddling my thumbs when I was introduced to a Brazilian guy. I encouraged him to tell me how great his country is.

After a stew and bread dinner, the gringos retired one at a time to their rooms until there were only five left: me, my Jeep-mates, and a pretty Scottish girl who stroked my arm hair as her boyfriend slept on his salt slab. "Scottish men don't have much body hair," she said.

Mary kept glancing at me in a peculiar way. We were on friendly terms inside the Jeep, but every time we'd get into a deep conversation Alex would insert himself and steer it in another direction with curt remarks. We'd never been alone.

Out of the blue she said, "I like how you have strong opinions. I'm not saying I always agree with them, but I like how you're not afraid of sharing." I think she was referring to when I told her that a man's value as a mate increases with age even as he gets gray and scraggly, since women don't only care about a man's looks. I told her I'd date a hot girl even if she was a janitor, implying that a woman's value exists mostly in her appearance, not necessarily her education or job. She protested at the time but we had a lively discussion about dating and relationships until Alex poisoned it with talk about anal sex.

I was still cross at the beefy gas incident even though Mary had no bearing on the outcome, unless the German girl's boyfriend was an invented boyfriend who didn't have the same affliction that I did.

"Oh and speaking of opinions, when you asked if I had beefy gas in front of the German girl, were you trying to be mean or were you just not thinking?"

"No no I didn't mean to say that. It was an accident. I didn't think you'd care if other people heard."

"That my ass emitted a bad steak dinner? You're right I should wake everyone up right now and tell them!"

"I'm sorry."

I made my point. "Whatever, it's done." We toasted and drank from our plastic cups.

Then in a low voice she said, "Maybe I was a little jealous." I didn't reply because Alex was right there listening.

It took three days to resolve the ambiguity. They weren't banging after all. The Australian woman threw more tinder on the fire when she looked at Alex and Mary and said, "Why don't you two just have sex already?" Alex was becoming noticeably uncomfortable that his failure to bed Mary was so out in the open. I sat back and watched the show, as Mary debated his merits and Alex talked real close to her mouth as if he was about to go for it in front of us. Mary responded by playfully slapping him across the face, something you'd expect from the way they tease and make fun of each other, but surprisingly he seemed offended.

"Never hit me again!" he yelled, while pointing his finger directly at her face.

He stormed out and she promptly gave chase. Later I walked by their room and a peek inside showed them to be in deep conversation. Perhaps he knew that something would have happened between me and Mary and decided the outburst would be needed to stop it? Or maybe he was so drunk that he couldn't hide how much he liked her.

I went to bed alone on my salt slab, which wasn't much better than a concrete slab. Before I fell asleep I fantasized about having a short love affair where the end comes in a flood of tears at a bus or train station. Addresses would be exchanged to send postcards and future promises made with a passionate kiss goodbye. After a few minutes I stopped and chided myself for even thinking about it.

VIII

I concluded that my latest round of stomach issues was caused by the recycled cooking oil that the shy cook Elena put into most of our meals. For lunch on the last day of the tour she served fried potato cakes that were profusely sweating oil. I knew it would destroy me but I was so hungry I couldn't stop myself from eating the most out of anyone else. I started experiencing awful cramps a couple hours later and whined about it to my Jeep mates, hoping for some traveler sympathy. Instead Alex said, "What you need is a nice tall glass of harden the fuck up."

The Salt Flat of Uyuni is the most stunning landscape I've ever seen in my life, but there isn't a whole lot to say about it. Twelve-thousand square kilometers of only white dotted with the occasional small mountain. A frigid snowy tundra without the snow or the cold, a winter wonderland in the warm fall. Surreal but monotonous. Our Jeep rode on the crunchy salt for over an hour, on ground made of naturally forming hexagon salt sheets. Underneath were layers of salt water that coated my skin milky white after it dried.

The flat horizon made for convincing perspective photos, like putting a can of Pringles in the foreground with people in the background to create an image of mini-humans standing on the can. I would have never imagined that a place like this existed on the planet, but after a couple hours the joy of the image began to wear out and I was ready to return to Tupiza.

Three hours into the five hour journey home, on a typical Bolivian single lane dirt road, we were met with a barbed wire gate at the entrance to a village. Several dozen villagers, mostly women, mingled around. A man came up to the Jeep to tell Mateo that this was a citizens roadblock. No one could pass. "The local ice cream shop only has two flavors and they wanted a third," I joked, before I learned there was no fast alternate route.

Mateo scanned the maps in his head and told us that the detour would take an additional twelve hours. Or we could wait overnight in the Jeep since the protest would end by daybreak. We all slumped in our seats. It was already five o'clock in the afternoon and we were on the verge of going mad from Jeep fever.

It was incredible how much power these locals have in closing a road—if we were in America the cops would be throwing people in the paddy wagon within ten minutes. It's too tempting as a Westerner to criticize the citizens for being "selfish" in their protest, but they're the ones who live here. As a guest in their country the only acceptable response was to give them my unconditional support, and lament my bad luck instead. We decided to take the extra twelve hour route.

On the way back to Uyuni we crossed paths with another tour agency Jeep that was headed right for the blockade. After informing the driver of the situation, he came up with a route that Mateo didn't know. It would take only six additional hours instead of twelve. We could be back in town around midnight and all we needed was some fuel. At the next village Mateo asked around and found an old woman selling gasoline from plastic barrels in a small hut that doubled as her home. I held the funnel inside the Jeep's gas tank and Mateo got the flow going by siphoning an oil-stained hose with his mouth. Off we went into the darkening Bolivian desert, the low orange sunset streaking brilliant red horizontal waves across the sky. We broke down only once because of minor engine trouble. I had my own sort of trouble: the potato oil sponges wanted to exit my body.

It was the same story. My gut sent wave after wave of contractions to expunge the toxins, and I fought back with meditation and deep breathing. We were in the middle of the desert and I could have politely asked for a stop at a large bush, but the modern man in me needed toilet, paper, and soap. So for five hours I sat there in silence, concentrating as tiny beads of sweat collected on the tip of my nose. During that time Alex's complaints increased in frequency and volume. He was "tired" and "sore" and "uncomfortable" and just wanted "to eat" and "go to sleep." What a pussy to whine about something that everyone was experiencing! With pure disdain I said, "What you need is a nice tall glass of harden the fuck up." His eyes twitched. I had my revenge.

Once back into town we pooled our funds together and gave Mateo a nice tip for his hard work. He let out one of his smiles and by the time he bowed his head to give thanks, I was already headed to the toilet to take the second biggest, most relieving watery shit of my life.

Twenty minutes later I met Mary and Alex in the lobby of the hotel we checked into. Alex ignored me, but I had already noticed a shift after the previous night at the salt hotel. He saw me as a threat and I understood (if anything I was flattered), but I wondered if Mary realized that she was sacrificing closeness with other travelers because of a desire to keep the boy toy happy.

After a brief recap of the tour over pizza, they fell into a conversation about previous drunken times they shared together. I paid my share of the bill and left early to be alone in my room.

IX

The nearest Bolivian town bordering Argentina was Villazón. After paying my $2 bus fare and watching a young teenage boy siphon some gas into the tank, I was on my way. And then an hour later it ended before we arrived.

There was another blockade, this time not due to a lack of ice cream flavors but paved roads. I was within walking distance, only three miles away from the Argentine border, so I grabbed my backpack and began huffing it. Eventually I decided it would be best for my back to hire an old man with a push cart, who was kept busy thanks to the protest. Seeing all the other men with push carts suggested that road blocks happened frequently.

The residents of Villazón weren't kidding around—they blocked both main and side streets with cars, trucks, vans, mini-buses, big buses, and ambulances. After getting over my bad luck for the second day in a row, I started to admire Bolivian protestors for getting shit done. American activists need to visit and take notes, because their email and fax campaigns look pale in comparison.

It took almost an hour to make it to the border, where an Argentine agent sized me up before stamping my passport with a three month tourist visa. I stepped foot into the city of La Quiaca ready to kiss the ground.

I went into an internet café while waiting for my bus to leave for Salta. The 18-year-old or so girl working the front desk caught my eye. *This* is how it would truly begin.

"Is there a super popular discotheque tonight where I can dance all night long?" I asked her.

"What day is it today?" she asked.

"Tuesday."

"No."

And that was that. Dry humor does a lot better at home, but that's okay. At least there was a girl to talk to.

The bus driver woke me up and told me we had arrived in Salta. It's been a little over two months. I made it through the toughest countries in South America. Now my body will heal, I will forget about wetting the bed, and I will end this increasingly uncomfortable sexless streak. I was the last one off the bus and when I went outside I saw a crowd waiting by the cargo hold to get their luggage. An old man was wearing a very familiar hat—my cowboy hat! I tapped his shoulder and he looked at me sheepishly before handing it back. No harm, no foul, because I've arrived in Xanadu.

SALTA & CHILE

I

I couldn't believe my eyes. There were grocery stores, real pharmacies, cafes on every other corner, clothing stores with name brands I knew, candy shops, and pet stores with baby chickens, doggies, and hamsters in the windows. Drivers obeyed traffic signals for the most part and there were no people yelling and selling plastic toys, no fare catchers hanging outside of 30-year-old buses.

Shortly after checking into my hostel, I stepped foot into a café that served real cappuccino and chocolate cake topped with rich *dulce de leche* made from scratch. The café even had free wireless internet and I stayed there for hours catching up on the latest pop music videos. My stomach wasn't feeling so hot but this was the happiest I had been since first arriving in Quito. The simple act of walking around and watching the beautiful, stylish people was a pleasure, and I was literally the kid in the candy store trying to choose which freshly made sweet to buy. My priorities changed. I decided to wait until after the weekend to see a doctor for the unrelenting pain, diarrhea and gas. If they prescribed me medicine, which they were sure to do, I wouldn't be able to drink.

I was already warned that the nightlife in Argentina would be schizophrenic. I waited with the two hostel bartenders, a French girl, and an Irish guy until it was an acceptable time to enter a club. All the Irish guys I met so far were outgoing with a fun sense of humor, without the bone dryness of the English or the crudeness of the Australians. They never turned down an invitation to go out. Once in the bar or club they bounce off the ceiling and put everyone else's drinking prowess to shame. This Irishman would be no different. It was in South America that I learned the stereotype of Irish people drinking a lot is not a stereotype. They can be passed out in a puddle of their own vomit with a hand reaching for more drink.

We arrived at Salon VIP at 3am. The club was a huge warehouse with two floors and ultraviolent lighting that gave an unfortunate glow to many teeth. I thought of the fire that struck a club in Buenos Aires a couple years back and killed 169 people. If this club is anywhere close in form I'm surprised more people didn't die. Too many intoxicated people, not enough exits.

The music was ear-splittingly loud, a combination of house music and *cumbia*, Argentina's answer to salsa that was slower and heavier on the bass. Unlike America, Argentina is a house music obsessed culture. There will be no grinding on asses here.

Before entering the club I told myself I needed to approach a lot of girls to end the cold streak. I wasn't going to sit around and wait for girls to recognize my exotic status and give me an obvious sign, especially when my "exotic" skin is just about identical to the average Argentine guy.

I leaned on the main bar with my new Irish friend and saw a group of five girls. We were already in a fun and playful mood so I didn't have to mentally think about what I had to do and how I was going to do it. I walked up to the girls and blurted out my tried-and-true Spanish opening line: "*¿Hola, habla inglés?*" It seemed to work better on larger groups where there was a higher chance that at least one of them speaks English, because if none of them do then a natural end to the conversation was reached. Two of them were learning English.

I highlighted the outsider status of my blonde hair, blue-eyed friend and we talked to them for fifteen minutes until they ditched us for the bathroom, never to be seen again. But the approach paid dividends when a girl walked up to me later and asked if I spoke English. She added, "I saw you trying to talk to those girls." We ended up dancing. Usually as I'm dancing with a girl and the night progresses, she gets closer to me or at least allows me to get closer, but this one maintained her distance. She got no closer to me than the instant we first exchanged words. Time out.

I went to use the bathroom and looked at my sweaty face in the mirror alongside several other guys fixing their shaggy hair, the hairstyle of choice for young Argentine men. Heavy drinking really does a number on the eyes and I looked ghastly in the bright bathroom lighting, like most everyone else. I debated if I should ditch the girl and try to talk to a new one, but the club was closing in ten minutes. It was her or nothing.

I fixed my hair and patted my face dry and then went back to her while the Irishman lingered around. Then out of nowhere came one of her friends, who for some reason was dying to meet the American. She had a more beautiful face than the girl I was flirting with, but with a couple (dozen) extra pounds her body wasn't as good. She began touching me and getting closer, hanging on my every badly-pronounced Spanish word. The choice was made. The streak would end with this chubby girl.

When the club closed the Irish guy and I followed the group, now four girls strong, into a taxicab. We hopped in without asking, not knowing where they were going. If we asked permission first they'd probably say no. They'd tell us they were going to sleep.

I sat in the front seat and the chubby girl got on my lap. I positioned her body in a way that much of her weight was against the door instead of crushing my body. The Irishman was in the backseat with three girls and during the commotion he caused, my girl started giving me kisses on my neck and cheek. But, inexplicably, she pulled back two times when I tried to kiss her on the lips. She eventually gave in but the kiss was a lot shorter and less sloppy than I imagined based on the attention she was giving me. Maybe she held back because her friends were watching?

The cab dropped us all off and at that point the game became one of endurance, to outlast the cockblockers before they succeeded in their mission. One girl vanished into a house while my original girl pulled the chubby girl into another cab. All that was left was a girl who the Irishman talked to a bit in the club. He won. He endured and he outlasted and he banged his girl at her parents place while I got nothing for my troubles except a long walk home. I felt like I got close, even though I really didn't.

I tried again the next night. I went out with a large group of doppelgangers from the hostel. Sadly the fun Irishman had left town. I was buzzed by the time I got into the club, but talking to girls didn't come easy like the night before. The previous night was an extension of having a good time, while now it was a tedious chore. I had to force myself. In two hours I talked to only three girls, and remained in the safe pack of gringos I didn't care to be with. When I returned to the hostel one of the bartenders was giving a topless French girl a massage on the couch. At the same time another bartender watched instructional videos on YouTube about how to give deep body tissue massages. Here I was going out to find girls while they sat and waited for girls to come to them. I gave them a thumbs up sign and went to bed. Later I found out that giving a thumbs up to someone in Argentina suggests you want something firmly rammed up their ass.

I was determined not to see a doctor until after the weekend, but I was in too much pain. My stomach would just twist and scream, regardless of how much food was in it. Luckily the hostel had a doctor on retainer. For no charge a female physician and her male nurse attendant came by the hostel into my dorm room. They asked me what my symptoms were and I told them what I told Zura. The doctor put her stethoscope on my stomach, listened for twenty seconds, and then said, "You definitely have an infection." No shit. The cure was ciprofloxacin, the same antibiotic I just finished two weeks earlier. Next thing I knew I was laying on my stomach with my pants down getting an injection of the drug directly into my left ass cheek. The needle must have hit a nerve because the pain traveled through my leg and stayed there for twenty minutes until it faded into a giggly sort of sensation like someone hitting my funny bone. I wasn't very optimistic the drug would help me.

It became clear that nightlife game for gringo guys revolved around the possibility of getting a one-night stand. It makes no sense to get phone numbers to try to court a girl when you're staying in town for only a few days. There is no chance of a first date at a familiar bar several days after meeting to begin a seduction that plays out for, as sometimes is the case, several weeks. I would have to play the sleaziest angle of game if I was going to get any.

I went out the night of the cipro injection but didn't drink. I followed the crowd to another club, one with a raised island platform for girls to shake their ass to house music. I found myself talking to a 16-year-old American girl, a self-described party animal with a cute face and eight piercings. She was here on a cultural exchange program, yet the only culture she seems to have picked up on so far is drinking.

For about a year before the trip, I complimented younger girls to anyone who would listen. I claimed that they have a more uninhibited and lively energy compared to older counterparts because they weren't yet dating pros who've completely internalized a character from *Sex and the City*. Young girls were the way and the light, I decided. Well there in front of me, under the influence of alcohol, was what I claimed I wanted, but I didn't do a damn thing about it. I couldn't make myself flirt with her and wasn't comfortable touching her either, no matter how mature, independent, and extremely developed she was for her age (big breasts).

I convinced myself I felt weird talking to her because of the feminist culture I grew up in, which was designed to make me feel guilty for finding a girl twelve years younger than myself sexually attractive. Or maybe I was scared of looking the fool if I was rejected by a kid. After we gave each other high fives goodbye, I turned around and saw the same hostel guy who was massaging the French girl the night before sucking face with a husky Dutch girl. Earlier he told me she was not feminine enough for him. I couldn't go after what I said I wanted and he went for what he said he didn't want. It bothered me that two men made firm decisions in their mind but went against them at the drop of a hat.

II

I decided to do something "cultural." I wanted to say my Salta experience was about more than just going to clubs.

I went to the local museum to see The Maiden, a 15-year-old girl from Incan times who was sacrificed to the gods on the Andes mountains and subsequently preserved by the cold. The curators built a little climax by first showing the artifacts found with her and her party—tools here, a gemstone bracelet there, and a short video about how she was recovered, including interviews with the scientists involved. Then I was shuffled into a dark room. There she was, preserved in a climate controlled glass capsule several inches thick, like she was about to be rocketed up into space, clothed in the same handwoven brown cloth she died in. The temperature console on her capsule looked familiar—it was made by the same company as some fermentation equipment I've worked on.

Other than her leathery skin she had the appearance of an indigenous native I'd see on a bus ride in Ecuador or Peru. The prominent cheekbones, large nose and forehead, dark olive skin, and jet black hair were all there. It was easy to get caught up in the moment with this dead little girl in front of me, and naturally I thought of death and the cruelty and shortness of life, but then a few minutes later I was back in daylight and the menu of a café was beckoning me to try their layered *dulce de leche* cake. I planted myself down at a sidewalk table and cracked open the daily newspaper to see how much I could understand.

III

Saturday night was a big deal at the hostel. The long grill on the roof was uncovered, cleaned, and greased for the big weekend barbecue, to be attended by twenty hungry gringos.

Fresh potato and eggplant salads were prepared downstairs in the kitchen. Grilled mushrooms and broccoli were cooked on the grill. There were big, thick pieces of the finest cow meat I have ever had, cooked at high temperature to darken the outside flesh while locking in red juice and tenderness on the inside. The meat was so soft it almost melted in my mouth like pieces of popcorn. There was also real pork sausage, not the pureed, packed hoof and ear cartilage leftovers from the cutting room floor. It was maple brown in color and wrapped in intestine casing that snapped when broken.

We gorged and filled our bellies at a huge cafeteria-style table as the chefs, who were also the bartenders, brought out cutting board after cutting board of animal meat stacked high, forcing us to eat more than we could handle. All of it was washed down with sweet red wine. I knew the meal would bother my stomach, which was only marginally better after the ass injection and subsequent pills from the *farmacia*, but I didn't care. It was one of those cases where the pleasure gained far outweighed the cost.

After no more food could be eaten and the last jug of cheap wine was consumed, an Irish girl moved from the wing of the cafeteria table to sit directly opposite me. She was a short brunette with long hair and a child-bearing figure. Her cheeks were slightly rosy. Other than a painfully gorgeous Spanish girl who was already taken by a nice guy from Norway, the Irish girl was the cutest in the hostel. Her accent was nothing short of adorable, and she had a way of speaking where her sentences would be capped off with a slight smirk on the left side of her face.

Like other Irish I met, she was committed to going out even though in this case she had to get up early. It was just us two headed to the club from the twenty that ate at the barbecue. Strange, considering it was a Saturday, but I wasn't complaining because there would be no chance of a cockblock from jealous friends. I smiled at my good fortune, especially since we were staying at the same hostel. It got even better when she told me her ex-boyfriend was Iranian. I couldn't be happier to know that he had a similar background as me, because that meant she had a type that I matched. This was turning into a sure thing.

We went to Twenty One, a one-level club with three girls for every two guys. Now with a cute girl on my arm, I got the attention from everyone in the club, even the guys. They looked at me first and then the Irish girl second, and I know what they were thinking: "What is he doing with a gringa?" After all I looked just like them. The Argentine guys probably thought I hit the jackpot, not having to deal with the "hysterics" of the Argentine girl, the definition of which I would find out soon enough.

There was no temptation to stray from the Irish girl no matter how many girls looked at me. I made my selection and was determined to carry it through. We settled at the bar and our faces got closer. When it was close enough that I could bridge the gap with just my lips, she pulled back.

I whined like a little bitch.

"I have the worst luck ever," I said.

"Why?"

"No, I'm just talking to myself."

"Why because I won't kiss you?" She smiled.

"No of course not, who said I wanted to kiss you?" I smiled back, brought alive by a suitable comeback.

"I want to kiss you but I have a boyfriend back home."

"That's fine."

"I can't cheat on him."

"That's fine! I understand. We can just dance."

"But I like you."

She wanted to have her cake and eat it too, to be able to kiss me without being disloyal to her boyfriend back home.

"Well how about this," I said, "you do what you want to do, and I'll do what I want to do. If it's the same then great, but if not then it's no big deal." I said this as my right hand was placed on her hip. She stayed still and we got closer. I brought up my left hand to the other side of her hip until her waist was wrapped around my arms. I could smell the cheap red wine on her breath. She didn't turn her head away this time and we kissed there against the bar.

The clubs in Salta have a weird system when it comes to the drink glasses. With your first drink you receive a glass that you're expected to hold onto for the entire night. Otherwise a small fine must be paid for subsequent cocktails and upon exit, usually $0.50. The effect of that policy can be seen in guys dancing with empty glasses in their back jean pocket. Those who lost theirs would participate in the great glass grab at the end of the night when the lights turned bright. The charge was too nominal for gringos though and they would pay the fine each time they went to the bar, glassless.

The Irish girl was a horrible dancer, to the point where I moved off the dance floor to encourage her to follow me back to the bar. She violently seizured with thumbs outstretched, causing me to think she was dancing to a song both 50% slower and faster than the one being played. She had a move where she bent her head all the way forward and randomly splashed her hair from left to right and back again. When she did this I couldn't see her face because it was held parallel to the floor. There were moments of flirting and kissing spaced between her solo ventures back onto the dance floor that I refused to tag along with. I didn't want the attraction I had for her to be lost by watching her dance.

We left the club at the 5am closing time, only a couple hours after we arrived. She was trashed but I still had my wits about me, as I had planned. I didn't want to get drunk and leave the possible end of the cold streak to mere chance, because it was chance that was wholly against me. I had to be aware of what was going on so I could properly adjust to whatever difficulty came my way.

We arrived back at the hostel. I expressed my desire to "snuggle" with her on my foam mattress in a room with nine other sleeping gringos.

"No I don't think that's a good idea. I have to go to sleep," she answered.

"How about for just a few minutes?"

"Plus there are too many people."

I persisted. "We can lay down in your room, doesn't it only have three other beds?"

"No there's still other people. I should really get to bed. I have to get up in three hours anyway."

Most reasonable men would give up at this point, but I sensed she really wanted to continue the night. She just needed a little bit of privacy.

"There's an hourly hotel nearby," I said. "We can just go there and hang out and sleep for a couple hours and come back."

"Hmmm. Okay."

Well that was easy.

Only thing was I didn't know the exact location of the hotel. I roused one of the bartender chefs from his drunken sleep on the couch and begged him to help me find a hotel nearby. I pointed to the Irish girl waiting in the hallway as evidence that this was an extremely urgent matter. He nodded his head and grabbed a scrap piece of paper. With a tired hand he drew a crude map with no street names, just lines that signified how many blocks I had to travel. Four blocks down and two blocks over.

I wasn't too concerned about his sloppy map because I was betting on an obvious neon sign to guide me and other couples inside. Once on the street we couldn't find a taxi. So began the walk to the hotel, the mood turning more awkward with each step. We arrived at the supposed street where the hotel should have been but there was nothing but shuttered shops. One block up and one block down it was the same story. I couldn't find a hotel and there was no one to ask.

Right when I was about to give up and head back to the hostel with my tired but willing date, an empty cab approached. We got in.

"*Hotel por la hora que es más cerca, por favor,*" I said.

"*Hay uno que es un poco lejos.*"

"*Está bien.*"

The Irish girl didn't seem to mind that we were taking this lengthy journey, but she was succumbing to fatigue. She dozed off with my arm around her. It was almost 6am.

Fifteen minutes later we arrived at the hotel. It wasn't what I expected: there were fifteen garages covered with off-white curtains in a large complex that seemed like a place where men bring their prostitutes, not their dates. I bit my lip and walked to the front desk while she waited in the cab, awakened when I pulled my arm from underneath her. She made no protest.

The female attendant behind the bulletproof glass was counting a large stack of cash. A man stood next to her watching the count and put his index finger up as if to ask me to wait. The snack bar next door was closed. I thought about the strong-handed way I got the Irish girl here and the prostitutes banging their gentlemen callers in the garages. I felt like a creep. I pushed too hard and was definitely taking advantage of a drunk, tired girl by bringing her to this dirty place. But I wanted to get laid, badly. I waited patiently.

The lady behind the glass finished counting and made eye contact with me. As I began to speak the phone rang and she told me to hold on. I walked away when the receiver met her ear. I went back to the cab and told the driver to take us back to our hostel.

I gave the Irish girl a kiss goodnight on the forehead. She could barely keep her eyes open. I didn't know whether to feel proud of myself or ashamed.

IV

The next day I ran into her in the common area. She convinced me to come have dinner with her and three other guys from the hostel. Whereas the night before I found her accent cute, on the walk to the restaurant it was painfully annoying. The conversation was stale and her humor not funny. I couldn't wait to join the others to be relieved of having to talk to her. It was an alcohol fueled chemistry, nothing more.

We sat down at the restaurant with two gay Swiss guys and a Dutchman, and didn't exchange another word for the rest of the night.

Three tables over, the Dutchman spotted two German girls staying at our hostel.

"I wonder if they are going out tonight," he said.

"Why don't you go over and find out?" I replied.

"You mean just walk over there and ask?"

"Yes, they seemed friendly when I saw them at the hostel."

He threw me a blank stare. He didn't know how to do it and needed me to give him explicit instructions.

"Go to the bathroom so it doesn't seem like the only reason you got up was because you wanted to talk to them. When you pass their table appear confused and tell them they look familiar. I'll bet they are not going out though. Gringos here don't go out much." The two gay guys couldn't care less about our efforts to get in with the cute Germans, but the Irish girl sat with tepid curiosity at our plan to talk to them.

The Dutchman spent at least ten minutes in the bathroom, probably mentally rehearsing the approach. I got worried because the last thing we needed the girls to think was that he had diarrhea. Finally he came out and went right for their table. The smile and laughs I saw from the girls were a good sign, but when the Dutchman came back he said they were staying in for the night. Hostel girls always had to get up early for some tour or excursion.

The gay guys and Irish girl said they were going back to drink at the hostel. Since the Dutchman and I were in the same boat, I asked him if he wanted to visit a club with me. He enthusiastically said yes.

We took a cab to Salon VIP, where a huge line wrapped around the building. "Fuck this let's bribe the bouncer," I said. I folded a fifty peso bill (about $16) and put it in my right hand squeezed between my palm and thumb. I walked up to the front, made eye contact with the bouncer, and with my hand out ready to give him a shake I said, "Me and my *amigo*?" He looked at me and the Dutchman for two seconds then said, "*Bien*." But he didn't notice the cash in my hand and let us right in without taking the bribe. My first attempt to bribe a bouncer failed in a very successful way, and the Dutchman and I gave each other high-fives in disbelief that that actually worked.

The club was mobbed and it was a sweaty journey to move from one area to another. I ran into the chubby girl I kissed a few days ago but this time around I declined a repeat. Instead I did at least seven *habla inglés* approaches, but the girls just ignored me. One group even made fun of me, or I think so because after rejecting me they all started laughing uncontrollably amongst themselves and pointing at my face. Where were girls from the previous night who were much hotter and couldn't stop looking at me? It seemed like it would be far easier to get a cute girl if I already had a cute girl on my arm, in place of, say, a Dutchman, who wasn't having much luck as well.

We leaned against a column overlooking the crowded dance floor and I fished for eye contact but got none. When I'm sitting in a café in Salta's main square I get some eye contact from girls who walk by, but if I'm in a club ready to flirt then no girl looks at me. They stare me down when I'm with another girl but not when I'm alone walking on a crowded sidewalk. It seemed like they are only gave eye contact when they were sure I couldn't do anything about it.

My eighth approach was the charm. A short, indigenous looking girl with a fleeting resemblance to The Maiden spoke some English and engaged me in light conversation. I introduced her to the Dutchman and judging by how much the side of her lips perked up, I knew she was more attracted to him than me.

The Dutchman was my polar opposite. I had long hair while he had short hair. I had a beard, he was freshly shaved. I had jeans and a t-shirt and he had a button-down with khakis (a very rare sight among gringos staying in hostels). She had a type just like the Irish girl had a type, but I was still mildly disappointed when I saw him making out with her not even twenty minutes later. It's nice that one of us got some, I suppose, but now the endurance of the cold streak was becoming too glaring and sore. I was supposed to be good at this. I returned alone to the hostel.

The next afternoon I ran into the Dutchmen at an ice cream shop. He told me he did not sleep with The Maiden. She lived with her parents, and he didn't try to go in. He seemed quite happy with the result regardless. For a split second I felt pleased with his failure, but that quickly turned to empathy when I thought of all the recent nights out where I came up empty. I wouldn't want others rooting for and relishing in my failure.

V

In the hostel I played ping pong for a couple hours against a South African guy. He told me about the once-a-year monster wave that roars down the Amazon River in Brazil, and how it carries so much jungle debris that boats and jet-skis must be hired to protect the surfers. Even though the competition became intense at times with profanity laced tirades, I enjoyed the camaraderie with someone I would have never met at home at the Starbucks in Maryland. I ended up losing every match (my opponent had been practicing ping pong for months in other hostels).

The Irish girl and her new Scottish girlfriend were floating around the table, pounding cheap beers. She warmed up to me by trying to encourage my sorry ping pong skills. After the last match she invited me to come out with her and her friend to a bar. For a second her accent was cute again and I felt an urge to finish what I started, but I was tired from so many nights going out and this would be nothing less than a four-hour affair. I told her I had to get up early. The napkin said it was time to briefly cross over into Chile, my fifth country, until returning back to Argentina.

VI

My first stop in Chile was San Pedro de Atacama, a tiny, sweltering desert town that catered to people like me with their canyon tours, mountain bike adventures, horseback riding, and so on, none of which I was interested in. My desert and mountain adventure needs were fully satisfied by the Bolivian Southwest. All I wanted to do in San Pedro was sandboard.

I took the do-it-yourself route. I rented a board and beat-up bike from a random shop in the center of town and was given a copy of a hand-drawn map that didn't seem to be drawn to scale. I was so used to signs pointing out tourist attractions that I expected several "Sand Dunes This Way" markers to guide me in. This wasn't the case and I got lost on sand paths in private property twenty minutes outside town with the board hanging out my backpack. Pedaling on sand is just as hard as it sounds—it felt like driving a car in the initial moments of rain, the tires spinning trying to find traction, except here you had two wheels instead of four.

I didn't lose hope in finding the dunes because the only reason I came to San Pedro was to sandboard. Failure here would be too crushing for my dented ego. I decided to follow a tour van into a narrow valley with twenty feet tall walls of rock on both sides. After fifteen minutes the walls opened up and I caught a glimpse of a large mountain of sand in the distance. I took the last swig from my small bottle of water and thought of a suitable newspaper headline: "Stupid Gringo Goes On Day Trip To Desert Without Sufficient Water, Dies." I couldn't have been the only one who came unprepared because right before the dune was a parked car advertising water, sodas, and snacks for sale. One gringo's mistake is another man's business opportunity.

I traveled down the sand road to find a dune more suitable to my inexperienced level. Not far past the giant dune I found the bunny slope where two German guys were making runs. I copied their style and left my socks on to protect the soles of my feet from the heat of the sand. I followed the foot trail, climbing up at a slight diagonal to soften the deceivingly steep slope of the dune. By the time I got up ten minutes later I realized why sandboarding was and never will be as popular as skiing: there are no lifts.

At the top of the dune I waxed the bottom of my board with a broken candle and laid it on the sand. I put my feet in the straps, visualized success with my eyes closed, and then made a little hop over the crest to let gravity do its work. Two seconds in I picked up so much speed that I freaked out and attempted a turn to slow myself down. Instead I fell head first into the sand, then tumbled down like a rag doll as the board escaped my feet and settled almost all the way at the dune's base. The German guys, watching me as they climbed for another run, gave me a thumbs up and I let out a meek smile. While the sand itself is soft and probably won't kill a man, the grains grated the hell out of my elbows and knees. The only real danger was twisting your ankle in a crash if the board straps stuck on while you rolled to a stop.

I managed to do six runs, two of which were somewhat respectable, before I could climb no more. The hour I lasted was much less than what I imagined (staying for the entire day and becoming so good that I could make 180 degree hops and slalom back and forth like an Olympic snowboarder). A few days later the carpet burns on my body healed, but I was still finding sand in my hair and ears.

VII

All that was in my way of Santiago was a twenty-four hour bus ride halfway down the country. I prayed I'd be seated next to a cute girl, a sensual Brazilian girl. I was going to will it with the force of my mental powers. I was slightly off, for next to me sat a handsome Brazilian guy named Rodrigo. He was 23 years old and just finished college a little over a year ago. He had lived for three months in India and another year in the United States along with visits to a dozen other countries. I carefully listened to him when he spoke of travel so I could pick apart how it changed his life for the better, an outcome that I wanted to happen to myself, but it wasn't obvious in his stories and observations. Instead he wanted to talk about girls.

After an hour of conversation things died out and the result was short bursts of conversation every twenty minutes or so. I can't read while moving because of my motion sickness so I coped like I usually did, napping and thinking and snacking on pastries I bought from vendors who climbed on the bus with their baskets of goodies. The Chilean desert offered little in terms of distraction besides the hope that the next metropolis I stepped foot into had the fun Salta vibe. I got off the bus with Rodrigo, surprisingly not moody like I usually was after such a journey. The rides were getting easier.

Santiago felt more like a city in the United States than South America. The mall and fast food culture was a letdown. Large department stores dominated the commercial district downtown, attracting customers with specials on cell phones and electric shavers. Hot dog stands and chain stores including McDonalds filled the spaces in between. The hot dog stands specialized in the *completo* ("complete"), mystery meat frankfurters loaded with mayonnaise and factory-made guacamole that was too bright in green color to be real. It was by far the most popular food I saw. I indulged in a dog related to the *completo* called the *Italiano*, whose only difference was a dash of special relish on top. Each bite came with a tiny piece of brown meat with a wallop of condiment. It was like I opened my mouth and let someone who hated me dump mayonnaise and mustard inside with a sprinkling of salt and pepper.

One can easily make the case that Chilean cuisine leans on the unhealthy side. Restaurants advertised the *lomo a la pobre* (literally "beef to the poor"), that consisted of fried steak, fried onions and french fries topped with a fried egg or two and sometimes slices of ham. It was common to see people puncture the yolk to allow it to dribble over the meat. The locals took to this meal like Americans took to the laboratory-made Pizza Hut pizza with the weird tasting cheese built right into the crust.

Hanging around the malls were chain smoking teenagers who had a look somewhere in between grunge and goth. Both sexes wore all black clothing with black dyed hair and thick eyeliner. Common accessories were dog collars and thick chains. Without a mall culture it's hard to imagine this type of tribe existing, because where there are malls there is wealth, and where there is wealth there are teens with too much money and time on their hands searching for something cool and different to do with it. I also saw the most homeless people in any South American city thus far, including one man in the bohemian, slightly upper-class Bellavista area who made aggressive cat noises whenever I passed him by.

VIII

Rodrigo decided to stay in the same hostel as me. It was filled with fresh arrivals—Santiago being a popular starting point for a journey through South America. In the kitchen, TV room or from my bunk bed, I'd tell other gringos how many times I'd been sick with pride, reciting each ailment as if I fought a glorious war battle. I made sure to throw in my grand plan of conquer: to visit every country on the continent, a not-so-subtle way of suggesting that my travel experience was more genuine or authentic. Yet there I was, firmly planted on the gringo trail, going to the same places and taking the same pictures as half the people staying in my dorm room. Where there are malls you have teenagers trying to be special by wearing dog collars, and where there are university degrees and cubicles you have confused 20-somethings trying to be special by going to exotic places.

On our second night in Santiago, Rodrigo picked up a guitar and like a jukebox played and sang popular American rock songs one after the other. Up to that point he never told me he played both the guitar and piano, learned from several years of music classes, something most people would bring up in the first couple hours of meeting another person.

Two Austrian girls flocked to his music and two more American girls eventually joined. Some guys may cry foul when a man picks up a guitar at a party, but it was fun to watch a circle of four girls close their eyes and gently sway to his music like he was Bon Jovi unplugged. It's a moment like that I wished I knew how to play the guitar, but then I thought of how many years of work it would take to get to his level. I don't regret learning how to pick up girls at bars instead, where all I need is words coming out of my mouth and clean clothing. I remembered when I used to do that somewhat easily, anyway.

Rodrigo stayed in to play guitar for his groupies while I tagged along with a bunch of Americans to The Circuit, a gay house club only realized after the cover charge was paid. I was a little annoyed that no guy hit on me and rationalized it by concluding that my heterosexual essence was too strong. At the next house club I was ready to make generalizations about Chilean girls. They were cute, just a tad chubby, but unable to compete with Argentine girls for the superficial beauty that I so greatly desired. Chile was significantly more expensive than Argentina but had inferior food, cafes, and girls. (This was all relative because compared to Bolivia, Chile was heaven-sent.) I looked forward to going back to Argentina.

IX

The next night Rodrigo finally put down the guitar and came out with two fresh Americans and myself to the Plaza Nuñoa square. The surrounding bars were the sit-down and people-watching variety that I noticed in Argentina, more for catching up with friends than picking up and getting laid. Unless you happened to sit right next to a group of girls that you wanted to talk to, it was impossible to work the floor and mingle. We didn't hike it all the way to this side of town to sit down at bars.

With Rodrigo leading the group asking for directions in his near-fluent Spanish, we arrived at Kmasu, a large club whose name was a play on Kama Sutra. The upstairs VIP room was hidden from the commoners, but every now and then I'd see a girl leave the guarded entrance for a dash to the bathroom, usually wearing a skin tight nylon bottom and bikini top bespeckled with dashes of glitter. My guess is there was some hanky-panky going on.

I accidentally asked a group of three girls if they spoke English in English instead of Spanish. Two of them did speak decent English and seemed quite excited to practice what they learned in class. The cutest one of the group, who looked more Brazilian than Chilean with her darker skin color and tightly curled hair, would be my project for the night.

The two Americans paired up and in a dark corner Rodrigo nursed a gigantic sore on his lower lip from too much time spent in the San Pedro desert without chapstick. The sore made it hard for him to flirt with girls and I don't blame him—it was a red crusty thing the size of a pinky fingertip. The antibiotic ointment he applied made it gleam in the darkness.

For the next hour I had a conversation that I've had with every other native girl who spoke half-decent English. I talked about my background, I asked about her culture, I told her about the highlights of my travel journey, and I made comments about what I observed in her country (the *completos*, in this case). There was also discussion of mundane details to fill airtime like her age, where she lived, and favorite American movie (*Titanic*). Every few minutes I'd take a break to talk to her friends to insure against the cockblock. She did warm up to me with more smiles and little innocent touches on my forearm, but she kept texting on her phone.

"What, are you texting your boyfriend or something?" I figured it was a girlfriend.

"Actually yes, he wants to know what I'm doing."

I noticed the wallpaper on her phone was that of a guy. Damn. I might as well go for the consolation prize—her friend. I did have some rapport with her, but no, I didn't want second best. Either I get the girl I want or I go home alone with my hand.

The girls weren't drinking, oddly enough. The cover charge came with one complimentary drink and that's all they had way back when I first started talking to them. How am I supposed to kiss a girl who has a boyfriend when she doesn't have any alcohol in her system? If a girl wants to hook up she'll drink, at least to give her the option of excusing regretful behavior. I was on drink number seven and it's a fact that no girl gets with a guy who is drunker than she is. It was hopeless. I used the bathroom and blotted out sweat and grease from my face using toilet paper. When I returned back to the circle the consolation prize developed a sudden headache. They left.

I found Rodrigo in the corner, long ready to leave. The American girl we originally came with got so drunk that her new make-out partner had to carry her to a cab. She promptly puked her guts out when it arrived at the hostel.

Rodrigo and I had a goodbye dinner on our last night in Santiago. He was going back home to Brazil and me to Valparaíso, west of Santiago right on the Pacific coast. I knew him for five nights, including one night on the bus, but not until the last night did I find out what he did (bank manager), and the only reason it came up was because he made a comment about not wanting to return to work. He never asked me what I did and I never told him, though it didn't matter because what I did before the trip would tell him nothing more about who I was besides what he already knew about me—my jokes, my beliefs, and my stories. I imagined when I returned home becoming even more annoyed by girls in bars who would ask me what I do after knowing me for only a couple minutes.

X

The beast roared back to life. It was asleep for nearly a week. I had shooting cramps in my midsection and my solids looked like clumpy tapioca pudding. It must be a parasite. Since anyone could buy drugs at the pharmacy without a prescription, I went on the internet to research anti-parasite drugs. Of the two most popular medicines, one is carcinogenic in mice and the other is mutagenic in hamster ovaries. The one Zura gave me is safest but could dangerously increase the level of nitrides in my blood. I decided to tough it out a bit longer, only taking the drugs if I found myself thinking "I can't live like this." I was close but not quite there.

It was fifty days prior that my stomach problems started in Huanchaco, Peru. I was familiar with the phrase "living day to day," but never understood what it meant until I found myself in the position of waking up every morning wondering how crappy the next sixteen hours would be. On the bad days, which were most days, I would fantasize about going back home, but I knew if I went home and didn't get better, if by chance a doctor couldn't find out what was wrong and the symptoms remained, I'd regret ending the trip early.

XI

I was surprised by Valparaíso. My expectations were so low I needed only to not get robbed to enjoy my time there (I didn't).

The city used to be an important stop for merchant ships traveling from the Atlantic to the Pacific, until the Panama Canal opened for business. Things deteriorated and the rich moved to the resort town of Viña del Mar a stone's throw away. But as luck would have it, many modern ships grew too big for the canal and Valparaíso became important once again. It didn't hurt that Chile's rising economy needed a port to export its wine, fruit, and industrial metals. The boom, bust, and boom again has given Valparaíso a character that blends the old with the new, set against a backdrop of rolling terrain with beautiful views of the city and ocean from no matter which hill you stand.

The century-old *ascensores* caught my attention first. They were funiculars, little trains that saved the time and breath of having to climb the hills. Vintage, rectangle boxes colored red and white made jumpy starts and stops on steeply sloped tracks, propelled by thick metal cables attached to spinning wheel motors. I've been to cities with funiculars before, but never to a city full of them.

It became a little gringo competition to go on the most *ascensores*, to be experts not only on the views they provided but on the nature of the neighborhoods they were in as well. It's at the higher elevations, at the top of the *ascensor*, that the streets would become a maze of curves and twists. What a pleasure it was to get lost!—to discover tiny artisan cafes and family-owned bakeries, to find myself going in circles as if blindfolded in a forest. It was important to take note of landmarks to guide me back, such as the turquoise house perched on the corner looking as if it's about to topple over, the large graffiti stencil of a man with a moustache painted on a decaying piece of concrete wall, or the shuttered row-house with a gang of feral dogs sleeping out front. My unhurried days in Valparaíso were spent studying the notecards in my little daypack, going from café to café, drinking two or three cups of coffee in short time while feasting on sweets made with the Chilean interpretation of *dulce de leche*.

I liked the waitress in one of the cafes. She had an hourglass figure and hair that went down most of her back, and seemed to hold eye contact with me one second longer than necessary. Unless she had lazy eye she was curious about the gringo patron in her café. I stared off into space to come up with a plan, the only problem being she knew no English and the Spanish spoken by Chileans sounded more like a distant relative of Spanish than Spanish itself. I was going to ask a couple questions to build rapport and gauge her interest before asking her out. I've never had success by taking wild stabs in the dark.

When it was time to pay the check I asked her for suggestions on where to go at night. I handed her my map and she marked a couple spots. I was waiting for her to mention her favorite bar but she didn't. Then I asked her which bars she goes to.

"I don't go out," she said.

Great. She didn't even ask me where I was from, the least she could do if she was just a bit interested. So I left, back onto the twisty streets for another walk that would take me to another café.

For the next hour I tore myself up reliving that simple encounter and why it didn't go my way. Usually it does. Not most of the time but a good percentage of the time. I lost count how many times I have been to a crowded Starbucks to share a table with a cute girl, only for the ensuing long conversation to end in an email address or number. Or the nights I spent in dive bars where I'd do a handful of approaches and walk out with a handful of numbers that turned into dates the following week. I left home at the top of my game, mastering and refining techniques that I figured I could use until the day I died, but dodging around the piles of shit left by the feral dogs of Valparaíso, I had to admit I didn't know as much as I thought. This was a different world, and instead of adapting to my new environment, I was just trying to import something that worked on a different kind of girl in a different place.

The reason why I wasn't full-on depressed was because the hostel guys were only hooking up with the annoying hostel girls, not the natives that I wanted. But then again is this why I came to South America—just to fuck? What a joke it would be to put my life on hold for good times and fast sex but leave with a heavy sack and a damaged stomach instead.

XII

I walked to the little nightlife zone next to the port and settled on a busy club called Cosmonova. I asked the bouncer if there were girls inside and he assured me there were, giving me an a-okay sign with his right hand. I paid a cheap cover charge and walked to the main room.

The reggaeton music was louder than the dozen people milling around warranted. I noticed a steady stream of fresh arrivals going into another room guarded by a bouncer, separated by what looked like a shower curtain. After getting a once-over from the bouncer, I passed by the shower curtain into the room. It was filled with guys sitting down in a semi-circle, fiddling with their phones, waiting for something. There wasn't one girl in there—another gay bar!

Back out in the main room I asked the nearest bartender what was going on, but it was impossible to understand her Spanish. Another guy overheard my question and in English he explained to me that "sexy girls" will be there, "very very sexy girls." That's when I noticed another room where only girls were allowed to enter, protected by a more proper curtain. It started coming together.

A couple minutes later I followed the Chilean guy back behind the shower curtain and there she was—an obese Chilean girl naked except for a pair of high heels and sunglasses, performing poorly executed moves off a chair. Most of the guys were taking pictures with their phones while the rest nodded their heads up and down to show approval for the low-budget strip tease. I wanted a chance at a real girl, not this.

I went back to the main area and fifteen minutes later the nudie show was over. Well I think it was over because a hundred guys flooded the main room. It was like who let the dogs out. Now hungry, they looked for a mate only to find none—the girls were still in their room enjoying their own show. It would have been better if they stayed there. What was eventually unleashed onto the men were the type of older woman that likes watching hairless men rapidly spin their dicks around in circles, possibly doused with whipped cream. There were one of them for every four horny guys. Numb, I left. I was growing accustomed to failure.

XIII

Viña del Mar is upper crust, the "vine of the sea." When Valparaíso struggled, the richest residents moved here and opened up trendy boutiques alongside towering condominium developments. The most beautiful girls in Chile can be found sun bathing on Viña del Mar's tiny sliver of a beach. Nearby was a row of vendors where I found the perfect complement to my keychain—a little wooden moai, the stretched head statues with the huge noses found on Easter Island. I was so excited about "Little Steve" that I returned the next day to buy a six-inch stone moai, which I named "Big Steve."

Big Steve was the most impractical thing a backpacker could buy, but it was tiring to be reasonable and efficient all the time. To relieve my loneliness I'd play out conversations between Little Steve and Big Steve in my head, with Big Steve teaching Little Steve about the ways of life and women. Little Steve would go out on his own and experience disappointment, but make baby steps of progress.

On the way to buy Big Steve I ran into Max from the hostel, a young German who always wore a Fidel Castro cap that was popular with gringos. He decided to tag along after I told him about the interesting market by the beach.

While I was haggling over the price of Big Steve, Max saw a Viña del Mar postcard with a photo of sea lions. He inquired about it with the vendor, who said that the *lobos del mar* were only a short bus ride down the beach. With nothing else to do and several hours to go before it was time to experience a weekend night in Valpo, we decided to undertake the journey to see the *lobos*. A half hour later there were still no *lobos*, but then my childhood television viewing paid off. I noticed a big rock island off in the distance.

"Don't sea lions hang out on rocks by the water?" I said.

"I have no idea," Max replied.

"I'm pretty sure they do."

"How do you know?"

"When I was young I used to always watch the Discovery Channel. Whenever they showed sea lions they were always hanging out on a big rock."

"Are you sure?"

"No, but where else can they be?"

"I don't know."

"I'm pretty sure they're there."

"How about if they're not?"

"Then it's your fault."

Squeezing his forehead he said, "Why is it my fault?"

"Well this was your idea."

"Yeah that's true."

And on that went for a while until we decided to take a risk and walk to the rock. It didn't seem far but objects in the distance appear closer than they are. One hour later the Discovery Channel was in fact vindicated and there were the lobos, sleeping soundly on little platforms that seemed carved into the giant rock just for them. Their fur coats were so shiny it looked like they were dipped in Bolivian cooking oil.

We climbed over a concrete fence and navigated over volcanic rock until we got the closest possible to the sleeping *lobos*, who didn't seem bothered by the pelican colony and their piles of white excrement nearby, streaks of it running down the rock to the water. Perhaps their relationship was symbiotic in some way, like those tiny little birds that clean crocodile teeth.

There was no one else watching the *lobos* but me and Max. The rock was not mentioned in Lonely Planet, so it might as well not even exist but to the locals. We crouched down and stared at the *lobos* for some time until high tide rolled in and forced us to move back. The sun was beginning to set, our journey taken a good part of the afternoon. Facing the west we watched the sun dip underneath the ocean, a small head turn away from the *lobos* and the pelicans. For a second I was able to imagine how it must have been like to discover the historical landmarks and the undisturbed animal colonies of the world before it was captured in inexpensive books sold to millions of people, before you could see pictures and videos of it with a few clicks on a computer. Whatever travel was about, whatever meaning it was supposed to have, this is what I wished it was, completely random and pure and calm.

XIV

Max and I went to Duff, a huge, three-story club with an average age of barely 20 years old. I was probably the oldest guy there, but not old enough where I felt like the "old guy in the club."

Max turned out to be quite the energetic firecracker. "We can't go home until we kiss girls," he said. "And I mean it!" Finally, a motivated wingman!

The first pair of girls we talked to was thanks to Max. He walked up to them and built some rapport with his proficient Spanish, then moved to dancing once the conversation waned out. He picked the cuter of the pair and I was left with the okay-looking friend. I wasn't too motivated to dance to Chilean rock music and barely bobbed my head to the beat. I felt like the old guy in the club.

The girls ditched us and we went to the bar where he continued his rapid-fire approaches, introducing me as his American friend with the really bad Spanish. It was a good cop, bad cop sort of vibe. There were three girls standing around, looking bored. I approached. "*¿Habla inglés?*" Talked to them for two minutes until they went to the bathroom. All the way downstairs were billiard tables and Max got in with a large mixed-sex group, but the cutest girls were taken. Next to the coat rack was a girl alone and I slid next to her. "*¿Habla inglés?*" She was waiting for her boyfriend. "*¿Habla inglés?*" Nothing. Bathroom break.

If I'm in a club bathroom with a gringo friend talking in English, there will be at least one native who understands our banter and asks where we're from. In the Duff bathroom I ended up meeting a Chilean who studied in Los Angeles.

"Chilean girls are tough," I said.

"Do you talk to the girls in English or Spanish?"

"I start off in Spanish. *¿Habla inglés?*"

"No no no that's wrong. Always start in English."

"They won't even understand."

"That's the point. You need to play up that you're an outsider right away. At least for the first three minutes speak in English only. It's different and exciting—they will laugh and enjoy it."

"Then after three minutes?"

"Start moving into Spanish. By then it won't matter because you got their attention. Always talk in English first."

Then I thought back to the night in Santiago with Rodrigo where I started in English by accident and got in pretty well with the group. Even though asking *habla inglés* already implies that I speak English, I decided that this random bathroom guy knew what he was talking about.

Back upstairs on the dance floor we ran into the same two girls we talked to initially. No guys were on them so Max went back in. His girl was much friendlier this time around, but she made him resort to playing elaborate cheek kissing games. Just when you'd think he was about to slobber on her face, she would reject him and turn away, only for Max to go for another cheek kiss. Then he'd ask her to give him a cheek kiss. It was obvious she liked him—why was she being so difficult?

Finally, after fifty cheek kisses, they went at it. I looked at my girl and thought "No." I'm not going through that for a kiss. I'd be supplicating to put in all that work for so little benefit. I wasn't even really attracted to her. The club closed and I didn't get my kiss and Max, giddy as a schoolgirl with an email address in his pocket, said he wasn't going to let me in the hostel. He got in my face and said, "You're going to sleep on the street with the dogs tonight!" Like he could enforce that, but I humored him anyway and said there were still girls on the street. It's not over until my head hits the pillow.

I talked to five groups of girls in just a couple minutes and didn't get a single positive response. Oops, I was doing it in Spanish. I approached the last pair in English, mouthing off a few sentences at fast speed without any hope they'd understand. They stopped walking and told me to slowly repeat myself. They wanted to understand. What followed was a mix of English and Spanish until next thing I look over and see Max giving his girl cheek and neck kisses. Then he asked his girl to give him cheek kisses back, and after only two dozen more they were making out. The girls dipped into a cab a minute later. I thought I put in effort but here was Max making me look lazy and passive. At that moment I missed American girls—they're ten times easier.

Now Max was high as a kite bouncing off the street while all I could do was grin and bear it. He was gentle though, and didn't protest when I expressed my desire to sleep indoors. I did learn a little piece of the puzzle that night and never approached another girl in Spanish again.

Before we went out, an Australian man in his 40s staying at the hostel told us a story: "The guys here are aggressive. I was on a bus and from the window I saw on the street a guy forcing a girl to kiss him by grabbing her chin when she tried to turn away. He put his other hand on top of her head to hold it in place." He went on to ask what came first—the chicken or the egg. "Are the guys aggressive because of the girls or do the girls resist because of the aggressiveness of the guys?" Since a man's game is based on what a girl is giving him, and every move or technique he has to come up with is in response to her, I'm forced to believe the former. I only had to look at the one-night stand for proof. Because many girls give out their number without any intention of seeing the guy again, it encourages guys to be aggressive and go for it all just a couple hours after they meet a girl. "Let me walk you home... I just want to make sure you get home safe... no really I don't mind... hey can I use the bathroom real quick... nice place how about a tour... oh cool I've never had this wine before... you like it when I pull your hair like that don't you?" When it comes to women, men are reactionary, not innovative. Max didn't give a hundred cheek kisses because that's how he kisses a girl, he did it because he knew the Chilean girls were frigid and needed to be forced into intimacy.

The napkin came into play. Since I wasn't having the time of my life, I had to leave for Mendoza in Argentina. I was happy to return to a country where the girls were cuter and easier, the prices cheaper, and the food less artery clogging. I remembered my first night out in Salta when I kissed the chubby girl in the cab and my Irish friend slept with her friend, and a couple days later when the Dutchman sucked face with The Maiden without a hundred pecks on the cheek. Things will be so much better in Argentina, I thought.

A DEAD BAT IN PARAGUAY

ARGENTINA

I

I arrived in Mendoza, Argentine wine country, and walked around the main promenade of shops before buying a small glass bottle of Coca-Cola. I sat down on a bench to people watch, and noticed something was off with the girls—they were so freakishly gorgeous and flawless that I felt like I was plunked down on a Hollywood movie set. They had large eyes, button noses, full lips, tanned complexions, slim bodies with curves, bubble butts, and hair grown since grade school. Every third girl younger than 30 years old could be a model if she wanted to, and walking around for twenty minutes during the day I saw more beautiful girls than I'd see going out in D.C. on Thursday, Friday, and Saturday nights—combined. There wasn't only girls with brown hair and eyes but blondes with blue and green eyes as well. I could live here, just for the girls, and rumor had it from other gringos at the hostel that a nearby city, Córdoba, was even better. Now was the time to put in that full Max effort to finally get some. It would be the beginning of the end of the cold streak, and I was ready to commit to make it so. I started researching cell phones to eliminate the luck factor of the one-night stand, fully prepared to date girls like I would at home.

My second night in Mendoza I had dinner with an Israeli guy who told me he struck out with the girls in Buenos Aires, but got his flag in Salta. He summed it up thusly: "Argentine girls are tough." Maybe it was tough for him because he wasn't trying hard enough? I figured all I had to do was approach in English and that would be sufficient. I listened to him with a skeptical ear because even though Salta wasn't especially easy, it seemed far easier than Chile. One thing we did agree on is that judging by the lack of drinking and flirty eye contact, Argentine girls don't make it very obvious they want to meet a guy in the club. With every Argentine girl we courageously walked up to it was like a craps shoot, versus a girl who at least recognized our existence and encouraged us with a glance or two before we opened our mouths.

The Israeli guy went on to tell me how rude his culture is and how even the American culture is a refreshing change from what he has to deal with back home. "I say *gracias* dozens of times a day, even for the smallest thing," he said, "but in Israel a word like *gracias* does not translate into Hebrew. When someone wants to say 'Excuse me, where is the bathroom... thank you,' in Hebrew it comes out like, 'Hey you, yeah where is the bathroom... okay yeah great.'"

He told me that in Israel everyone is trying to screw everyone else and it's a big deal to always be getting a good deal. I noticed this with Israeli travelers who were the only ones that tried to bargain with the posted nightly rates in hostels, a topic that was brought up in hushed tones among other travelers. And it wasn't uncommon to meet an Israeli who paid 20% or less for a tour than I did.

"How did you get that deal?" I'd ask.

"I bargained. They know I will tell a lot of other Israelis," they'd say. I did not see any bargaining skills by American Jews.

We drank at a café on Avenida Villaneuva, the nightlife zone full of restaurants and bars. But there on a Tuesday night it felt more like a quiet relaxation zone. We asked our server for a bar and she sent us across town to one that turned out to be for transsexuals, probably on purpose since we did try and fail to hit on her. All the gays milling around freaked out the Israeli.

"You should be flattered," I said. "It's nice to know that you are wanted by someone, even if it's a guy. It's like being invited to a party that you don't care for going to."

"I'd be humiliated," he said, deadpan. I started laughing but then stopped when I noticed that his poker face didn't flinch.

He went on about an entire country that crossed his comfort zone. "In Thailand there are a lot of lady boys and you have to be careful.

Check if they have hips and definitely make sure they have an Adams apple. Sometimes it's very hard to tell." He went on about the art of picking out lady boys from a crowd.

"You seem to know a lot about detecting transsexuals," I joked.

"Of course, I'm homophobic."

Two times during the night he mysteriously alluded to an incident that happened to him in Thailand, but refused to give details when asked.

After just one beer we called it a night and walked back to the hostel, our mini-friendship coming to an end because he was leaving the next day for Chile. It was futile to exchange email addresses with someone who wasn't going in the general direction I was, since nothing more than a couple short emails would result from it.

As beautiful as the girls were in Mendoza, I didn't want to sit on my hands until the weekend with the hype surrounding Córdoba flying around. To kill some time before my overnight bus there, I played pool alone in the hostel, slowly getting the angles right. After an hour a cute, brown-haired Swedish girl in hiking gear challenged me to a match. She said it with such eagerness that I knew she was good, and sure enough she proceeded to whip me four times in a row. But I still talked trash.

"I'm just taking it easy on you."

"I want to give you the confidence that comes from beating a man."

"Let me know when you want to play for real and I'll stop messing around."

"I don't want to hurt your sensitive girl feelings."

She either laughed or squinted her eyes to form a death stare. There was chemistry. She was touching me and we kept up the back-and-forth with her telling me how much I suck and me telling her that I'm ten times better than my actual performance. I think it was a hint when she asked me for a place where she could buy a nice pair of jeans because she was ready to "take a break from hiking to go out."

Within thirty minutes we were talking a lot closer and maintaining stares without words. I had to think back a long while for the last time I had sexual tension with a girl like that. Definitely not on this trip. I debated tossing my bus ticket and staying just for her, but I was afraid I was setting myself up for a disappointing fall. I imagined how shitty I would feel if I altered my plans and nothing happened. On the other hand I wanted to take a risk and put the work necessary to build something—anything—with a girl that I liked. If it didn't work out then who cares? At least I gave it a shot. The chances I'd see her again if I walked would be slim.

I got her email address. We swore to meet up in Buenos Aires where I boasted I'd beat her for real at pool. I fantasized about her long and hard on the ten hour bus ride to Córdoba, and not just about sex but more romantic things like long walks on the beach and spooning. I was starved for companionship, an emotional bond. I thought I made the right choice because in just ten days I'd see her again and wonderful things would happen.

Or so I thought. I did not anticipate staying in Córdoba for a month. It wouldn't have killed me to spend one extra night in Mendoza.

II

I decided to develop a strategy for getting goddamned laid in Argentina. Before I left Mendoza I wrote a bulletproof nine step plan on a piece of paper that included tips such as "Forget everything you know about eye contact—don't wait for it, don't expect it," "Speak English first," and "Pursue innocent daytime conversations by asking for directions or the time—ask her out if she asks you questions." I stuffed the plan away deep in my pack, never to be referenced again, but it was a good sign that I was using my big head to make needed changes. I honestly believed that girls would throw themselves on me because I was American, but now I knew this not to be the case. It was time to give it absolutely everything I had.

People were already heading out to work when I arrived in Córdoba early in the morning. I never could sleep well on the overnight buses so when I checked into the Tango Hostel I took off my jeans and shirt and dozed off. I was out for about two hours.

I was in a large bar that had the feel of Leprechaun Bar in Baños, with its woodsy theme and mixed crowd of gringos and locals. I was hitting on girls like usual, not really getting anywhere, when one girl walked up and asked me to dance. Dancing turned into grinding and I got quickly aroused—too aroused. It felt like I was going to blow my load right there on the dance floor with my crotch rubbing up against her ass. I squeezed my pelvic muscles as hard as I could to stop the orgasm. Then I woke up, in the middle of ejaculating in my boxers. Thankfully everyone else was asleep. I changed in the bathroom then tossed my soiled undergarment into my pillowcase laundry bag. It was my first ever wet dream, in the company of four sleeping gringos. Just when the paranoia from wetting the bed in Bolivia began to wane, I went back to grabbing my crotch immediately after waking up in the morning, a habit I'd keep for months.

This dream was easy to figure out. I was backed up like a clogged hostel toilet. Without privacy I had to sleep every night with a swollen sack. It's as if my body said, "Well if you're not going to take care of it, I will."

The wet dream didn't dampen my spirits, and only one day after writing my girl strategy I was pumped to go out. Unfortunately the specter of toxic meals past wouldn't have it. At dinner with a Spaniard and Uruguayan couple, I got violent stomach cramps and could barely touch our *parrillada*, a meat meal of sausage, steak, and various other bits from the cow I have not seen before like heart and tripe. It looked like they exported the good parts of the cow and served us the leftovers. The Uruguayan guy still couldn't get enough. With mouthfuls of ecstasy he kept repeating *"Muy muy buena."*

I valiantly fought the pain but two creamy scoops of ice cream afterwards sealed my early exit from the party. I went back to the hostel and sat on the toilet until my legs became numb with an evacuation that was my third worst in South America. I felt bad for the English girl sleeping just two feet away from the bathroom door, but there was nothing I could do. While camping out on the toilet I wished I had come to Argentina first.

III

In a couple days my stomach improved and I hit a club called Dorian Gray. It featured relatively famous DJ's for its small dance floor, along with a closet of a side room playing American 80s and hip hop music. I went with a group of male gringos who didn't know how to approach girls.

The night started when I talked to three girls using my English-first strategy. After taking an eternal three seconds to recognize the language, the girls put in effort to cut through the music to understand what I was saying. I was making progress, I like to think, until a drunk gringo I came with put his crotch on one of the girl's asses and tried to grind her American-style to house music. The girls promptly walked away. Approaching alone in a loud club is only slightly more preferable to wetting the bed, but I had no other choice. If I did it alone I couldn't blame anyone else if I didn't succeed.

Before I came to South America I went through all three units of the Pimsleur language program. Each unit had fifteen hours of audio lessons that taught me Spanish through a call-and-response system. Native speakers repeated sentences like, "I am from the United States," "I would like to buy a beer," and "Where can I find the bus station?" With the addition of a textbook I was on my way to Spanish proficiency, but since I was still speaking more English every day thanks to staying in hostels, the progress was a lot slower than I had wished. I couldn't tell a story in Spanish and had trouble making jokes without using obvious physical humor. It was like my personality was locked up in a cage and all I could do was hope that it was somehow leaking out into the ether.

It was with this lean Spanish that I communicated with Daniela and Sofia, fraternal twins who spoke not a word of English. They were curvy, beautiful young women with absurdly long wavy hair, oval faces, huge breasts, dozens of jingle-jangle cosmetic bracelets on their arms and a necklace or two draped from their necks. Daniela had a lighter complexion than Sofia and was also more confident, but Sofia was shy and awkward in a cute, endearing way. Their third friend was just as beautiful, but as fate would have it I first talked to the sisters and not the friend, far away from the gringos I had since ditched.

Having never before met an American, they were very curious about me and asked all sorts of questions, most of which I couldn't understand. There was a lot of nodding and smiling, but with the music pumping the silences weren't at all awkward. They invited me to come with them to the closet room. It was impossible to decide which sister to go for because they were giving me equal amounts of attention. No hot-blooded man could distinguish between their equal beauty and sweet personalities. I prayed that one of them would pick me instead by giving me a deep look or an intimate touch, but as hour three approached I was still unsure. I had to pick, and if I picked poorly then I would get nothing. I felt like Indiana Jones who had to choose the correct Cup of Christ to drink from or he would die like the Nazi guy before him.

I picked Daniela, because her ass was a little bigger.

I moved closer to her and away from Sofia. I danced with her. I put my hand on the side of her hip. I shared my drink with her from the same straw. The loud music was my savior because all that we had to do was chat for a minute and dance for ten. She invited me to come with her sister and friend to an after-hours club next door, where she bought me a fruity daiquiri. I insisted on paying for it but she got angry and shoved my money back into my jean pocket. Like her sister she was 21 years old, a college student working part-time to pay tuition bills. No other girl in South America had bought me anything so I took this as a very positive sign.

I grabbed Daniela's hand and led her through the club. She didn't resist. I tried to get close for the kiss but she maintained her distance, probably because her sister and friend were hovering around. I caught Sofia giving me strange looks. We all left the club at 8am. On the sidewalk in front of the club I put Daniela's number into my new prepaid cell phone with Sofia watching.

Two days later it was time to initiate contact with a text message. Texting girls was a new game to me because at home I would pick up the phone and call, a far more efficient system where plans could be made in two minutes as opposed to being drawn out for several hours. My first text (in Spanish) was simple: "Hey it's Roosh. How are you?"

She responded in thirty minutes, long enough to make me sweat a little, but with enough exclamation points that I was encouraged. She ended the text with a *beso*, a kiss. The sex fantasies I had been having about her for the past two days kicked into high gear. I saw no reason why she wouldn't be my next Argentine girlfriend.

I asked the bilingual hostel cook for help in asking her out. In Spanish he suggested, "If you are doing nothing tomorrow, how about we get something to drink?" But to me that was like asking, "If you're not going to be a loser tomorrow…" I asked two of the hostel maids for advice as well but their suggestion made me gag: "I had an amazing time with you the other night. When can I take you to dinner?" Instead I sent the following: "If you are free tomorrow, how about we get something to drink?" Solid plans weren't made before I went to bed, but I wasn't at all concerned. I didn't know at the time that pretty much all Argentine girls end their text messages with a *beso*.

The hostel maids at Tango were all female college students, a nice change from the typical maid who would have more in common with my grandmother than girls I saw at the club. By day they cleaned the room, usually barefoot, making idle chit-chat along the way. To humor them (and myself), I'd lay Big Steve on the pillow before heading out for the day, and when I'd come back in the afternoon he'd be tucked into the sheets. If Big Steve had an especially rough night I'd place him face down. At night the maids helped cook the communal meals by peeling carrots and preparing stews, going by memory instead of a cookbook. It may be a tired cliché to want a girl who cooks and cleans, but it was a tremendous turn-on watching them mop and then bake with an apron. There has to be something hardwired into my brain that causes me to positively respond to a woman who knows how to maintain a house. If only baking wasn't seen as old-fashioned back home.

IV

A Canadian guy checked into the hostel and within the first hour bragged that he had sex with twenty girls in thirty days in Rio. He told me it takes almost no work to get laid and that it's a completely different world from Argentina. "In Brazil," he said, "the girls will stare at you and all you have to do is speak English and you will have sex with her." Alarm bells went off in my head because the kind of guy that is prone to exaggeration is one that tells you numbers of girls he's had sex with without you asking.

If he was telling the truth, it wasn't due to his appearance. Compared to the guys staying at the hostel he was average looking at best. He had large bicep muscles but a small chest to match. His smile was charming but his face had sharp, angular edges. His hair was thinning.

A Swedish guy staying long-term at the hostel was dating a local girl who brought out a friend. (There were five guys staying long-term at the hostel, five more than any other hostel I stayed at.) The Canadian quickly pounced on her, giving no one else a chance. He grabbed her face within ten minutes to kiss her and then brought her back to the hostel a few hours later. He got laid on his first night in Córdoba, and here I was texting like a wuss, still trying to get a date with Daniela.

I watched him for the next couple days and quickly noticed that he was always in the mood to hit on girls. Regardless of his mental state or the time of day, if there was a cute girl in the room he was on it. His unlimited energy level was freakish, and I was beginning to see how he could get tons of ass through sheer numbers and will alone.

His game was simple enough: touch a lot and constantly talk about sex. "It looks like you need to get laid," he'd say to girls. A couple times I overheard them telling him he thinks of sex too much, but with a tone that made it hard to tell whether they actually disliked it or not. He asked one of the hostel maids to show him her "fat ass" and she took him to a room upstairs and did as instructed. The other hostel guys and I started following him, trying to absorb his energy, gradually believing that he really did fuck twenty Brazilian girls in thirty days. Someone came up with a nickname for him—Predator. Within a few days of his arrival half the guys at the hostel were trying out his cocky sex talk, eager to learn more.

A clique of horny guys formed. Besides Predator there was Samuel, a tall Canadian with a dry sense of humor and a penchant for storytelling, and Caleb, a New Zealander (Kiwi) who had the build of a rugby player and liked tackling guys when drunk. He also got a kick out of taking pictures of gringos while they were asleep. There was Luke, a young Australian Judo master amazed at the quality of Córdoba's pickings, determined not to leave the city until he got his Argentina flag, and finally Marcus, an Englishmen taking four hours a day of Spanish classes. He found it impossible to study in a hostel where the party sometimes began before dinner.

Three days after Predator's arrival, Caleb and I went to a club called Mitre. We worked the crowd, keeping our options open by talking to groups of girls and gracefully exiting in the search for better, a search that could continue indefinitely in a place like Córdoba where it was more common for a girl to be beautiful than not. We settled in with a group of three cute girls who absolutely loved us. They insisted on taking our pictures and asked for our names, our jobs, where we were staying, how long we were staying, and if we had girlfriends. When they went to the bathroom we double checked our pockets for condoms, excited at the prospect of what was to come, but they never returned.

As the night went on and more Argentine guys rolled in, the girls became less friendly. Our energy dissipated. We couldn't find any of the girls we talked to earlier. It was impossible to hear human speech after three hours of loud music blasting our ears. I told Caleb our best option left is to hit on girls outside in front of the club. He agreed. It seemed to work, initially anyway, because at least we could hear, but girls lingering in front of the club are always on their way to somewhere else, and we were never invited to join. Caleb got tired and left but I decided to stick around. The streak would not end by giving up.

I talked to a pretty girl and her friend on the sidewalk while the sky went from black to dim blue. We saw an erratic driver collide into a parked car and then drive away. I wanted to kiss the girl, but then she told me was only 17 years old. At 5'8" tall she had the body of a girl five years her senior. She didn't seem like she was seventeen.

It was impossible for her and her friend to find a cab so I offered to walk them home a couple miles away. They didn't mind, but then it started to pour. We stopped walking and waited in the canopy of an apartment building. I continued the conversation while her friend tried to hail a cab. Finally after twenty minutes of waiting an empty cab stopped right in front of us. The friend jumped inside and left the door open, yelling at my girl to hop in. Then I went for it. I looked in her eyes, wet my lips, tilted my head to the right, and moved in. At the last second, right before our lips were to meet, she turned away and gave off a childish giggle. She ran into the cab and that was that. I thought I would feel ashamed for trying to kiss her, but I didn't.

V

My Canadian dorm mate Samuel did something that skyrocketed the amount of respect I had for him. With extremely limited Spanish knowledge (much less than me), he called a girl he met at a club with crib notes on how to ask her out gleaned from the internet and one of the hostel maids. I was there when he made the call and it was just as awkward as I imagined it to be, with long pauses and badly spoken Spanish, but he managed to set up a date for later in the evening. I was sweating bullets just sending text messages to Daniela. It had been exactly one week since we met and I could not get her out. I'd given up.

I went out with Luke for a drink at a quiet sit-down bar, where he taught me that in Australia the word for banging is "rooting." He was seven years younger than me and seemed interested in picking my brain when it came to flirting with Argentine girls, but with no solid success under my belt I didn't have much to tell him besides not to fish for eye contact. After our drink we took a cab to Dorian Grey. Fifteen other gringos staying at our hostel were there to greet us. One in particular, an English guy I talked to for a quick minute, was making out with one of the hotter maids at the hostel. I always thought that the maids would be harder to root than other girls, but I guess there is a reason why those girls know English and work for meager pay in a place where there are always a bunch of exotic guys rolling through.

I saw a large group of young girls and went in alone with a few words in English. All were seventeen or eighteen and celebrating a birthday. They took a liking to me and I felt very comfortable talking to them. Two of the girls in the group pulled me aside and asked if I wanted to go dance in the closet room. I obliged. We danced in a tight triangle only a few feet away from where I spent much of the last time with Daniela and Sofia. Now the debate was on—which one to pick? Before I could make a decision who shows up but Daniela and Sofia.

I instantly knew I picked the wrong sister judging by the huge hug Sofia gave me. Daniela only gave me the standard single cheek kiss. With my attention diverted to the sisters, the two young girls lost interest and went back to their group. Did Daniela tell Sofia that I texted her and tried to get her out on a date? She must've—they're sisters. I was nervous I wouldn't have a good chance at Sofia if she thought she was the second pick, so I came up with a brilliant cover based on the fact that when I got Daniela's number, Sofia got mine at the same time. I told Sofia, "I contacted your sister because I gave up on you after waiting two days for you to contact me." The lie was so good even I believed it. I liked Sofia more all along. We were always at war with Eastasia, not Eurasia.

For the past week, the Predator had been teaching us moves. The first fought cockblocking. He said, "If you don't want to get cockblocked, simply make out with your chick. Chances that the chick will then let herself get pulled away by a friend will be much lower." It was a simple but novel way of looking at the problem because until then the only way I'd fight cockblocking is by entertaining the cockblocker to make her happy. The second move was the waist pull. "Put one arm on the girl's waist, pull her dangerously close, make firm eye contact, smile, and build up the tension until you release it by loosening the grip." He said the key to this move is the intense eye contact. The third move, also simple, is for isolating the girl away from her friends. "Just say you are going to the bar to get a drink and if she wants to come. If she likes you she'll say yes." The best ideas I have ever encountered are the ones that had me wondering why I didn't think of them first.

I asked Sofia if she wanted to come to the bar with me to get a drink. She said yes. Once at the bar, after the bartender handed me my $3 vodka and Speed (Argentina's answer to Red Bull), I pulled her real close, made laser eye contact, held it for three seconds, and then loosened my grip. She stayed close. With our faces only a few inches apart and my hands around her waist, I went in for the kiss. She turned her head. If this was the first time it happened to me then I probably would have freaked out, but I had a strong feeling it was coming.

I took slow sips of my drink and kept my hands on her waist. I waited five minutes, and then went in for the kiss again. She turned her head once more, but this time much slower. I caught the corner of her lip. I felt close. I just had to hang in there. For the third time I waited only two minutes. The tension was too great to wait any longer. I smiled at her, then went in once more. She closed her eyes.

Cold yet affectionate wouldn't be a bad way to describe Argentine girls. Sofia couldn't keep her hands off me after we kissed and I thanked the gods for not punishing my mistake in picking the wrong twin sister. My hunch was that if I wanted the best, warmest parts of an Argentine girl, I would have to kiss her first.

We took a taxi to my hostel. She declined to come in.

VI

The Predator struck again. He banged his Argentine girlfriend all night long, parted ways with her the next afternoon, then went to the park with Luke to pull seven stunning teenage girls back to the hostel's common area. It was legendary. And he had to leave town just a couple hours later! There was no chance he'd be able to do anything with the girls from the park, so why'd he do it? I had to ask.

"I just can't help it," he said. "When I see a cute girl I have to talk to her." He wasn't a complicated man.

We were all bummed by Predator's departure, and decided it was our duty to keep his spirit alive by continuing his work. By then we had developed a daily routine where we'd spend most of our time with each other, starting from when we got up in the afternoon. We'd eat some toast with *dulce de leche* and then shoot the shit in the patio for an hour or two, reviewing the previous nights' events and cursing the girls who ditched us for the bathroom after making it seem like they were ready to take us home. Then we'd pay a few dollars for a day pass to the gym to bulk up, followed with juicy barbecued chicken at a carry-out place one block away. Gym and chicken, it was called. After that we'd spend the late-afternoon walking around, bullshitting, or studying Spanish on our own. The drinking would begin in the hostel at night around dinnertime (9pm) and continue in another loud club. We dedicated our lives to getting our Argentine flag, and with the Predator's energy and moves inside all of us, failure was impossible.

Failure was possible.

A day after Predator left, Marcus dragged Luke and I to the university food court to hit on girls. After purchasing bottles of water and finding a seat, we were struck by how at least three out of four students walking around happened to be female, as if a horrible civil war wiped out the city's stock of men. No less than half the girls were beautiful.

For our very first attempt I started the conversation in English with a basic question: "Where is good to go out at night?" The girls tried their best to explain names of clubs while we joked around to show personality. When they asked our ages Luke kept saying "two" in Spanish. I asked where I should go to find a nice girl for marriage who knows how to make *media lunas*, little mini-croissants that were a popular breakfast food, catching the attention of the girl whose back was facing us. She finally turned around and for a second we collectively held our breaths—she was the prettiest girl we've ever seen in our lives. If she really knew how to make *media lunas* I would have considered marrying her. Yet there was no sweat on our brows or shaky voices coming from our throats, because by that point we had each talked to a couple dozen beautiful women. We had beautiful women experience.

The conversation eventually phased out but we deemed our attempt a glorious success and started hitting on girls everywhere, especially parks. It resulted in more than a dozen numbers between the five of us in under a week, but all would eventually get stuck in text messaging hell. That's exactly how it was playing out with Sofia. It took nearly thirty text messages over the span of three days to arrange a date. It was so bad I wondered if she used texting as a way to entertain herself while she worked.

For our first date we had planned to meet beside the fountain near the mall she worked at. She was twenty-five minutes late. An Argentine guy once told me that his people see time more as a "cloud" than a "line," so I tried to let it roll off my back. When she did walk up I was struck by her femininity—her super long hair, necklaces, bracelets, earrings, rings, high heels, and tight clothes. Her nails were long and polished and everything about her said "real woman." She embraced a hyper-feminine role that was becoming a rare sight in America. I remembered my first date with Stacy, the American girl who I was dating before I left. She rolled up in flip flops, something that would never happen in Argentina. After I made a comment about them Stacy replied that they were "comfortable." If I had showed up on a date in flannel pajamas saying they were comfortable I doubt she'd want to see me again.

At a nearby restaurant Sofia and I talked about our families for a while and when that died down I went on and on about my previous travels. To kill time I drew a map of South America on a napkin and wrote down every city I've been to on the trip so far: Quito, Tena, Baños, Riobamba, Cuenca, Huanchaco, Huaraz, Lima, Cuzco, Puno, Copacabana, Potosí, Tupiza, Salta, San Pedro, Santiago, Valparaíso, Mendoza, and Córdoba. After writing all that out, I was surprised at how much ground I had covered.

I jumped at her suggestion of visiting a bar her friends were hanging out at—it would take some pressure off having to speak. Many times I broke out in English knowing she wouldn't understand because I had so much trouble telling her things I wanted to in Spanish. She would just hold my hand and smile, as if telling me she understood my frustration. The bill, including dinner and a bottle of wine, came out to $30.

I counted how many guys checked her out on the walk to the next bar. It made me feel good that I pulled a desirable local girl without using money, or even language, apparently. It would be like seeing a hot blonde at home with a scruffy Colombian guy who spoke laughable English and had no job. I thought of the damage I could do if I was fluent in Spanish, and hit the notecards harder than ever the next day.

At the bar I sat next to her on the couch and wrapped my arm around her thin yet curvy body while she talked to her two friends. All I wanted in life at that moment was to put my dick inside her. I fooled myself into thinking I was close but all we'd done was kiss.

It had been just over three months now since I had sex, the longest I've gone without it since my early 20s. But I was still careful about displaying affections only to match hers. If she knew I was desperate and having wet dreams then it would be over. After two drinks at the bar she walked me back to my hostel. On the way we passed by an hourly motel and I jokingly tried to steer her to the door. She shook her head sideways and said, "No, I'm difficult."

VII

Three days later, after gym and chicken, I went to Sofia's store as she was getting off. Six other giggly girls were there to meet me and they made me feel like the queen of the ball. Since I knew those introductions were coming (it was her suggestion to come to the store), I made sure to shower and wear a clean shirt.

We walked around town for an hour, got ice cream, and sat down in the park—the same park I came to hit on girls with the guys. Then she called her friends and we headed to an apartment for an informal get-together. It was me, one other guy, and five girls. For years since Claire and her friends in Georgetown, I tried and failed to get back in with a group of hot college girls. I succeeded again in the best possible place I could hope for.

We listened to music, looked at photos, drank, ate barbeque chicken and fries, smoked weed, and ate cake and puffy pastries. They wouldn't let me pay for anything and I had to resort to sneaking out to buy bottles of beer. They took time-outs from their conversation to slowly explain to me what they were talking about since I could only pick out bits and pieces. Sofia would also take a break every now and then to give me a kiss or a touch to show she wasn't neglecting me. I relaxed on the couch, watched my new friends, my new girl, and let it all soak in.

At the end of the night Sofia walked me back to the hostel and this time I dragged her inside to show her off to the guys. They all expressed their approval after she left. Other people's opinions of someone I'm dating shouldn't matter, but it felt good that my peer group gave their thumbs up. Only one thing bothered me: Marcus engaged her in small talk with Spanish that was far better than mine. I wanted to be able to communicate with her like he did, so I went to his language school and signed up for five days of four-hour lessons.

VIII

One night I went with the guys to El Sol, a medium-sized warehouse club. All the practice I had done on the girls was beginning to show. I could start conversations very easily and long gone were brutal rejections right off the bat. My phone was filling with prospects and it was just a matter of time until something came through (the law of averages deemed it so), but things were a lot harder than I felt they should be. Taking things to the next level was still a huge challenge because girls either kept disappearing to the bathroom or flaking out on dates. I figured something was missing from my game. Maybe I needed to be more aggressive, or stir more jealousy, or just learn more Spanish.

I was beginning to understand why I was so unsuccessful until Córdoba: it takes time in a town to make friends and find a nightlife niche, things that make meeting a girl much easier. If I visit a city for a night or two then my only chance is with the low-hanging fruit, but the longer I stay and the more I integrate myself into the town, the easier it is to get with girls who don't just want to have a one-night stand.

Someone new came with us to El Sol: Ronald from Tallahassee. He hated his name and preferred to be called Tennessee. Tall and built with sagging eyes and a resemblance to Lenny Kravitz, he had a habit of twirling his short dreadlocks while he spoke. He told us he has been continuously traveling for five years, reflected by his holey clothing and canned corn diet. To survive he'd walk by outdoor cafes and ask people for the food left on their plates, and sometimes he'd shack up with girls he met along the way until they got sick of him and kicked him out. A couple years back in Denmark he was homeless for a month and got arrested on purpose to be fed and sheltered. He was born and raised in the United States, but his accent was unlike anything I'd heard—it sounded like a fake English accent with Spanish-sounding intonations, the result of studying several languages and being away from home for so long. He replaced the Predator as the most fascinating character in the hostel, though the degree of fascination depended on how drunk and high he was.

After a night of drinking at El Sol, I walked back to the hostel with Tennessee and Caleb.

"Argentine girls fucking suck," Tennessee said. "They're bitches, stupid whores."

"What do you mean?" I asked.

"They just act stupid. I have no idea why they come out when they're not trying to do anything. They get off on making you feel like shit. Fuck that I just want to go back to Brazil. Fuck this."

"Why don't you go back?" Caleb said.

"Because if you spend six months in Brazil you have to spend six months out. I have to wait. I should have stayed illegally. I don't know why I came here."

"Everyone keeps saying that Brazil is paradise," I said.

"Bro, compared to Argentina, Brazil *is* paradise. The people of Argentina are the worst in South America. The biggest racist assholes in the world."

Tennessee convinced the manager of our hostel to let him sleep in the hammock out back, one that he actually installed several months prior when he passed by Córdoba on his way to Chile. Everyone was paying $8 a night for a dorm bed but he paid less than half that to sleep outside. On his first night he got locked out and had to urinate in a flower pot.

The next morning we woke up to disaster. Samuel's camera and iPod were gone and another guy's wallet was missing. Someone came into our room in the middle of the night while we were sleeping and grabbed what he could from the two guys who slept closest to the door.

Samuel lost all the photos from his two month long trip, and for fifteen minutes he pounded his foam bed yelling obscenities while throwing things across the room. A handful of guys tried to calm him down. I lost count of how many iPods I'd heard get stolen in hostels. Everything had to always be locked up.

Eventually the finger was pointed at a French guy who was the only one to check out the previous night. Everyone agreed it was probably him, though there was little motive since he already had one of those expensive SLR cameras. The person who was first to lay blame on the French guy was Tennessee. With his weak financial status he had the greatest motive, but no one dared accuse the coolest guy in the hostel. It also happened that Samuel looked up to him most. I didn't tell Samuel that I wouldn't rule out Tennessee because, after all, I had no proof. As a bluff I should have suggested that everyone in the hostel empty their bags, taking note who put up the most resistance.

Two days later Tennessee had an especially bad night out where he got rejected by a handful of Argentine girls. He checked out in the middle of the night and took his hammock with him. A couple guys asked me if he paid his bill. I wondered that myself.

IX

Sofia took almost five hours to respond to a simple text message. I've always believed it's important to get sex out of the way as quickly as possible to not get strung along. Before sex I have little power, and the more it's delayed and the more I have to invest in a girl, the weaker I become. I felt like I needed to pull out a bold move with Sofia so she knows I mean business. Maybe I should slap her ass in public, something I saw an Argentine guy do to his girlfriend inside a café around lunchtime. Or maybe just feed her more drinks so she comes with me into the love hotel, a much harder feat than simply inviting a girl back to my place for a drink. In front of the love hotel there's that do-or-die moment where she must make the decision to have sex with me or not, but in my own place that decision doesn't come until half her clothes are off and she's already deep in the moment.

At the hostel I started hitting on another Daniela, a cute maid that worked twice a week. She was young and quite shy, not having talked to me for the three weeks I'd been at the hostel so far. But we hit a stride after a bottle of Brahma beer with a fun conversation in English stereotyping gringos. We were sitting down, the back of my hand barely touching her knee, when Samuel ran up to me. "Dude, Caleb passed out upstairs and puked all over himself! You gotta come upstairs and see this!"

"Oh my god really? Daniela I'll be right back."

I ran upstairs to see Caleb putting pomade wax in his dirty blonde hair. Samuel laughed it up. The gag was slightly amusing, but something I would have expected from a seventh grader and not a traveler buddy of mine. When I went back downstairs Daniela was already busy with another group and didn't even look at me. I was so mad at Samuel I didn't talk to him for a day, eternity when you're living in the same room.

In hindsight he probably did me a favor. Tennessee mentioned that Argentine girls like it when their men put out an aloof vibe, and you can't be more aloof than excusing yourself to laugh at a guy covered in puke. Maybe the reason why the girls always ditched me for the bathroom was because I was giving them too much attention. And maybe it's the same reason Sofia was taking her sweet time in getting back to me. When I got a text message from her that said she wasn't coming to the club of the night, Peekaboo, I took that as a green light to forget about her. I messed up and there was no use trying to salvage things.

It took over an hour at the club until I was talking with Daniela again. She encouraged the conversation any way she could, almost ignoring her friends that would swing by every few minutes to talk to her. She maintained steady eye contact and didn't excuse herself to use the bathroom even once. My hand found its way to the small of her back and I estimated she would turn her head only twice before staying still for the kiss. I went in close to test the waters, our cheeks just a few inches apart, when I glance over her shoulder and see Sofia and Daniela entering the club. I pulled back.

I knew Sofia wouldn't walk directly up to me since that would go against an Argentine girl's style, so I stayed the course and continued flirting with Daniela the maid but at greater distance. I wasn't sure if I should go for this new girl I haven't even kissed yet or continue my investment into Sofia, which just an hour ago I concluded was a lost cause. But Sofia wouldn't have come unless she wanted to see me. I'll have my cake and eat it too.

"I think we should hang out sometime," I told the maid.

"No."

I figured she heard me incorrectly or didn't understand what my question was. I tried again: "No, I mean I think *me* and *you* should get a coffee or a drink soon."

"No, I do not want to hang out with you."

I furrowed my brow in a vain attempt to understand out what was happening. She just stood there staring at me, with no hint that she was joking. That same night Caleb was working on a girl who he flirted with before, a friend of one of the hostel maids. At Peekaboo she complimented his looks several times and asked to dance with him. After a couple hours of dancing he went in for the kiss and she said, "I don't want to kiss you." This behavior frustrated us, but as long as we wanted to get laid without paying for it, all we could do was take it. If the maid doesn't like me, she doesn't like me—I'm not going to beg her. I tried my best and it wasn't enough, so it was time to try on another girl.

I started scanning the club for Sofia when the maid put her arm around my waist and brought me in closer like she wanted to kiss me. She was doing Predator's move! I looked at her, stupefied, when a girl I had never seen before tightly grabbed my forearm and said my name. The maid instantly released her grip and I squinted at this new girl trying to figure out how she knows me and why she's cockblocking. She said her name and it hit me—it was Sofia's friend that I ate chicken with in the dorm. I didn't recognize her because she had on makeup and clubbing clothes. The maid stared me down, fuming that I'm talking to this other girl, but I had to make the decision to let her go. She was too crazy, even by Argentine standards. She stormed out of the club without saying goodbye to her friends, and all future attempts to chat with her was met with curt responses. I guess there is a such thing as too aloof.

I followed the friend to where Sofia and Daniela were standing. I walked up to Daniela first. I played off what happened. "Yeah that girl I talked to works at the hostel," I said. "She was telling me about other cities in Argentina to visit."

"Okay."

"You know, your sister Sofia is very difficult. Very difficult."

"Why?"

"I don't know. The text messaging thing is weird. I don't know what she wants."

"Okay."

"In the United States it's so much easier. Girl likes guy, guy likes girl—they go out. I like your sister but I don't know."

"Do you know who I am?" she asked.

"What?"

"Do you know what my name is?"

"Yeah, Daniela."

"No, I'm Sofia, that's Daniela." She pointed to her sister standing five feet away.

I looked back and forth at the two sisters in disbelief. My shoulders slumped and I could only stare at Sofia with my mouth halfway open. My sloppy game was inexcusable. She said it was okay, no big deal. My mix up, combined with witnessing another girl flirt with me, seemed to pique her interest and we were going at it within minutes. The amount of aloofness was just right. But she still didn't want to come with me to another club. It was another night that I got nothing.

X

Luke's Australian friend Ethan joined the hostel. Not to take away from his game, which was in fact very good, but he had incredible good looks along with a gym-chiseled body (he eagerly joined in on our gym and chicken outings). His blonde hair and blue eyes made him quite a catch in South America. If he couldn't get laid then it definitely was a problem with the girls and not us.

On his first night out he struck out badly like everyone else.

Even while failing it was incredible how much we were learning in such a short amount of time. At home I'd go out once a week but in Córdoba it was five times that. All successes, no matter how minor, were discussed among the group so that the experience of one became the experience of all. We tried hard to fight the girl bathroom escapes and developed a strategy that included opening in English, showing aloof disinterest, and acting like a dick. Everyone was especially interested in the dick component, where we'd ramble on in English even if the girl didn't understand and question why she didn't know more English since it's "a popular language." We learned to tell girls that we thought Argentines were weird and made sure never to comment about their beauty, which we were becoming used to anyway. The strategy was working and we got even more phone numbers and make-outs than before, but the love hotel still eluded us all.

At a random bar with Ethan, Caleb, and Samuel, I saw three girls about to pass by us. Out of habit I said, "Do you guys speak English?" It turned out that one of the girls was an English teacher. They were on their way out so after a quick conversation I exchanged numbers with the teacher. A drink later I texted her, asking where she was, and she responded almost instantly. I made the guys come with me to meet her at a club two blocks away.

At 29 years old, the teacher was a lot older than the average Córdoba girl, but on the plus side she had blonde hair, green eyes, and a gigantic ass. Unlike every other Argentine girl I met she didn't smoke. I talked to her at the club while Samuel stuck around to get drunk, eventually kissing a beast.

I brought out the Predator's moves. I asked her if she wanted to come to the bar, and then pulled her close with my right arm. I went in for the kiss, but she turned her head away. She turned away a second time when I tried again fifteen minutes later. Finally, after two hours of talking to her in the club, we kissed. Later I walked her to a cab and tried to get in, but she wasn't having it. She told me to call her.

XI

Ethan got laid on his fifth night. He went to a bar with Luke and there next to them was a girl sitting alone. She spoke English. He talked to her for three hours before walking away with her number. The next night he brought her out and she was a beautiful, young college student, typical of what I'd see in the university food court. I had earlier told him about the love hotel that I pretended to steer Sofia into, and that's where he took her. He told me it felt sleazy and weird with the buzzing red lights and humping couples next door, but the girl didn't mind at all. This was how Argentines have sex. We laughed about it and I asked him if he was going to see her again. "Nah I don't think so," he said.

Predator and Ethan cracked the code and I felt close. Samuel and Luke were also close, but Marcus and Caleb were having trouble. Their energy and will was fading and time was running out.

XII

I warned Ethan about the cocktail party the hostel throws every Saturday night. For a small amount of money we could consume all the fruit daiquiris we desired. I told him they were very strong, that the liquor was hidden by copious amounts of sugar, but he didn't listen. I gently urged him to slow down but he told me to relax. Within an hour he was slurring his words, right as two girls knocked on the door to see him and Luke, part of the original seven that Predator brought back from the park. With Luke leading the way it looked like something was finally going to happen—the girls were done up and came all the way to the hostel to see them, and Luke's girl was looking especially good.

I said a joke right as Ethan took a sip of his fifth slushy drink. He failed to hold back his laughter. Not only did the sip come out but all the other drinks roared from his belly and ejected from his nose and mouth onto the patio floor, collecting in a slimy red pool. The hostel crowd erupted in laughter while his date's face went from sweet innocence to utter disgust. No one was surprised when the two girls declined to join us at the club. Ethan was too drunk to care but Luke seemed disappointed.

On our way over to the street corner to catch a cab, Caleb did his thing where he lifts me up, rests me over his shoulder, and spins around in the middle of the street until we both fall down. The louder I yelled the faster he spun, and all I could do was spread out my hands to brace for the crash. Caleb and I were becoming close and we had just made plans to hang out in Punta del Este, Uruguay for New Years. Both of us were talking about the crazy times we'd have there, a sequel to Córdoba. With the guys around I forgot about my stomach problems, which wasn't all that better from what I was experiencing in Chile.

By the time we got to the club I had been texting Sofia and the English teacher for the entire day. I wasn't sure which one would come through (if they would at all), but I was ready with a condom in my back jean pocket. There were at least fifty more where that came from.

I hit on a group of four young girls with the now slightly sobered up Ethan, and though the girls were friendly, I imagined how long it would take to get with them. Probably hundreds of text messages followed by numerous hang-outs with other friends and nights of only make-outs with nothing more. I didn't want any more numbers. Ethan's and Predator's girls must have been exceptions. A part of me began to believe that even with our optimized strategy, all we were doing was approaching girls until we found the easy ones (by Argentine standards anyway).

At 3am, just one hour after we got to the club, I got a text message from the English teacher. She wanted to see me. I was having an amazing time with my friends at the club, at the peak of our rapport built from weeks spent together, but the streak had to end tonight. They understood.

I got into a cab and met up with her at a bar. We had two rounds of drinks while kissing on a corner couch. The bar closed and we walked out, when I suggested we "relax" somewhere.

"Where?" she said.

"I think I saw something around there." I pointed in the general direction where the love hotel was. There were actually three love hotels within a block of each other, and I decided to skip the one Ethan visited a couple nights before. We walked to my first choice and several couples were loitering around the entrance. "How about we go inside and relax," I said.

"Okay."

But the hotel was completely full. It was Saturday night and every couple in Córdoba wanted to get laid. Lucky for me there were the two hotels right nearby. We walked inside the second and they were full too. Then we walked to the third one, the one Ethan went to, and I couldn't believe it—completely full!

At that moment I believed in god because only an omnipotent being had the power to stop me from getting laid after all I'd done. I bought a cell phone. I talked to tons of girls. I optimized my approach with many hours of reflection. I danced to music I didn't like. I poisoned my body with barrels of alcohol. I endured sharp stomach pains and nonstop gas. I destroyed my ears with loud club music. There was nothing more to do except throw my hands in the air, stare at the sky, and cry. How stupid was I to come to South America just to get laid! I was an idiot and a failure.

I plopped myself down on the curb and put my head down between my knees.

"Do you want to wait?" she asked.

I looked up at her. "Wait?"

"Yeah the rooms are by the hour so I doubt we'll have to wait very long."

"Oh, okay, yeah. That's a good idea." I stood up and regained my composure. Just like that I was back in the game.

We went back to the first hotel and got a number. We waited in the lobby listening to Argentine soft rock with other couples nearby. I couldn't believe it was going to happen.

Our number was called and we went into a room that smelled like jizz, a faint bleachy smell. The door closed, the clothes came off, and I had my way with her. I pulled her long hair and slapped her round ass and rammed my dick inside her as hard and far as I could. I felt like I just lost my virginity.

The phone rang, waking me up. It was the old man from the front desk telling me I'm out of time. I put the English teacher in the cab and walked slowly to the hostel. For one day no one could bring me down from my high.

XIII

Almost everyone left the next day. Samuel left for Brazil, Caleb went back to Buenos Aires to meet up with friends, and Luke and Ethan went east to Rosario on their way to catch a flight to Patagonia. Only Marcus and I remained.

A handful of new travelers checked in to replace the guys who left, but it just wasn't the same. The perfect storm of good times, pussy chasing and friendship was over. In short time we became the best of buddies, raising Córdoba to a mythical level that had less to do with Córdoba than it did our relationships with each other. The girls allowed men from different ages, cultures, and upbringings to bond as if they shared the same blood.

For the next couple days Marcus and I mourned the change. With our Spanish classes complete we accepted that our time in Córdoba had come to an end, but I still had unfinished business.

I set a date with Sofia, something I thought would be a one-on-one affair, but she brought her sister and two friends. My Spanish proficiency went through the roof thanks to the classes and I was able to tell the girls a couple funny stories in Spanish without flailing my arms like a monkey. I kept the drinks coming, but I knew it would be impossible to drag Sofia to one of the love hotels. She definitely was not a sex kitten like the English teacher, who started taking off my clothes the minute we entered the motel room.

Sofia easily declined an invitation to hang out with me at the hostel and hopped into a cab with her sister. Our kiss goodbye was weak. I made one last attempt the next day to get her out, alone, but got no reply after two hours. In frustration I sent *"Como quieras,"* which is the best translation I could find to "Whatever." She didn't respond.

For my last night in Córdoba I went to an American-themed restaurant (they had onion rings) to meet up with the English teacher. The waitress was young and cute and for the first time I felt that I could do much better. In fact, I didn't even like the teacher. She didn't have a sense of humor and would make fun of other people she'd see in public. I took her to the love hotel anyway and ravaged her as best as I could, but felt nothing when we said our goodbyes.

The happiness from breaking my sexless streak lasted only a few days, and I felt like I was back to where I started. While I will always treasure the time I spent with the guys, I can't say that all that work to get my Argentina flag was worth it.

XIV

I headed east to Rosario with Marcus to join Ethan and Luke for one last night before they traveled south to Patagonia. With more than half the continent left to explore I had to quicken the pace. We tried to relive Córdoba, only for one last time, but it was of no use. Girls would talk to us only to reveal they had a boyfriend, or they'd pull their bathroom escape artist move. Ethan got slapped across the face when I jokingly pushed his hand on a girl's ass (he didn't have to squeeze!), and Luke lost us and had to jog a few miles back to the hostel because he couldn't find a cab. He refused to resort to the local method of throwing himself on the hood of one to get the driver's attention. Marcus was so dismayed he fled back to Córdoba the next day, and the Australians left shortly after him to catch a flight. It was definitely over.

As if on cue, my stomach roared back to life, partially thanks to a chicken *empanada* I ate that had as much cartilage as meat. Within a couple days the shit coming out of my ass had the consistency of sludge, and in the shower I noticed my hair coming out in clumps like I was a cancer patient. I was convinced I was going bald.

I sent an email to Stacy saying I was thinking of her but she didn't reply. I called the other girl I was dating and left a message on her cell phone but she didn't send me an email to acknowledge it. I called my mom and she cried, begging me to come home. For two days I vegetated in front of the television and did nothing except wonder how I would finish my journey, and if I would be able to eat and shit again like a normal human being. I wanted to go home.

Before Córdoba I had planned to rent a room in Buenos Aires, the last destination on my napkin, and live there for a couple months to hit the clubs and bring girls back to shag. But I no longer had interest in doing that. I decided to forget about the napkin and follow Luke and Ethan into Patagonia, to take a break from clubs and cities. I needed to get inspired or else I'd never finish the trip.

XV

I got on my first South American flight all the way down to El Calafate, in the area known as Patagonia. For a place spotted with glaciers the weather was mild when I arrived, with a temperature hovering around 50 degrees. After checking in to my hostel I signed up for a glacier boat tour.

A bunch of other gringos and I stood on the deck of a boat as it steamed along the Perito Moreno glacier's 150-foot high face. The glacier itself was a thick sheet of ice that slowly flowed between two mountains into a lake. On its way there it picked up minerals from the land and deposited them into the water, giving the lake an opaque turquoise color. Bitterly cold wind blew off the top of the glacier onto my face, and I froze my ass off while others asked me where my jacket was. This was unplanned, I said, a spur of the moment type thing. I'm off the napkin, thanks.

Every ten minutes or so a car-sized chunk of ice would fall off from the glacier. People with gigantic cameras worth more than my entire pack hurried to take a photo before the splash settled.

On the boat I met Peter, an American lawyer from North Carolina who was traveling for only ten days. "Typical American vacation," he said. He told me of his experience in Southeast Asia where he contracted a parasite so bad that for one month he couldn't eat solid food. Everything would just come out as liquid from his ass or mouth.

He thought he was going to die but after some treatment at a university medical center he was back to normal.

He convinced me that I had a parasite camping out in my intestine. The reason my symptoms came in waves, according to Peter, was because of the parasite's life cycle. After a dormant breeding stage the adult had baby parasites that would resume shredding my insides. It made sense to me.

That night, after ordering pizza, I heard my name called. I turned around and there were Ethan and Luke. I immediately joined their table. We talked for an hour over goat cheese pizza, but with nowhere to go after eating we couldn't do our main bonding exercise of hitting on girls. I'd see them again in a few days in Buenos Aires.

I found myself hanging out with some teenage guys when I saw a pretty girl, around 21 years old. She was much younger than me but older than the guys. I made an attempt to seduce her but gave up quickly when she wasn't acknowledging me. It was like I didn't even exist. Then one of the teenagers walked up to her and performed weird hand motions in front of her face, like he was trying to hypnotize her. It looked ridiculous and I was laughing so hard I started crying. I was thinking of good ways to make fun of him when he returned to the group after getting rejected, but he didn't fail. He was making out with her, licking her face, and she loved every second of it. I was embarrassed that I got out-gamed by a kid. I stewed with my head down, glancing up every few seconds to see if he was still kissing her. Then I got curious. After he walked away I went to her for the second time and copied his exact same moves. I moved my hands in crazy patterns until she fell into a trance, and then I kissed her too. I couldn't believe that worked. Then I woke up.

This dream confirmed that I see a girl's brain as an annoying obstacle, as something that must be figured out like a math puzzle. The right solution, in this case hypnotic hand movements, must be applied to the girl's brain with finesse so sexual pleasure can be achieved. Happiness and good times should follow.

XVI

I filled each day in Patagonia with a tourist activity. After the boat tour of the glacier I went on a day trip to Torres del Paine across the border in Chile. I spent fifteen hours on the bus, two hours at border control, and only one hour at Chile's most popular national park looking at mountain and lake views. It was foggy and rainy and I took only two photos. It was the first time I got fleeced on a tour, but I deserved it for thinking I could experience a 600,000 acre park on a packaged day tour that serves a stale sandwich and bag of chips for lunch.

The next tour was on a catamaran to look at more glaciers with two-hundred other tourists, mostly families. Thick mobs of people camping out on the deck made it difficult to get a clean shot of the glaciers, which weren't quite as magical with people unapologetically shoving me out of the way. I'd rent a boat and do it myself if there wasn't a risk of sinking with all the icebergs. While my travel strategy had its own flaws, as the ass sludge and red itchy bumps on my body could've explained, there is nothing like an aggressive tourist horde to take out the uniqueness and tranquility from an experience.

I gave up on the tours and hung around the hostel, where two Argentines shared my bedbug infested room. (Some mornings I'd wake up to blood stained spots on my sheets from bugs I rolled over in my sleep.) I decided to start a conversation with the trusty "So where are you from?" Next thing I know I'm having *mate* with them in the huge common area, complete with wooden tables, chairs, and walls that gave it a pleasant vacation lodge feel. All that was missing was the stick of marshmallows roasting in a large fireplace.

Mate, pronounced MA-tay, is a species of holly that grows in the southern parts of South America. To prepare it in beverage form you pack the plant's dried leaves at a slant inside a cauldron-shaped gourd made of wood. Gourds range in size from a small human fist to a softball. The leaves are wetted with a small amount of water to allow easy placement of a metal straw with a built-in screen at the end. Then hot water is poured in until the rim and the liquid is sipped, free of leaf particles. If the water is too hot, the straw will singe your lips since it heats up to the temperature of the liquid. *Mate* tastes like an extremely bitter tea, almost like coffee, and is said to have a ridiculous number of health benefits. Because the gourd is good for a couple dozen pours, most Argentines carry it with a thermos so they can continually sip throughout the day. Most grocery stores sell thermoses near the dozen or so brands of *mate* for sale.

Along with the huge bottles of beer that one person can't possibly finish on their own before it gets warm, the Argentines have a culture of sharing and community that is only dependent on your luck of getting an invitation. My Quilmes beer is your beer, my *mate* is your *mate*, like weed smoking almost, but sip-sip-give instead of puff-puff-give. The best way to get to know an Argentine is through beer or *mate* (they smoke weed, too).

With nothing else to do in El Calafate, I traveled a couple hours away by bus to El Chaltén to see more glaciers and hike on a few trails. El Chaltén is how El Calafate (their names were mixed up by just about everyone) looked a decade ago, without paved roads and internet cafes. It's a modest village with a handful of luxury hotels and restaurants, all of which will change in just a short matter of time. It will get more commercialized and El Calafate will get more commercialized, and hundreds of thousands of people will be herded onto even bigger boats to see the glaciers, until the glaciers melt and there is nothing left to see.

Getting off the bus at El Chaltén I forgot to grab my cowboy hat. The hat was such a pain to carry separately from my pack that a part of me was relieved it was gone. I didn't have the courage to throw it away because I had made the hat an important symbol of my journey, with my attachment to it representing my longing for home or something of the sort. But it was just a hat.

As luck would have it, the bus driver found the hat and returned it to the hostel. This was the second time it found me.

XVII

I hiked to Capri Lake. I considered putting heavy weights in my backpack to make the hike more interesting, but it would be embarrassing to my family if I got lost and died. "Gringo Perishes Just Ten Feet From Trail Carrying Pack Stuffed With Weights. Possessions Donated To Local Orphanage." Other travelers I had met told me that hiking is about reconnecting with nature and getting away from modern life with its pollution, machines, and crowds, but to me it's just walking on dirt and looking at trees. Hopefully that will change as I age.

A day after my first hike I returned to the supermarket and stocked up for another on a different trail, but the wind was too strong and I quit twenty minutes in while still within sight of the town. I returned to the toasty warm hostel and studied my Spanish notecards when I noticed an Israeli girl at the table next to me glancing over. After a month in Córdoba I forgot what it's like when a girl I don't know keeps looking at me.

I made some sort of generic comment to her and she invited me to her table to play cards with her two girlfriends. They were playing *yaniv*, a simple but addicting game where the point is to lay down the lowest card total before anyone else. But if you declare "*yaniv*" when someone else matches your count or has something lower, you get the big "*asif*" and a large point penalty. I mouthed off the whole time by making subtle comments like "I can't wait to *asif* you" and "I want to *asif* you so bad." Playing *yaniv* with trained female soldiers was more interesting than the pitiful hiking I attempted earlier. Drinking *mate* with the Argentines was more enjoyable than the glaciers. My happiness seemed to come from connecting with human beings. Henry David Thoreau is rolling over in his grave.

During the time we played *yaniv*, I was mindful that these girls have training in how to kill men, specifically brown men from Middle Eastern countries (all Israeli citizens are required to serve a two-year stint in the army). They could cleanly carve me up with little knives in their pockets and not flinch when my blood splatters on their faces. It was no surprise the girls were much more cynical and sarcastic than average. In the process of learning how to destroy armies, a part of their femininity has been destroyed as well.

Later that night two other Israelis joined the group, one guy and one girl. The girl was pretty but terribly boring and might as well have been a mute, except for when she wanted something. "May I take?" she'd say as she was already taking beer from my bottle. By the time I joked "no" her glass was half full with no sign of stopping. When I retired to bed I forgot my jacket on the chair. It was gone the next morning, leaving me with just t-shirts in Patagonia.

I exchanged email addresses with the original Israeli girl who invited me to play *yaniv*. She was very receptive to seeing me again, but too bad it won't happen, just like with the Swedish girl who crushed me in pool. It barely mattered because it's been only two weeks since I reset the clock with the English teacher. There was no cold streak pressure or urgency, no mountain to climb. It'd be another month before I cared. The travel love affair was obviously not going to happen. This wasn't turning out to be like the movies where your exotic soul mate grows up in an entirely different culture than you. No, she went to the high school a few miles from yours. I accepted it, and was more than pleased when Stacy emailed me recent photos of herself.

XVIII

I rode with Peter the lawyer to the airport and sat next to him on a plane to Buenos Aires. We talked about girls and how most guys cripple their sex life by falling for one girl and then being the only one in town that doesn't get to fuck her. I told him my theories about approaching, being aggressive, and why it's important to get sex out of the way as quickly as possible. I did this only because he was asking me questions. Otherwise I'm not going to presume a man is a failure with women by giving him unsolicited advice.

"Okay what's a good opening line?" he asked.

"Say you're at a bar and there is a girl sitting next to you," I said. "A good line is this: 'You look like you're having the most fun here out of anyone.'"

"Say it again."

"You.. look.. like.. you are.. having.. the most fun here.. out of.. anyone."

"That's good."

"Yes it usually opens a girl. It doesn't feel like a line."

He took out a pen and piece of paper to write down the things I was telling him. Eventually he said, "You should write a handbook on this." I laughed and then felt compelled to give him a disclaimer. I told him that this worked pretty well on American girls back home, but I was struggling abroad. I was just beginning to adjust and my pathetic results even made me question how much I really knew. That didn't matter to him and for the next hour I told him everything he wanted to know. We parted ways at the end of the flight.

A week later he emailed me with good news. He approached a backpacker by teasing the Canadian flag on her bag: "Are you really Canadian or an American trying to pretend you're Canadian?" He turned on the charm, focusing on humor, and took her out later to drinks. Though he wasn't as forthcoming with sexual details as I would've been, I think he got something out of it, at least a blow job.

Once a man sees what is possible, and makes just a few changes, a whole new world opens up where he finds opportunities that he couldn't see before. His brain gets rewired.

XIX

It was hard to get excited about Buenos Aires, and I'm not sure if it was because of the city itself or my post-Córdoba low. It struck me as a big, smelly dump with a couple safe enclaves for tourists to go to clubs and dine in restaurants with organic vegetables and free-range chicken. It was the same shit: poor people, aggressive vendors, rip-off taxis, pollution, and military statues built during a time when dictators ruled with an iron fist. A handful of gringos had previously told me that Buenos Aires was "a cheaper version of Spain." Now I doubted if they actually had been to Spain.

A DEAD BAT IN PARAGUAY

I stayed at a party hostel in the rich Palermo area of Buenos Aires. In my room were three Australian girls. I told them that my hair was falling out and they reassured me, saying that when hair gets long it looks like a lot falls out after showering. I busted the balls of one of their friends who was staying in another room by asking her if it's possible to volumize her hair more so it doesn't look so thin and flat. She gave me a look like I just strangled her hamster to death and said, "I don't even know your name." In cases like this I can pinpoint the exact moment when a girl becomes attracted to me.

I went to have dinner with Ethan and Luke and their three friends. A woman with a stack of newspapers came to our table and in English said she was homeless and selling them to support herself. Without looking directly at her I brushed her aside with a hand motion.

The dinner was nice but with three new characters I couldn't monopolize my friends' time like I could before. We didn't have any idea where to go afterwards and decided to call it a night. This would be the last time I'd see Ethan. I gave him a hug and we vowed to meet again someday in Córdoba, but I already knew how it would play out. Out of sight, out of mind.

I returned to the hostel where the Aussie girl with the thin hair was flirting with every other guy in the place. I tagged along with a big group that included her to Asia de Cuba, a new club in the developing Puerto Madero neighborhood that had new condos and American chain restaurants like TGI Fridays. The cover was an astronomical fifty pesos ($16), five times more than for something comparable in Córdoba. Inside I was predictably greeted with posing, table service, and VIP sections.

A few songs in I found the Aussie girl and flirted with her a bit, when she turned halfway around and started talking to another guy. I wasn't going to stand there like her obedient puppy dog and wait for her to finish the conversation, so I walked away. Then she did something that no Argentine girl would ever do: she sought me out halfway across the club and grabbed my arm, asking where I went. Finally, a girl who puts in effort by chasing a man who is willing to walk away. She was by my side for the rest of the night and back in the hostel we went into a dirty bathroom and fooled around a little. I went to bed with a heavy sack, already used to it existing in a seemingly permanent state of distention. I was lucky to get myself off once a week on a toilet bowl.

The next day I was sitting at the hostel bar with my laptop when seven Brazilian girls came in. They encircled me after dropping off their packs in the room. Before I had the chance to think of what to say, one of them asked me where I was from. For the next two hours they kept the conversation going in such a way that I had to put in very little effort. The young guys in the hostel noticed this and tried to get into the conversation by offering us cookies and slices of pizza.

That night a founding member of the Predator group was returning to England to resume work. Marcus finally escaped from Córdoba's grasp and was in Buenos Aires for a couple days, staying with his two friends who taught English. We had a couple drinks at a pool hall then walked to a house party where the topic of Argentine girls came up. Both of his friends commented on how tough they were, and Marcus and I could only nod in agreement. At the party two more gringos confirmed our experiences. Turns out that what I thought of as a cold streak was a hot one compared to what these other guys have gotten— nothing. Not a damn thing.

With so many Argentine girls at the party I almost wanted to put in one last surge to be the first gringo ever to hack the matrix, but talking to them was like pulling teeth. The highlight was when one very large Argentine asked me for my name before I asked for hers. For her, this was probably going overboard in showing initial interest. Not feeling well from the latest cold I caught on the plane ride over, I left early and wished Marcus the best. Of course we vowed to meet again someday in Córdoba.

XX

The Argentine bartender at the hostel told me two important things about his culture. The first: "There hasn't been a sexual revolution in Argentina." The second: "Girls have been trained that they aren't worth anything if they are easy." That would explain their unrevealing dress, lack of sexual suggestive dancing, and maddening head turns. His information helped me connect the dots, but the boat had already sailed. The motivation was gone. If I had to do it again I'd have the mind of a caveman and simply approach a huge number of girls until I find one too horny to turn her head away when I go in for the kiss. Problem solved. No sweating or planning or analysis required. They want you to beg them, just like the Chilean girls Max had to beg. I couldn't do that.

"This trip is not what I expected," I told the bartender.

"Why not?"

"Look around. Travel is just about gringos getting drunk and partying," said the man who voluntarily checked into a party hostel.

"It doesn't have to be that way. I don't travel like that. I pack a tent and sleeping bag and sleep in city campgrounds. Each city has one. This job barely pays my living expenses so I need to work while I'm on the road."

"How do you find a job?"

"I juggle at intersections. It pays for my food and bus tickets. Instead of going to clubs at night I meet other campers and we drink beer together. And the girls who camp are a lot more friendly than the ones you meet in clubs here."

"How about if I don't like camping?"

"Then I guess you're stuck with these gringos," he smiled.

"True. I keep running into the same gringos because we use the same guidebook. There was a girl I met in a beach town in Peru who I saw months later in front of a Córdoba bar that was in the book."

"That shouldn't happen. South America is a big place."

I'm convinced that at some point in the future, guidebooks will be seen as the pinnacle of modern society. In the palm of your hand you have information on thousands of cities, townships, beaches, museums, parks, restaurants, hostels, hotels, motels, clubs, bars, cafes, jungles, campgrounds, train stations, trolley stations, and bus stations. It condenses huge continents into digestible bits so that wherever you are you'll never be far from a city that has been succinctly reviewed and critiqued by another human being.

Even if you ditch the book, you'll still end up in the same places where other gringos congregate—places that are in the book. If you look up hostels on the internet, chances are you'll come across ones that are in the book. You can't escape the book. The only way to jump off the gringo trail completely is to go to the tiny towns the book deems too pathetic to be included, but this would mean having to speak the language. Most gringos cannot order dinner in anything but their own tongue.

A hundred years ago there were no guidebooks or bank cards or tourist areas or *semi-cama* buses with pillows and blankets. There was no travel insurance to bail you out in case of trouble. There were no signs in English. Travelers of the past carried silver and gold and figured things out as they went. A journey that takes me six months took them years. I'm sure there was a day when you had to be intelligent and sharp to travel, but that day has passed, and now all you need is some money and the book. The tourist network will do the rest, holding your hand from one city to the next. Otherwise gringos would perish—they simply would not survive. Something would get them and kill them.

I wasn't a traveler or a tourist but a sheep, with my ear tagged, following all the other sheep, polluting the environment with mountains of shit and plastic water bottles, sleeping in hostels with sheep from Australia and Ireland, getting drunk in bars located in the richest parts of town. I saw and experienced what the book told me to see and experience and during the moments in between all I tried to do was get laid. The benefits of perspective and learning about others cultures had been pushed aside. The first poor kid who wanted to shine my shoes affected me, the fiftieth I told to fuck off. But I couldn't quit the gringo trail. I would never stray from it, as much as I hated it, as bitter I would become about my method of travel. The real unknown is too dangerous and hard.

XXI

I woke up early for a $30 "volunteer" tour of an Argentine *villa*, a slum on the outskirts of the city. (They are called *favelas* in Brazil, *barrios* in Venezuela.) Barefoot toddlers in nothing but diapers roamed around like they were lost, sometimes crying, and shirtless hooligans gawked at the girls in our group. The residents were much darker than what I saw in rich areas like Palermo and Recoleta, and turns out most were immigrants from Bolivia, Paraguay, and Peru. No one ran to us and begged for donations, wailing in pain for help like I would see in television advertisements for world aid organizations.

Lopsided houses were constructed of aluminum sheeting and discarded materials. It seemed like a modest thunderstorm would cause widespread devastation. There were strong metal gates on every door, surprisingly, probably to protect the television set that everyone had. Electricity was illegally spliced from power lines. The sewage system overflowed whenever it rained, and we were told the smell was unbearable for a day or two afterwards. The ancient Romans would have been offended. On the bright side, this particular *villa* provided residents with free drinking water and meals.

After a short tour of the slum we went to the community center to play games and help kids with their homework. I drew Christmas trees with a quiet little girl, which felt strange since it was sweltering outside (seasons are flipped in the southern hemisphere). I made her laugh by adding things like hippopotamuses, giraffes, and fire trucks to my Christmas tree. The other kids were positive and playful and I couldn't guess by their attitude that they lived in a slum, but I'm not going to kid myself and say I made a difference. The little girl forgot about me in a couple days.

Education was stressed but it's just a matter of time until the parents put the kids to work or there is an accidental pregnancy. Unless someone from the outside comes in to pluck them out, or they are lifted with skilled job training and opportunity, they are doomed to breeding and poverty. The powerful and the rich who can make a difference in her life choose not to, or the poor themselves choose this way of life. In this *villa* the job to better the lives of the little girl and her friends, one pair of shoes and one textbook at a time, is left to a woman who lives in the slum herself. She sees hope where I see none.

XXII

A Dutch girl with Romanian ancestry checked in to my dorm room. She had a voluptuous body with toned arms and legs and large, perky breasts that defied gravity. Her face was okay but it was the body I wanted. I was inspired to work to get it. While she was busy sightseeing I laid in my bed thinking of a way to get her out, and in she came to invite me to join her and her friends at a salsa club. I still despised salsa, but I would be an idiot to turn down an opportunity to wrap my tentacles around her. I figured we'd eventually relocate to another club and then back to the hostel for quiet sex to not wake the others. Only thing was I missed a big warning sign. She said, "I love to dance."

We went with a large group from the hostel. At the club she danced with random men but it was to salsa and I already knew the deal with that. I felt like a pimp that I'm letting my bitch dance with other men, knowing she'd be right back.

After about an hour, there was a small performance by some guys in white suits and I watched it with my hands resting on her body. She said she wanted to come to the next club with me, but fifteen minutes later she was still dancing with other guys. I exerted my pimp hand by walking up to her and saying, "Look I'm ready to go. Are you coming with me or not?" She paused, obviously torn. She could stay and shake her ass without committing to any man, getting enormous amounts of attention doing what she loves, or she could leave with me. She decided to stay. I was enraged, not because she ditched me but because I wasted two hours of my Thursday night on a girl who was never serious about hooking up in the first place. Poor me, all led on like that.

In dramatic fashion I said goodbye and stormed off, and went alone to a club recommended on the hostel bulletin board. In Buenos Aires, one of the largest cities in the world, I ran into Samuel bobbing his head to the house music. And with him was Tennessee! He was stoned out of his mind, standing in the middle of the dance floor with his eyes closed.

Samuel and I milled around the bar, talking to some girls without much success, then made plans to hang out the next night, a Friday. I stayed out longer than I wanted because I didn't want to return to the hostel before the Dutch girl and let her think she ruined my night. When I finally did get back she had just finished changing into a tank top and soft cotton pajamas. She whispered something to me about her feet hurting. I sat on her bed and moved closer, but she reminded me how she had to get up early.

XXIII

Samuel came by the hostel and tagged along with me and the Brazilian girls to a club called Sunset. On the way there, in a large party van provided by the hostel, I asked which cities he visited.

"I went to Florianópolis for three days and Rio for a week," he said.

"Well? How was it?"

"I had a blast. Brazil is so different from Argentina. The people are so positive and friendly. The buildings are colorful. The weather is great. And the food is better, with all these fruits you've never seen before."

"How about the girls? Did you hit?"

"Yeah, two girls. It was ten times easier than that bullshit we had to put up with in Córdoba. I wish I could've stayed longer, but I booked a flight and couldn't change it."

"So it's true then what the Predator said?"

"Yeah pretty much. Brazilian girls love gringos. As long as you don't hang out in the rich areas, you'll get far if they just hear you speak English. Girls here don't care if you're a gringo or not."

"Well there are Brazilian girls here," I pointed out. They were in the seats up front, laughing and talking loudly amongst themselves in Portuguese.

"No, I like the ghetto *favela* chicks with a little bit of black in them. These girls are white and rich."

I liked one of them and made a weak attempt in the club to dance with her, but she wouldn't stick around for long and I didn't care to chase. There are the girls you'd bang but not work for, and the girls you'd bang and do whatever you could.

Drinking with Samuel put me in a great mood. I got motivated and decided to try for another Argentine girl. I would use all that I learned from our days in Córdoba and make it look easy. I approached two girls by the small bar. One of them gravitated towards me and rubbed my back like I was a baby needing to be burped. Finally, a freebie! I stayed put, talking slowly in English, and she inched closer. Ten minutes later she said, "Well, I'm going now. It was nice meeting you. Goodbye." She walked off. I was dumbfounded but I took it. Once the sun came up I gathered with Samuel and the Brazilians in a McDonalds parking lot to wait for our party van back to the hostel.

The next night I went with Samuel to Crobar, located right next to a park that serves as a gathering place for transsexuals. Samuel was still dreaming of Brazil so he stood around like a log, his 6'5" frame towering over everyone else, Jack Daniels drink in hand. It was up to me to make something happen.

I saw two pretty girls by the bar. One of them looked like she had had plastic surgery, her face stiff, frozen in time. I wanted to be the first guy of the night they talked to than trying later when a shield would develop and they'd have no problem flicking me away with contempt. The ensuing conversation with the plastic surgery girl went well, but after ten minutes I looked over to Samuel, still the log, and told him I'm ready for them to dip to the bathroom. Sure enough, at the fifteen minute mark, it came.

Shockingly, they returned.

I danced with my girl. She kept touching my hair, which I had back in a pony tail, while my hand rested on the top of her ass. I took pictures of her surgically enhanced face. The vibe was positive and fun, unusually so. When I went to the bar I didn't even think twice about buying an extra drink for her and her friend to share. She asked me for my email address and phone number. When it was time for another drink I told her I'd be right back, and went to the bar about ten feet away to get a screwdriver. We had been talking for almost two hours. There was no wait at the bar and I got my drink and paid for it in about two minutes time. I turned around and they were gone, nowhere to be seen.

I was so mad I wanted to throw my drink into the crowd. I wanted it to smash on some girl's head and I wanted her to bleed and cry. How much worse would I feel if I bought them another drink! God I was so stupid. Every night these girls disrespected me and played me like a cheap toy, and I kept going back for more. I leaned against a column, stewing in anger. But near me was a girl that kept looking. A Chinese proverb I had read somewhere popped in my head: "The temptation to quit will be greatest just before you are about to succeed."

I said something in English and she liked it, even though she couldn't understand. I said every Spanish word I knew to keep the conversation going as long as possible. Then Michael Jackson's song "Thriller" came on. I know how to dance to Michael Jackson. I grabbed her hand and gently pulled her to the dance floor. She declined. Okay, okay, I get it.

Samuel was long gone. While trying to find a cab on the street, a hideous transsexual pawed at me and wouldn't let go of my arm until I snatched it away.

Whenever I saw a happy Argentine couple holding hands or making out in a park, I couldn't help but imagine how much shit the guy had to go through to get her.

XXIV

I walked to the nearest convenience store to buy a drink to go along with a medium pizza I was about to eat by myself. I hadn't yet put together that dairy was making the beast growl.

An older woman waiting in front of me looked familiar. She had to be at least in her 50s. It's a strange feeling to find someone familiar that you couldn't have possibly met before in your life, but I had in fact met her. Her bags gave it away. She was the woman who tried to sell me newspapers at dinner with Ethan and Luke.

I forgot who talked first, but next thing I knew I'm telling her about the countries I'd been to and she is telling me about how she loves the Persian culture. I don't think she recognized me. She was curious about why I quit my job to come to South America and I told her that with

ARGENTINA

each month I was slowly forgetting why I did it. "When you're away from something for a long time it seems like you only remember the good," I said.

I had some pocket change so I was ready for her to ask me to buy a newspaper, which I was happily ready to do. But she never asked. I felt ashamed. People say you find out things about yourself when you travel, but it's not always good.

XXV

Motivated to cure my lingering stomach issues, my sludge, and my anal itch, I called four Buenos Aires doctors. All I needed was one of them to do some stool tests and he'd find the parasite or whatever I had and give me medicine and I'd be fine. I only got answering machines. The front desk at the hostel told me to go to a private hospital, but that was out of the question. Too expensive and nerve-racking.

I went to a pharmacy to buy an anti-parasite drug (the one that is carcinogenic in mice), but back at the hostel I read the indications on the internet and discovered the dosage varied for different conditions as much as fivefold. I didn't know what I had. So I went to another pharmacy, to not arouse suspicion, and bought the same anti-parasite drug I took in Peru. Only six pills, two a day, with the lone side effect of neon yellow urine. I rationalized this to be the right move since I already knew my body tolerated the drug well.

Later I met up with Paula and her friend for lunch. They were taking advantage of the strengthening Brazilian *real* currency with a weekend getaway in now cheap Buenos Aires, which I began calling Malas Aires. I was surprised to learn she was still seeing the Irishman she met in Cuzco the night I was stuck in bed with salmonella.

We talked about Brazilian culture. She told me how for New Year's Eve Brazilians wear a color that represents what they want for the following year. White is peace, the most common, but people often accessorize with colors that stand for things like money or love. Paula told me that while she normally wears white, her underwear is the color of something she really wants. Something to look forward to, colored underwear that is, if I ever find myself on the beaches of Rio for New Year's.

That night the Dutch girl asked me out on a date. She was very forward so I had a feeling it was a trap, but I was excited at the chance to isolate her away from salsa music. I met up with her at the obelisk downtown, the Buenos Aires version of the Washington D.C. Monument that was once wrapped in a gigantic condom for AIDS Day. We sat down and talked when the log randomly walked by and said hello, his hostel being only a block away. I was content to stay and people watch, but she was itching to do "something."

We strolled along a pedestrian walkway. With her fluent Spanish she found us a good deal for a *parradilla* meat-fest. It was the first and last time I ate blood sausage—cow blood filled in emptied intestines and cooked to a pâté-like consistency dark red in color. She had a ravenous appetite, and I could actually pinpoint the moment my attraction for her diminished when she put the last piece of disgusting blood sausage in her mouth, rolled her eyes in the back of her head, and said, "So so good."

Besides her obsession with dancing (she was accomplished in several forms), a problem I had with her was that she was too smart. She spoke six languages, came from a family of lawyers and doctors (she was a lawyer herself), studied meditation, practiced yoga, graduated college two years ahead of her peers, and had worked for internships where she contributed more to the world's volume of knowledge than men twice her age. How can I defile a girl in bed that I admire? She didn't care for my radio show humor anyway, and wanted to have deep, serious conversation about how to bring different cultures together and solve the world's problems.

After dinner we walked back to the obelisk and sat down. Not ten minutes in she asked me if I wanted to go dancing. No thanks.

The next morning I moved to a tiny twenty-bed hostel in the San Telmo working class neighborhood on the other side of the city, for what would be my last week in Buenos Aires. The only reason I had stayed in the city so long was to kill time before meeting up with Caleb in Uruguay for New Year's.

ARGENTINA

With no noise from hooting and hollering Australians, I was able to sleep like a baby for the first time in months. There was no conceivable reason for me to get up in the morning since I already finished visiting sights my guidebook recommended.

Sometimes the two younger sisters of the hostel owner would cover the front desk for a few hours at a time. I would have many fun conversation starters in my head to use, but would hold back due to my prior experience with Argentine girls. I knew that because of their culture they would respond frigidly and withhold interest for quite a while, and not just sexual interest but interest in me as a person. Even though I was always milling around the hostel, cooking and eating and watching television, they acted like I was invisible.

If I grew up in Argentina I can only imagine how different I would be, maybe enough that I'd go up to girls and pull their hair like I'd seen guys do in clubs. This is the country where the phrase "Beauty isn't everything" must have been born. It is everything, but only for a short time.

The anti-parasite drug didn't work.

A DEAD BAT IN PARAGUAY

URUGUAY & PARAGUAY

I

I took a ferry from Malas Aires to Montevideo, the capital of Uruguay. Its seedy casinos gave it a derelict feel at night, but were extremely convenient for exchanging money. Pieces of old newspaper collected against buildings near gamblers down on their luck, and gangs of teenagers hung out on monument steps smoking and drinking. They were more smiley than their Argentine counterparts.

On my first night I went alone to the old city center. I walked around checking out the scene, trying to decide which bar I should go into, when I saw five girls about to walk past me. I said the first thing that came to my mind: "Do you know if this place is a bar or club?" They giggled at my English and invited me to join them at another bar. I approached a lot of girls in Argentina on the street but this never happened, and they never showed cleavage like these girls did. They were all about 17 years old.

At the bar I bought them slushy alcoholic drinks that came in oversized plastic tubes. I didn't want to drink alone. They all had childbearing figures, but I defaulted to being the pleasant, nice gringo, almost like their big brother. One of them was a pretty Brazilian but I did nothing because the circumstance has to be right for me to go after a young girl. I have to be desperate and there has to be a lack of audience, neither of which was the case. I left at 5am and kissed them on their cheeks. The Brazilian probably thought I was not a real man.

Tired of the polluted cities, I stayed in Montevideo for only two nights.

A DEAD BAT IN PARAGUAY

II

Punta del Diablo is an isolated beach on Uruguay's southern coast. The paved road into town turned to sand well before I could see surfers bobbing up and down in the ocean, waiting for a wave. It's the kind of place where if a shopkeeper doesn't have change for your big bill she lets you take the goods and pay her later. Everyone is sipping *mate*, slowly walking around like tortoises, people watching. There is no internet café to follow the news and get a sense of time, no car horns or aggressive vendors.

There were two hostels in town and I checked in to one of them. A friendly Irish girl invited me to sit with a group of her friends and two American girls. The conversation was about common birth names and Hollywood celebrities they wanted to have sex with. It was Christmas Eve. I sat there in silence with my Patricia beer, which smelled like raw ground beef, wishing I could be with my family instead.

Everyone whooped it up and made cheesy grins for the camera until they headed to another bar a little after midnight. I relaxed alone on a hammock but felt a painful sting on my right arm. I had been bitten by an exotic double-fanged insect. I waited for signs of my impending death such as dizziness or a swelling throat, but nothing happened.

My new bed was packed in with nine others in a space that usually saw half as much. Bags owned by mostly Irish and Swedish travelers covered the floor, making nighttime trips to the bathroom a dangerous undertaking. I had to get out of the hostel.

The first thing I did when I woke up was ask local merchants if they knew about *cabañas* (cabins) available for rent. I got lucky at the phone shop—the clerk knew an elderly woman who had a small cabin available for only $6 more a night than I was paying at the hostel. It was a shabby little shack—the windows didn't lock properly and the toilet was tricky to operate, but I had my own kitchen, bathroom, and dining room table. It was perfect.

I wondered why other gringos didn't do what I did, but then again Lonely Planet conditioned us to put in as little work in finding accommodations as possible. Just showing up is usually enough because if one hostel is full then there will be another across the street.

But asking random natives who don't speak your language for a room with no guarantee that you'll get one? Forget about it.

In the shack I wrote in my journal, cooked omelets, studied Portuguese, listened to house music with portable bookshelf speakers I had bought in Chile, and jerked off like I was eighteen again. If I could only afford to get a private room everywhere I went, but with no more fat paychecks being dropped into my checking account every two weeks, I was stuck with dorms.

My social interaction needs weren't met like it was when staying in a crowded hostel, so I made friends with the surf board rental lady and the shopkeeper's kid, who I lit fireworks with at night. I put in effort to get to know them that I wouldn't otherwise if I already had gringo friends. I wondered if a trip staying in private rooms would be a better, more "real" experience than a trip three times as long in dorm rooms.

On the beach I was tired of watching surfers catch waves and not me, so I asked the surf board lady to give me a good deal on a rental. I wanted to experience the magic of waiting in the water and riding a wave to completion—a lonely, introspective act that seemed to fit the mood of the trip. Unfortunately, without lessons the best I could do was wipe out on one wave in two hours. It wasn't as simple as looking at other surfers and copying them.

My first night in the shack I walked a few steps away to one of the town's only bars. I could pull a girl and not worry about where to take her, but there were no girls besides the bartenders. One was a 27-year-old Brazilian with a cute face and the other a 19-year-old Uruguayan with a better overall package. I chatted with them for most of the night and felt like I was in Venezuela again when I frequented the same restaurants to build something with the waitresses. The more I butchered their language, the more charming they found me.

The next night I went back to the bar and the vibe with the Uruguayan was strong with lots of long eye contact and flirting, but she wouldn't get off until 7am and my bus was leaving two hours after that. I brainstormed and came up with the brilliant plan—kiss her while she was on duty! That proved to be impossible. The manager was hanging around and there was a three foot wide bar between us. I asked her to take a drunk picture of me with a cocktail umbrella in my hair and then

I left. I would have stayed longer if I didn't already reserve a bed in Punta del Este where I would reunite with Caleb.

I lost the cowboy hat for good. I placed it on my pack while waiting for the bus and a gust of wind blew it away. Several hours had passed before I realized it was gone.

III

Punta del Este was different from all the other South American cities. Teenagers in trendy clothing and oversized sunglasses walked out of summer condos, taking pictures of themselves in prefabricated poses or checking their phones every two minutes. Skinny girls wearing booty shorts flew by on roller blades like they were auditioning for a cameo spot on Beverly Hills 90210. Roads were well-manicured with thoughtful landscaping in the medians, and every fourth car was a Mercedes-Benz or oversized import with a tag from Argentina, Brazil, or Paraguay. Restaurant windows displayed menu prices that were five times higher than Montevideo, next to WiFi stickers I hadn't seen in months. All the wealth being displayed made me realize my place on the world's totem pole. For the first time in the trip I felt poor.

Since there were no real sights to take pictures of or kill time with, I decided to take surf lessons. My instructor was a young Uruguayan girl who had piercing gray-blue eyes and a magnificent body finely tuned from years of surfing. Her attractiveness was both a blessing and a curse, because while she was great to look at, I worried about things I wouldn't have had she not been so attractive, like how my ass looked from behind in a wetsuit and if my crotch bulge was respectable enough. But she was a good instructor and I stood up on the board pretty quickly.

It's tempting to discover something and declare that's what you've been looking for all along. I couldn't resist to do that with surfing. There was nothing like sitting and waiting and paddling for a wave that picks up my board, and hurrying to stand for just a few seconds of exhilaration. I went to the internet café and read surf tips and wave reports, and watched videos of professional surfers tackling thirty-foot monsters. I asked other travelers if they surfed and knew anything about Brazil's waves. How much I envied the little 10-year-olds who got such an early start, surfing like experts with their superior balance from having a low center of gravity. After a couple hours of lessons I decided that surfing would be my new purpose in life.

IV

I emailed Caleb first thing when I arrived in Punta, but two days passed and I got no response. He was with a large group of friends. I was bothered until I met someone else, a curly-haired Italian staying in my room named Beppe. He spoke fluent Spanish and English and came to Punta to find a bartending job in the famed La Barra club district a few miles north of town. He printed out a resume and went door to door asking for a job, and on the first night he landed one. It was the first time I met a traveler who got something besides basic hostel work like setting up breakfast or manning the front desk.

A couple hours before he was due for his first night on the job, we sat on the patio with three Argentine girls drinking Fernet mixed with Coke, an abomination of a liquor that is more bitter than Campari. Other guys were around but the girls liked our humor, especially Beppe's, who knew how to accentuate his stories with a range of facial expressions that made him exciting to listen to. He'd say the punch lines in Italian and we understood even though we didn't.

The girls all lived in America for half-year stints. We were able to talk about cultural differences and their love for shows like *Friends* and *Simpsons*. Because of this they said they were "cool" Argentines, and I had to agree. I wondered if they were easy as well—if my brand of sexual norms filtered down to their psyche after exposure to the sex-obsessed American culture.

An American guy eavesdropping on our conversation about dating said "American girls are all easy sluts." I found myself defending American girls, calling them "horny" instead. While there are many things about American girls that I don't like, such as their materialism, coldness, and obsession with celebrities, their easiness is definitely not one of them. My experience in Argentina made that very clear.

Beppe went to work, leaving myself, the American, a jovial Dutch guy, and the Argentine girls. Out of the girls there was the skinny, pretty one who needed the most attention; the taller, meatier one who was quiet and reserved; and finally the homely duckling who seemed like she would make an compliant girlfriend with attempts to please her man. I kept my options open, which is one way of saying I didn't get enough interest from any of the girls where I could make a good decision.

We took a bus to La Barra and then walked down a dark country road on our way to Crobar (a common club name, apparently). The prettiest Argentine broke away from the pack to get directions from passing cars, until she just got right in one. We didn't see her for the rest of the night, and before her disappearing act she had said nothing to her friends. I was almost happy to see this happen because it validated my observation that Argentine girls love disappearing, apparently even on their childhood girlfriends. And the weird thing is that the remaining girls didn't care. Their apathy said this is something normal that happens all the time. It's definitely not normal with American girls, where there would be much drama and frantic phone calling. "Oh my god where are you—are you okay?!"

Crobar was mobbed and only VIPs were allowed in. We wandered around La Barra. The American settled on the homely girl and the Dutch guy ditched for another club, leaving me with the tall one. The math was good, the selections were made, and nine times out of ten at least one of us is going to get some in this type of situation. We walked around aimlessly and bought booze from a gas station, drinking it on the sidewalk with obviously underage teenagers. Two hours after leaving the hostel we still hadn't gone inside a club. Eventually we gave up and decided to head back to the hostel. The American seemed to be making headway with his girl and I to mine. It was time to isolate.

Almost at the hostel, I said to my girl, "Hey this bench looks comfortable—do you want to sit down for a few minutes?"

"No thanks. I'm a little tired," she said.

"Okay."

Eventually we got to the hostel door.

"Do you want to take a walk to the oceanfront?" I asked. It was only one block away.

"Umm no that's fine."

"Okay."

Once inside the hostel she went right to bed. I wasn't mad because she didn't disappear on me or disrespect me, as I didn't disrespect her. Nothing to get riled up about it. I gave it my all, but she didn't want to buy what I was selling. It was clean. The American guy didn't get anything either.

I noticed it was very common for Argentine girls, like the tall one, to rest their hand on my forearm early in the conversation. If an American girl did that then I would take it as a huge green light and escalate the encounter by touching more and getting closer, but apparently that's not a green light for the Argentines—it's a test to see how eager I am. Ramping up after had been nothing but doom. The aggressiveness that is so rewarded with American girls are duly punished by the Argentines, but I didn't know how to be passive unless it was with a girl I didn't want.

V

My body was destroyed from surfing. My knees and palms were raw from wipeouts in the sand, my right foot was scraped and bruised from kicking a stone hidden in the sea bed, and my face was bright red despite putting on sunscreen nonstop. My calves screamed in pain with every step, my arms were so beat I couldn't lift them above my shoulders, and my back was as stiff as my foam trainer board. But I felt happy to be pushing myself in ways other than getting laid. It was just me and a big piece of plastic in the ocean, away from the gringos and crazy Argentine girls, waiting for the water to lift me up. After riding a wave I'd turn around to face the ocean and feel the same as when on the rock with Max, when we watched the *lobos* sleep as the sun set in the background. My spirits were coming back. I was tired of moping and feeling sorry for my stomach and my luck.

VI

Brazilians invaded the hostel. An extremely friendly Brazilian couple sat with me on the patio for two hours, educating me about their country. They went out of their way to tell me where to go and how to stay safe, and taught me useful phrases in Portuguese like "*Que porra?!*" (what the fuck).

Two Brazilian girls milled around. They were performance artists who worked in casinos and hotels to cover their travel expenses. They juggled and twirled fire, among other acts. One was very aware of her sexuality but a bit old at thirty-eight. Her petite friend was twenty-two and much more my type but she couldn't speak a word of English. All she did was smile a lot. She was the type who stops to smell a small flower garden in front of someone's house and then take pictures. It was enchanting, though if she was ugly it would have been annoying. Without a way to communicate with her I talked to the older Brazilian more and more, who didn't bother to translate for her younger friend.

I was feeling stubborn and told myself it would either be the young one or nothing. I'm not going to go after a girl just because she likes me. While a noble idea on the surface, considering the language barrier and the fact they were both leaving the next day, I questioned my decision the next morning when I woke up alone with my dick in my hand.

During the time I was getting nowhere with the Brazilians, Beppe was fucking the pretty Argentine girl doggy style in the hostel bathroom. He had quit his job after only two nights (he didn't appreciate that they put him in the service bar), and went out with the Argentine girls to a bar. The story came out the next day in bits and pieces while on the beach. Just like with all the previous Argentine girls he had sex with, he said all he did was be fun, make jokes, dance, smile, dance some more, twirl her around, and wait for the right moment to strike.

"Alright you gotta tell me the secret to these Argentine girls," I begged.

"There's no secret. They're just like any other girl."

"Maybe Italian girls but not American. They're ten times harder than American girls."

"Yeah American girls are pretty easy. They get very turned on by just an Italian accent!" He laughed. "Well with the girls from Argentina you have to be patient. When it's time to make a move the feeling will change—she will give a different, more intense look."

"What do you mean more intense?"

"It's hard to explain but you just know. She tries to look through you. She moves slower. You just feel it."

"Sounds subtle."

"Yes it is, and only when that happens can you make your move. It's pretty easy really."

His strategy was too simplistic. I had the feeling that he didn't know all the right things he was doing.

That night we left the hostel for a house party in a rich suburb. It was New Year's Eve. Along with us were his Venezuelan lady friend and her two girlfriends from England. On our way to the bus station, Beppe stuck out his thumb and we hitched a pick-up truck for half the way. For the other half we caught a cab, and the driver was in such great spirits that he didn't charge us for the one mile ride. I was touched and gave him the full cab fare since taxi drivers usually do their best to rip me off.

We couldn't find the house so Beppe walked up to someone in the shadows to ask for directions, but turns out it wasn't a person but a dog. The girls and I were laughing while the dog was following Beppe, who was cursing at it in Italian for not having the proper directions.

We found the house—more like mansion—and joined about fifteen other people in the backyard drinking beer, Fernet and Coke, and red wine. The music became louder and Beppe danced by himself with ridiculous arm movements. He danced with a large potted plant by squatting over it, followed by running in circles around the grass with arms outstretched like he was an airplane. He'd burst into Italian song and jump in the air to clap his feet. He opened his eyes so wide they were bulging from his head, making him look possessed. People couldn't stop watching him and he made friends with just about everyone.

English girls are usually on the colder side, but the cuter of the two was extremely warm and friendly to us both. While chatting her up I noticed she had her eyes on Beppe. When the garden sprinklers came on everyone ran for cover, but he stayed put and ran barefoot on the yard in random patterns, soaking himself in the process. He grabbed the cute English girl's hand and ran around the lawn with her. She loved it and couldn't stop laughing. The rest of us stood amused on the sidelines, staring at this crazy Italian guy with his jeans rolled up to his knees, sucking an English girl into his world. Not only did he deserve her more than me but he was so mesmerizing I wanted to sit back and watch to take notes. I'm completely comfortable with my heterosexuality, but if I was gay the sprinkler scene would be the moment where I'd want to have sex with Beppe. He emanated an energy that would take everything out of me to reproduce.

There were a couple other guys at the party whose energy was just so low and weak compared to Beppe, so stiff-like. They were going from girl to girl, spitting game with a warm drink in their hand, sometimes making progress but usually not. Then it hit me like an intestinal parasite—those other guys were me. I touched as part of a plan, Beppe touched as part of some fun game. I told a story that I knew would get a good response, he told a story to share who he is. I got girls by being aggressive, he got girls by allowing them to get aggressive. My game was inferior compared to his.

The Argentine girl he had had sex with in the bathroom, Lelu, showed up unexpectedly with her two friends. I still don't know how she got the address. They greeted each other and Beppe turned to me when she went inside the house to use the bathroom. He gave me the same *what the fuck do I do* look that Keane had given me several months ago in Huaraz.

"Who do you want?" I asked.

"Mary." He wanted the English girl.

"Then go for her then."

"But it's not a sure thing."

"True, but it's pretty close to it. She loves you, just keep doing what you're doing and take her to the bathroom."

"How do I get rid of Lelu?" he asked, rubbing his chin.

"Just do what they do to me all the time—disappear!"

"Where am I going to disappear to? I'm screwed."

"You're being a sissy. Hey maybe you should go for the threesome." I ran out of helpful advice.

"That's not going to happen."

"Do you like Lelu?"

There was silence.

"Okay that means no. Go for Mary. She's cool and she likes you. Lelu will get over it, don't worry."

"Alright I'll go for Mary."

But Lelu wasn't going to let Beppe slip away. She literally threw herself on him when she came out of the bathroom, clamping down on his torso so tightly that he had to peel her off. I'd never seen an Argentine girl do that before. Beppe was weak now from all the alcohol and couldn't resist. Even though he told me he was going to go for Mary, the selection was Lelu. The lure of the sure thing is too powerful for most men.

Poor Mary. There she was, ready to receive Beppe in all his glory, but here this girl comes from nowhere to steal her New Year's hookup. The pain on her face was obvious. It was like a doctor had just told her she was infected with genital warts. The cauliflower kind.

Beppe couldn't even go to the bathroom without Lelu yelling his name every ten seconds, completely oblivious to everyone becoming annoyed at her. He worked her up to such a frenzy I didn't know a girl could behave so desperately, Argentine or not. I thought the Predator opened my eyes, but then I met an Italian man named Beppe. Without even coming across as a player he is the best I've seen.

There was one point in the night that piqued my curiosity, when Beppe mimed like a street performer for the party-goers. I turned on my digital camera and looked through the photos I already had of him. All his poses were unique. There was one with his arms in the air, one of him pointing at the camera with his head tilted, one with his legs spread far apart, one looking up at the sky, and one where he is holding a girl's hands above his head. Then there was his surfer pose, his muscle man pose, his hysterical face pose, and his serious, thinking man pose. His face always had the perfect expression. If I didn't know any better I'd say he was an actor.

I left the party and saw Lelu straddling Beppe on a neighbor's yard. She was in love with him. Beppe may be right about his strategy on Argentine girls, for waiting for the subtle signs, but it was his personality that did all the heavy lifting. It was potent and could not be reproduced. All I could hope for was to take one little piece from it. Even though the party was just a so-so sausage fest, with Beppe it was a night of revelation.

VII

Caleb finally did get in touch with me, but his replies took so long it was impossible to make plans. If I wasn't distracted by Beppe's brilliance, I would have felt like a fool for changing my travel itinerary for only one person who proceeded to flake on me. Long-distance friendships are futile, only good for the occasional email.

I left Punta del Este on New Year's Day headed for Puerto Iguazú in the northeastern corner of Argentina, home of arguably the most magnificent waterfalls in the world.

VIII

It was a mistake to travel on a major holiday when buses ran less frequently. After the two hour ride to Montevideo I had an eleven hour layover. Everything was closed except for a diner. I sat down on a chair and watched a muted television set. Then I took a six hour overnight bus ride to Salto in the north of Uruguay followed by a five hour layover, where I slept like a homeless person on the bus station floor. Then a one hour bus ride to Concordia in Argentina followed by an eight hour layover. After depositing my bag in Concordia's bus station, I walked around the city until I found a bench to nap on for two hours, one over from a real homeless man. I was so tired my mind could only process lower order thinking—I couldn't even concentrate long enough to read the fluffy pages from my guidebook. That's a bad state to be making important decisions, like whether a taxicab driver's face is honest or not. The final bus ride took twelve hours, bringing the total voyage to forty-five hours. For the first time I was able to fall asleep sitting completely upright with my neck hanging limp off to the side. I was a soldier, Delta force.

In spite of the girls, a part of me was glad to be back in Argentina, a country I stayed in long enough that it felt familiar upon my return. A day after getting my three-month Brazilian visa I paid a visit to Iguazú Falls, right on the border with Brazil. Dozens of waterfalls fell from giant cliffs like the Devils Throat, whose whitewater splashed on tourists standing on metal scaffolding. More scaffolding connected to other lookout points of the falls, from sweeping overhead views to eye-level platforms right next to water crashing into the river. Roaming around were lizards and a half-squirrel, half-raccoon looking animal that rummaged through tourist trash. The power of the water and modest number of tourists made it an enjoyable scene even with the subtropical heat, much better than Machu Picchu—that overpriced, overhyped pile of stone. Many travelers had argued that the reason I didn't enjoy Machu Picchu is because I skipped the four-day Inca Trail, but if that's the case then the Inca Trail should be admired for greatness, not Machu Picchu.

After a tour of the falls I went out with two South African potheads. We drank in a bar where I quickly discovered I paid a dollar more for the exact same beer they got. I didn't care about the money but I wanted to let the bartenders know that I wasn't a stupid gringo. When I nicely confronted them they acted confused, making up some claptrap about prices being different depending on if you order outside or inside. They gave me the price difference.

One of my new friends echoed a view I'd heard before. "Travel is selfish. It's hedonistic to visit a country just to say you did it, to laze around and drink and sightsee and make little attempt to connect with the culture. I admit that what I'm doing is selfish."

It seemed like a reasonable conclusion on the surface, like calling Buenos Aires a cheaper version of Spain, but I failed to see how it's more selfish than working a typical job at home to sustain a first-class material lifestyle of consumption—a lifestyle that not only is unsustainable to the environment but unattainable to most people of the world. Replacing getting drunk abroad is no different than getting drunk at home, though at least now your dollars are going into a country that is a lost less well off than your own. I figure it's a wash on the scale of selfishness.

We walked to a club where the bouncer made up a cover charge after asking where we were from. We eventually got in for free but I didn't stay more than five minutes—it was too loud and as much as I would've liked to pump another Argentine girl, without Beppe around to inspire me the motivation to undertake the laborious process just wasn't there. My mind had already moved on to Brazil, and word of a new Brazilian club opening right in town got me excited. Both Brazil and Paraguay were just a couple miles away, and the point where the three countries meet is actually a tourist attraction.

The following night I drank with the South Africans at a quiet bar before going with them to La Barranca, the Brazilian club celebrating opening night. The cover charge was $10. Now I hate covers as much as the next guy, but outside were tons of nicely dressed Brazilian girls. No Argentines in sight. Still, the South Africans were chafed and wanted to go back to the shithole from the previous night. I had to make a decision: go with the guys to the lame club or go alone to the Brazilian club.

I bid them a sad adieu.

Within just a couple of minutes out on the patio I started talking to two tall Brazilian sisters. They wore skimpy halter tops and mini-skirts that left their bits exposed to the humid air.

Their demeanor was nippy and far from encouraging, but it's rare that I walk up to an attractive girl and she instantly turns on the bubbly vibe. They started warming up to me when a huge meathead rolled up and gave a hand sweep motion telling me to fuck off, similar to what I did to the homeless woman in Argentina. "No, he's American," one of the girls said. "He's cool." He apologized and I learned he was the boyfriend of one of the girls. Perfect, it was like I had a wingman.

I was rusty and out-of-practice. A meekness took hold, and for the first half hour I didn't touch the single sister at all. I went to the bar once and forgot to ask her to come with me. I also forgot to zoom in close and look her deep in the eyes. During the conversation I thought of how I needed to be more like Beppe, but it was useless to try and copy an essence. I was back doing the same low energy game.

After at least an hour of talking to her I needed to use the bathroom. I said, "I need to use the bathroom real quick." I took a piss, fixed my hair a little bit, and then came back. But they were completely gone. *Que porra!*

Maybe I should have explicitly told her that I'd be back. Would that have made a difference? I thought it was implied. The boyfriend and sister were arguing for much of the night—maybe they had to leave abruptly? I tried to look on the bright side but I couldn't find it. All I could do was declare this yet another bottom, a "turning point" where things would suddenly get better. I wonder if this type of optimism in the face of pain or repeated failure is human nature. The only other option is to give up. At that point I still believed I could finish the trip. I was about to dip into Paraguay and after Brazil there would be only five more countries—Colombia, Venezuela, Guyana, Suriname, and French Guiana.

IX

The ride to Asunción, the capital of Paraguay, was of the Ecuadorian variety where the bus stopped for anyone sticking out their hand. The usual solicitor crowd came aboard, including women in pink and white maid dresses selling delicious cheesy cornbread snacks called *chipas*. Next to me was a young mother who popped out her huge breast every now and then to feed her baby. I looked when I could.

Paraguay is the second poorest country in South America behind Bolivia, and I doubt it's a coincidence they are both landlocked. I noticed the poorer the country I'm in, the more likely I'll meet travelers, usually female, who like to romanticize about poverty. Repeatedly I had been told how even the worst-off South Americans without running water and other basics "are so happy." That's when I'd start asking questions. How do you know they were happy? Were you with them all day for an extended period of time or did you just interact with them for a couple minutes? Do you think there are parts of their lives that aren't happy, and possibly something a person such as yourself might consider suffering? Do you just expect someone living in poverty to cry all the time and not have the capacity to make laughter with a rich Westerner who gives them positive attention? If you genuinely believe they are happy, why haven't you signed up to relinquish your Western way of life and all its unnecessary trimmings for a happy existence in a slum without running water and paved sidewalks? Do you think if they had the choice they would rather live like you, or continue living as they are? My barrage quiets them down, as if they are finally forced to think about what they've been parroting. The lighter version of "poverty is happiness" is when someone stresses how they took the "poor bus" because they wanted to do as the locals did, as if the poor ride it because they prefer it. Only the rich can afford to pay to experience poverty.

Almost in Asunción, my bus got stuck in traffic. I looked outside to see what turned out to be a typical Paraguayan scene: locals shooting the breeze over a drink of cold *mate*, women selling sandwiches, a policeman on foot patrol playing with his cell phone, and sketchy characters carrying random goods like Lexmark printers and inflatable pool toys. My eye caught one man slouched on a bench. He was wearing an orange apron with the name of a bingo game I saw advertised on billboards as "So Easy." Thick stacks of cards bundled with rubber bands weighed down his left hand. A muscle spasm in his neck caused him to continuously bob his head up and down like a pigeon. Whenever someone walked by he would timidly raise the hand full of bingo cards up to his chest, revealing his emaciated arm, but would fail to make the sale each time. He never spoke and when he blinked it was for two seconds too long, almost like he didn't want to reopen his eyes. It was 100 degrees out and he sat there baking in that ridiculous bright orange apron, drenched in sweat, defeated. He had a miserable existence and it will always remain miserable, just like the others I've barely allowed to register in my thoughts. I shouldn't have stared at him for so long because now I remembered all the others—the 5-year-old homeless girls who ask me for money and her shoeshine brothers covered in polish and filth, the family living in plastic bag tents digging through trash next to the bus station, and the group of elderly men setting up camp underneath a busy bridge to live out their last days. They will all suffer and die in pain. If I accepted the human suffering I witnessed every day then it would've been impossible to continue.

That night I sat in my hotel room in Asunción, stared at the wall, and broke down. I cried like a baby. It's not fair they're dealt such hands. I wanted to help them and make a difference, but eventually the same petty bullshit that worries me will return, and I won't do a damn thing, and nothing will change.

X

It was late Sunday afternoon. I went out for a walk but everywhere was closed. My paranoia was well-practiced by now and I looked behind me every two minutes. I noticed a man with a sharp gaze walking at my pace with his hands in his pockets. The city was so desolate we might as well have been the only two men out. I made a left turn and he did the same. I made another left turn. If he followed then I would run. I looked back, half a block ahead of him, and he stood at the corner. We watched each other. Thieves work on the element of surprise—take that away and their advantage is small. Like a bear chasing two men in the woods, I only had to be stronger than the most obvious target. There was no shortage of gold-wearing tourists who didn't think twice before unfolding their poster board maps in shady parts of town, and it's only when they weren't around that I was in any real danger. The man went off into the other direction.

During down times on long bus rides I mentally rehearsed what I'd do if mugged. If I didn't have my pack on and someone pulled a knife I'd just bolt—there would be no way he'd catch me. My long legs were worthy of a sprint. If he pulled a gun I'd give him whatever he wanted, but if he asked me to follow him in the car I'd take a chance at escape. I had heard stories—third-hand of course—of thieves in fake police uniforms kidnapping gringos and tying them up for days while their bank cards were drained, sometimes killing them in the end. If the thief ordered me to follow him with the barrel of his gun pointed at me, I'd shift to the left, pull his wrist towards me with my left hand to get him off balance, then grab the barrel of the gun with my right hand and twist it towards him to loosen his grip. All in one lightning fast Bruce Lee move. Then I'd have the gun and point it at him, and he'd apologize with his hands in the air and run away. The only problem is what would happen if I failed. Or maybe I'd wait until he got distracted and then run in an unpredictable zigzag pattern. It's extremely hard for an untrained shooter to shoot a moving target. Gringos like myself should practice self-defense moves in the hostels with rubber weapons. Actually I like that idea—a hostel with a dojo instead of an overpriced restaurant-bar.

On my second night in Hotel Miami, suffering from my seventh or so cold of the trip, I caught a show called *E! Wild On* featuring highlights of the "hottest" Spring Break parties. I watched girls grind on crotches, get soaked in wet t-shirt contests, make out with just about anyone regardless of sex, and drink until they passed out and needed to be carried off by a friend. They were out of control and extremely horny, their night a failure if they didn't suck face with at least one other person. I had not seen this type of sexual behavior in South America, and I don't remember the last time I saw a drunk girl *not* from the United States, England, Ireland, or Australia. Dear God: I will never, ever utter the term "slut" in derogatory fashion again. I will use it as a compliment instead. I will never fault girls for choosing a mate based on purely sexual reasons, for I have been the benefactor of such a decision on many occasions. Please send me something easy but exotic.

Sincerely yours, Roosh.

It wasn't hard to convince myself that my cold was actually a mild case of dengue fever, the mosquito-borne disease making a comeback in South America thanks to standing water collections in suburban garbage heaps. I didn't have the fever but I did have intense body soreness, and for the first couple days in Asunción when I woke up it felt like I had been hit by a *chiva*. It took a good ten minutes to work the painful creaks out of my limbs and back.

I decided to stay in and get healthy for wonderful Brazil. It was a shame really because there weren't many gringos around and the girls were surprisingly attractive, owning to their *mestizo* background—half-indigenous and half-Spanish. A significant number of them color their hair dirty blonde, which gives a nice contrast to their tan skin. My hunch is that the hair coloring is a display of status for them, unless there is a cheap way to do it with a bottle of hydrogen peroxide without looking like a cosmetic school victim. Paraguay broke the trend where the poorer the country, the uglier the girls.

XI

I got up in the middle of the night, tossing and turning like I usually do when sick, but with my right hand pushing against something. I was awake but not fully aware. For my entire life it has been very safe to assume that except for maybe some small bugs, there would be nothing on my bed that I didn't go to sleep with. I forced myself to open my eyes. The left side of my face rested on a sorry excuse for a pillow and my right eye could only see darkness. I moved my hand up a few inches, grazing against a soft, furry lump. It was sleeping with me.

I jumped backwards off the bed and ran towards the front door and hit the light switch. My eyes burned in the light. I crept to the bed and got within a few feet of the black mass. It was a rat—a black rat bigger than my fist. I flipped out. I flailed my arms like a girl and made whimpering sounds on the way to the bathroom. I scrubbed my hands then took off my boxers and inspected my naked body for any signs of bites. I found nothing. I tried to calm down. I went back towards the bed, hoping the rat would be gone, but it was definitely dead. I found no hole it could have entered from and my window was completely closed. I double checked the front door and it was still locked. It must've been here when I checked in, snacking quietly underneath the bed on my cracker crumbs.

My room had an extra twin bed where two days earlier I smashed a nickel-sized bug with a newspaper, its brown insides squirting out onto the pillow case. I covered the rat with a sheet and turned over the pillow on my new bed and tried to sleep. I wanted to leave the hotel but it was too dangerous to be strolling on the streets of Asunción at that hour. I dozed in and out, waiting for the sun to come up.

In the morning I took a closer look at the rat and instead of a tail it had wings. It wasn't a rat but a bat. It was hanging upside-down on the ceiling as I slept until it decided to drop dead beside me. I'm not a superstitious man and I don't believe in omens, but based on my luck it was a short matter of time until I was attacked by living animals. I'd wake up with one of my eyeballs hanging out of my socket and a creature nibbling on my optic nerve. I'd snatch my eye back and move it around like a camera, still able to see.

I had to leave. I packed my bag and told the nice lady at the front desk I wanted to check out, casually letting her know about the bat. "Oh, by the way…" She asked me if I was checking out because of the bat. I lied to her. I said I planned to leave this very morning at 8am with a dead bat coincidentally on my bed. Otherwise she would push for me to stay in a different room. I just wanted to go to Brazil. The only reason I was in Paraguay was just to say I stepped foot into it. So I could notch my belt.

I had a two hour wait for a bus back to the three borders area. I bought a couple pieces of *chipa* and just like many other bread products I ate in Asunción it contained bits of dirt. I wondered if they put the dirt in there on purpose to provide essential minerals like iron and zinc. Then I went to kill time in the bus station's internet café, where I remembered that bats carry rabies. Within seconds I'm reading how most people in the United States who die of rabies get bit by bats in their sleep without realizing it. Small bats have teeth like little pins so it's easy not to feel it.

It was entirely plausible that the bat chose me as its last victim. I weighed the chances of the bat having rabies versus if it bit me or not, but the problem with rabies is that if you get infected and begin to show symptoms, it's a guarantee you will die. I had to get the vaccine. I found a private hospital in my guidebook and showed a cab driver the address.

I didn't know the Spanish word for bat or rabies. The receptionist in the front desk had to find someone who knew English to translate that I woke up next to a dead bat. They seemed perplexed that I came in even though I wasn't bitten. Shouldn't they know that bats have teeth like little pins and I may not have felt it? The doctor who examined me said I had nothing to worry about and that I didn't need to get the shot. I didn't think he knew what he was talking about. If I died of rabies he wouldn't care or be held responsible. He wasn't an expert on rabies like I was after reading about it for twenty minutes on the internet. The only way I'd have peace of mind is if I got the shot, so I told him that's what I wanted.

It wasn't in my stomach like I thought but in my upper arm. I would need four more injections over the next month. I went back to the station to catch a bus to the border and then a cab to Foz do Iguaçu, the town nearest the Brazilian side of the falls. I didn't have Brazilian *reals* so the cab driver played off my conversion rate ignorance and tipped himself an extra $10.

Even though I got the vaccine only eight hours after being exposed to the bat, I was still worried. How about if the vaccine didn't work on me? How about if the nurse didn't administer it correctly? How about if it was expired or counterfeit? The possibility of having an illness that is certain to kill messed up my mind, and I couldn't resist going on the internet and reading everything ever published about rabies. I read about the German traveler who got bit by a dog in Morocco and died two months later. I read about how in Pakistan the rabies vaccine has a high failure rate. I had no idea what kind of vaccine I received. At that point I would have welcomed dengue fever or malaria with open arms. Now I had a great burden to carry for the next several months where any fever, body ache, or flu symptom will be the initial signs of rabies and imminent death. Getting the vaccine was supposed to give me peace of mind, but it did nothing of the sort.

There were no distractions in Foz to take my mind off the rabies. I went out to eat lunch, spent hours on the internet reading about rabies, went out to eat dinner, then read about rabies some more. I called my sister and dad and they both said I was crazy to worry about it, especially since I got the shot, but they didn't know the shot wasn't always perfect. They didn't know the details. After two nights of self-inflicted mental torture, I booked a bus to Rio de Janeiro, a city that I had been hoping would be the savior of the trip (the previous savior was Buenos Aires).

The twenty-four hour bus ride to Rio was on a basic bus. There was no in-flight movie and no music. It was only partially full and the seat next to me was empty. There was nothing to see out the window. After two hours on the road I started to feel dizzy and lightheaded and, incredibly, my mouth wouldn't stop salivating. I had to keep swallowing spit. I couldn't believe it. I had rabies. I panicked and convinced myself that I was going to die. I curled up in my chair, closed my eyes, and begged and pleaded for this not to be it. I was ready to renounce my atheist beliefs and bargain with Him for life. I'd dedicate myself to the church if it meant I could survive. I truly thought this was my end.

I needed to find a hospital that could pull off the same experimental treatment as on an American girl who was the first person ever to be treated successfully after showing symptoms of rabies. Sure she had to be put in a coma and rehabilitation took over a year, but at least there was a chance. I even imagined myself fighting with the doctor to look up the treatment and administer it on me because I still had "a lot of living to do." But after a short while something interesting happened: my mind wouldn't let me linger on my upcoming death. It reminded me that I was still alive. I was dizzy and salivating, but I was still alive.

"Calm down, it's impossible to catch rabies two days after a bite," I said.

"How do you know?" I replied.

"Because all that shit on the internet said on average it takes around a month."

"Yeah you're right. But maybe I'm the exception?"

"Exceptionally crazy. You're a fucking wreck, man."

"I know. This sucks."

"Just go home. Book the ticket. It's done."

"No... but Rio..."

"Too late. You won't enjoy it now. Shoulda went there first. Oh, don't forget we gotta get another rabies shot the day we arrive."

I'd calm down for a couple hours until the morbid thoughts would return, and I was back in the chair, curled up, fantasizing about how many people would attend my funeral. My stomach was cramping and emitting copious amounts of gas and noise. My body was tired. I was tired. There had been moments I greatly enjoyed, but I can't deal with so many dips. I'm not strong enough to deal with them. The fun, outgoing vibe I thought I had was fading into the background. Either I head home or let my bad travel luck destroy me, maybe get me killed. I missed home. It had only been five months, but I felt like it's been years.

A DEAD BAT IN PARAGUAY

RIO DE JANEIRO

I

In the middle of the night, Brazilian police came on the bus and searched everyone's carry-on bag, though not the luggage underneath. One man had a box full of cigarette pack-sized blocks wrapped in pieces of black garbage bag. A policeman with a plastic gladiator shield on his shoulder poked the blocks with a knife. I fully expected him to take some white powder out and taste it, but it turned out to be nothing and my *Goodfellas* fantasy came to an end. If the policeman had searched me I wouldn't have been bothered because I wasn't aware of my rights, but in my own country without probable cause I'd tell the pigs to stop wiping their ass with the Constitution. The treatment I was willing to accept depended on my knowledge of the law.

I had made reservations at the Mellow Yellow hostel in Copacabana, where Luke and all his other friends were staying (Ethan was back in Australia). Dizzy but no longer salivating, the first thing I did after I checked in was go on the internet and see if the rabies vaccine had any side effects. Sure enough, dizziness was a symptom in 5-40% of people. I wasn't going to die after all, but with four more shots over the next month, I was afraid that I was going to be dizzy the entire time. As if having a bubbling ass wasn't enough, now I had to sit down after very short amounts of time walking to catch my bearings.

I went to a private hospital in Copacabana to get my second rabies shot. The nice lady at the front desk said I needed to go to another clinic, but it was closed so I needed to "wait another day."

"But I'm supposed to get the shot today," I said.

A DEAD BAT IN PARAGUAY

"One day shouldn't matter."

Doesn't she know that rabies fucking kills! What a reckless woman! I insisted and she told me to go to a public hospital nearby.

There was a long line of human suffering. Mothers were crying over their sick children and the elderly sat on the floor fanning themselves with newspapers. A girl's shorts were soaked in blood and she had to get in the back of a line that spilled out onto the sidewalk. The door to the examination room was manned by a security guard, and no one could enter unless they showed the proper paperwork, no matter how much they begged and cried. On the bright side, public hospitals in Brazil offer free care.

After waiting in line for an hour, the bureaucrat at the front desk told me I was at the wrong hospital and gave me directions to the one thirty minutes away in Barra, Rio's take of a typical American suburb with strip malls, parking garages, and *cul de sacs*. I was too tired and discombobulated to figure out which buses to take to avoid $70 in cab fares.

There was no line at the third hospital. Right when I was about to give my passport at the desk, an old man wheeled in a teenager on a hard metal chair. The teen, probably his son, was going in and out of consciousness with his eyes flickering into the back of his head. It looked like he was dying, but there was no nurse or doctor rushing out to treat him. I let them go in front of me. The old man showed some papers and received a print-out. He had to nicely ask others if the boy could take their place in line for examination. No one said no.

I was sent to the *sala de sutura* room where two English-speaking nurses helped me fill out a form describing my rabies encounter. They were very pretty despite the room's harsh fluorescent lighting. Predictably, I imagined having sex with them. They were about to give me the "vaccine," hot three-way sex. Instead they sent me to the injection room where I got my shot without incident. This shot and the next three were free and I thank the Brazilian government for their care. The vaccine series would have cost at least $1,000 back home.

I ran into Luke when I returned to the hostel. He asked me if I wanted to go out with him. I was in no condition to go out, but I said yes. The alternative was to lay on my dorm room bed with twenty-three other people and think of death. I needed to be distracted.

I pounded some Benadryl, which helped relieve the dizziness, and we went to an Irish pub called Shenanigans in Ipanema, the beach just north of Copacabana where the girls are more beautiful, the shops more expensive, and the men more flamboyant. The bar was filled with white gringo men going apeshit over a Cowboys and Giants football match on television, paying scant attention to the native girls in the crowd. Luke and I shared a table with two of them. One branched off and talked to other people she happened to know while her friend stayed and shared a hot fudge brownie sundae with us, a horrible compliment to the beer we were drinking. She carefully fed me a piece like a mother would feed her little toddler a spoon of applesauce. Luke went off to the bar to hit on a gringa, leaving just me and her.

She had a German look owning to that ancestry, with misty blue eyes and a cherubic face. She responded to my game in the same way that I expected, her eyes opening wider whenever I teased her. I asked her if she wanted to get some fresh air in the balcony. She agreed, and within a couple minutes we kissed. There wasn't a single head turn.

She left not long after that but not before I got her number, which reminded me that I needed to get a cell phone. By the end of the night quite a few Brazilian girls were making out with the gringo guys and I made fun of Luke for going after the only gringa in the place. Though Shenanigans was not a big bar, I didn't see hooking up on this scale in Argentine clubs six times as big.

Just a day earlier I thought I was going to die. The rabies scare had passed. Now I just had to deal with the symptoms of the vaccine, which while uncomfortable and annoying were manageable, more so than my stomach problems. I began to accept the idea that the trip would come to an end much sooner than I had planned. No longer did I look forward to revisiting Venezuela, getting to know Colombian girls, or going to those three small countries in northeast South America that no one ever goes to. I had little energy or will to explore the rest of Brazil, a country almost as large as the United States. I decided to stay in Rio until Carnival and then see how I felt after that.

II

Luke and I sat down to hammer out the logistics of banging a Brazilian girl while lodging in a cheap hostel. First thing we did was buy a pre-paid cell phone with a local number. Now I could keep in touch with Paula and Joana, and call girls like the one I met at Shenanigans (I called—she was busy for a long long time). Second thing we did was ask a Brazilian guy at the front desk for a cheap hourly hotel nearby. He handed us an address on a piece of paper while his female coworker gave us a dirty look.

Luke and I walked over to the hotel to make sure it existed. Once we visually confirmed the hotel, we sent text messages to our phones that contained the address. Now if we had a girl all we had to do was show it to a cab driver.

The last thing we did was get pumped about being aggressive. There would be no hesitation to approach girls and we would screen them based on their easiness instead of amazing personality traits. We had to get our Brazil flag out of the way first and then maybe after that we could find love. Neither of us wanted a repeat of the mostly lonely Córdoba nights with only each other's interesting but non-sexual company. There is nothing like planning to get laid to turn it into a cold, mechanical undertaking, but it works.

We taxied over to Lord Jim's, a tiny, dark English pub that featured a cover band named ZoomBox. The stage was the size of two sit-down booths. The band members bumped into each other while playing American rock songs mixed with Brazilian classics.

I pushed Luke to talk to a group of three girls drinking at a table, but he didn't last long enough for me to come in. Some time later, while we sat in a dark corner drinking our beers, one of the girls from the same group gave him a marathon five-second stare that ended with a big smile. Not only did Luke feel uncomfortable by the stare but I did too, even though I wasn't the recipient. I told him to get up and go talk to her before she was approached by another guy. He did, with me closely behind him.

I was the angel on his shoulder (or devil, depending on your perspective), and after fifteen minutes I leaned over to his ear and said,

"Ask her if she wants to go to the bar with you to get a drink." She said yes. "Don't forget to the do the Predator arm move," I added as he walked away. They began kissing after the bartender served him his *caipirinha*, immediately after the arm move. Her two friends didn't want to have anything to do with me (they didn't even ask me where I was from), but I did my best to distract them like a clown so Luke could have some private time with his girl. I didn't mind sitting on my hands for most of the night because of the story he told me on the cab ride over.

In Florianópolis, a beach city south of Rio, Luke worked on an Argentine girl for three nights. She resisted his attempts to bang the first two nights and it came down to the final night. He was with her at a party, along with his Australian friends and her Argentine friends, but for some reason she got flustered and disappeared. She told Luke that she was on her period and nothing ended up happening. Later that night in the dorm, one of his friends thought Luke was sleeping and bragged to another that he fucked the girl in a bathroom during the hour she disappeared. Luke didn't do or say anything.

I told Luke his friend was full of shit, that with what we know of Argentine girls the chances his story was true approached zero, but it's impossible to know what really happened. For a week the betrayal was simmering in his mind and he questioned not only his failure of getting with an Argentine girl but the value of his friendship as well. Whatever did happen in Florianópolis, the night in Lord Jim's was his. He took the Brazilian girl to the hourly motel we visited earlier and gave it to her twice until his time was up.

I was happy for Luke's success, which made him quickly forget about Florianópolis. Now the pressure was on me to get my Brazilian flag out of the way.

III

I counted four gringos in Mellow Yellow wearing "I Survived The Death Road" t-shirts. The death road is a cliff-hanging one-lane dirt road outside La Paz, the capital of Bolivia. It has been marketed as the world's most dangerous road thanks to the few dozen people who fall off it each year and die. The Bolivian government has embraced the label since even the world's largest cheese ball is sure to attract tourist dollars. More death would only add to its allure.

Sensing opportunity, fly-by-night entrepreneurs began renting out mountain bikes to gringos to take the "tour" of riding downhill. A guide from the agency teaches you how to hold the brakes and that's that. No athletic ability required. I wonder what locals who have lost a relative on the road and are forced to use it think of the tours.

Sadly quite a few gringos have fallen to their deaths, and because of consent forms the tour agencies are not held responsible. I looked down on these t-shirt wearers because they were bragging about something that is famous for causing needless loss of life, but then again here I was—at least up to recently—trying to visit every country in South America, partly for bragging rights. That's the only reason I went to Paraguay. My death road was just longer and more drawn out, and perhaps even more foolhardy. It was a stupid goal to make.

IV

A Swedish girl checked into my twenty-four person dorm room and the first thing I said from my bed was, "Welcome to the hottest dorm room in the world!" It had no air conditioning and we were in the middle of Rio's summer. Every morning I woke up on sweat-soaked sheets grabbing my crotch, thinking I wet the bed, and a few times my dick was hanging out the pee hole of my boxers. After peepshow mornings I tried to see if the attention I received from girls in the room increased or not due to liking what they might have seen, but in the end I couldn't tell any difference.

I had no end goal with the Swedish girl and was just in a chatty mood. She asked me if I wanted to get something to eat and we hung out for a couple hours, inspecting local gyms and walking on the beach. In a bar it makes sense to have a plan. You're talking to this girl at midnight and in one hour you want to make out with her, and then one hour after that you want to take her somewhere else, but when it's one o'clock in the afternoon that's not possible. You can't plan to make out with her after your mid-afternoon snack well before the sun goes down. Instead you must be off-the-cuff like Beppe, the fun and cool guy that girls gradually get into, setting things up for nighttime where the action happens. The Swede asked me if I wanted to check out a samba club with her sometime soon.

Luke and I had a double date of sorts at a bar with two girls we met on the beach. Even though they sat there drinking with us, dressed like adult women, it came out that they were only 16 years old. Twelve years younger than me and five years younger than Luke, who told me that they were still much too young for him. In Brazil the age of consent is fourteen, unless a parent complains whereby you'd get a charge akin to statutory rape. It's eighteen if you don't want to get in any sort of trouble. I looked it up. The girls were nice and taught us a few Portuguese words, but neither Luke or I made a move.

A couple days later I found a Portuguese tutor after shopping around for classes. The guidebook wasn't kidding when they said learning Portuguese in Brazil was expensive. In Argentina the cost was $5 an hour for group classes, but here it was $23 an hour for individual tutoring without the option of learning in a group. I got a recommendation from the hostel to book Bruna, a private tutor who charged $17 an hour. I was dropping $100 a day in Rio and looking for any way to save besides having to cook my own meals.

Portuguese is five times harder than Spanish. There are sounds that I could not make no matter how many times Bruna told me to repeat it, especially the "ng" nasal sound that is a large part of speech in Brazil.

"It's just like talking through your nose," she tried to explain to me.

"But I've never talked through my nose before."

"Just try harder!"

I couldn't get it. And trying to write down the English equivalent of these sounds was fruitless because there is no English equivalent, unlike Spanish where besides the rolling "R," most sounds can be reproduced. Too many Portuguese sounds are in between English sounds, like the "ba" in Copacabana. It's between an English "bah" and "buh" but definitely not a "beh." I can hear the word in my head pronounced perfectly, but I simply cannot form it with my vocal faculties.

I learned a good chunk of my Spanish through a textbook without a tutor, but for Portuguese that would be impossible, and besides, the bonus of having a tutor was learning more slang, curse words, and culture, like the differences between southern Brazilians and northern Brazilians. (Northern Brazilians have more African and less European ancestry, and are poorer from a lack of industry, though they have the most beautiful beaches.) Bruna also recommended some juices I should try like *caju* (cashew juice), adding to my already daily habit of *açaí*, a purple fruit found in the north of Brazil. It's the most popular drink in town, made by blending powdered sugar and *guarana*, another Brazilian fruit loaded with natural caffeine. Because of its milkshake consistency, it's eaten with a spoon.

The Swedish girl asked me if two other Swedish girls could come to the samba club with us. I didn't mind as my interest in her had already waned. One of them was a six-foot tall basketball player with platinum blonde hair and creamy white skin. She was 19 years old and exceptionally shy, the type that seemed to only have sex after dating a guy for months. She went completely against the type I thought I had—petite, tan skin, dark hair, and holder of a gigantic ass, but I wanted her nonetheless. The more I traveled the more my type went out the window. There are too many flavors of ice cream to try.

We all took a cab to the samba place and there we heard the sounds that make up the samba *batería*: the *surdo* (big bass drum), *caixa* (snare drum), *agogo* (Brazilian cowbell), and *chocalho* (metal steel shaker), among others. Samba music is both upbeat and sedate, fitting as a backdrop for either vigorous dance or bedroom pillow talk. On the dance floor, Brazilian women jiggled and vibrated their bodies as if they were being electrocuted. Their feet moved rapidly in seemingly random patterns, but there was an overall beauty to the dance that suggested a complex technique. They smiled while doing it.

As the night went on the original Swede became visibly annoyed, maybe because I was giving more attention to the basketball player. I was still stuck on going for the girl I wanted and not the one that wanted me, though that decision in South America always resulted in failure. But I'll never get what I want if I don't go after it.

Beyond some light joking I didn't get anywhere with the basketball player. She didn't drink so it was completely futile without alcohol to impair her judgment. The three Swedish girls left the club a minute before Luke arrived. We decided to check out a bar in Ipanema.

On the ride over we approached a police roadblock. A very rotund policeman, who looked like he just got out of bed with his shirt untucked from his trousers, peeked inside the cab and asked the driver who we were. The driver said "gringos." The cop responded by asking us to step out of the cab and empty our pockets. We put our hands on the hood of the car while he patted us down. Just like on the bus ride into the city, I didn't feel violated because I assumed this was standard protocol for most people who live in Brazil. At home this would be outrage, in South America it's adventure, a story.

If I did have drugs on me the going bribe is said to be around $500, though for locals it's only $50 after some bargaining. I was told by natives that if I get caught with marijuana my best bet is to go to the police station and pay a fine that is less than the bribe, but then again I'd do pretty much anything to avoid the prospect of staying in an overcrowded, violent Brazilian prison, the likes of which I saw in the movie *Carandiru*. With a dozen men stuffed into my cage, I conservatively estimated I'd be raped at least four times a day.

At Emporio bar in Ipanema, there was a mass of gringo men barely able to stand, trying to score some easy sex by slurring gibberish to the few girls there. Their game was getting drunk. I left after ten minutes.

V

I reunited with Paula. She took me to an outdoor samba club in Lapa, the old working class section of town, where we caught up on happenings since last seeing each other in Buenos Aires. On weekends the streets of Lapa turn into an outdoor party fueled by Skol beer, sold by vendors wheeling around cheap styrofoam coolers.

"I must say I feel pretty safe in Rio," I said.

"Safe? Here? Are you joking?"

"I mean compared to other cities I've been to like Quito and Lima. Rio feels a lot safer."

"No Roosh it's not safe. Every one of my friends has been mugged. Actually I was mugged last year. I was in a market during the day with some friends, taking pictures with my camera. A man came from nowhere and put an old gun to my face and tells me to give him the camera. The gun didn't even look like it would work so I held on tight, but my friends yelled at me to give it to him. I did and he ran away."

"During the day?"

"Yes. It's very common. If you live here it will happen to you. Ask any Brazilian if they've been robbed and they'll tell you stories. Be careful, it's not as safe as it looks."

Later she got on the topic of Brazilian girls, something that perked me up since I was still in hunt for my flag. She said most of her friends have only had one or two sexual partners coming out of college, that while Brazilian girls are not as conservative as Mexican Catholics, who remain virginal in their mid-20s, they are more conservative than Americans.

"The idea that Brazilian girls are easy," she said, "comes from the *favela*, where it's a dream for the girls there to be taken out by a rich man for a meal that costs more than her monthly salary. The sex is secondary or even lower because the *favela* girls are exposed to it at an early age. It's their fault there is a stereotype that all women in Brazil are easy and crazy about sex."

I wasn't sure what to believe. The Brazilian girls I had met so far seemed very curious that I was from the United States, more so than the girls in Argentina, but then again the only fair way to compare girls from different cultures was to account for their socioeconomic class. It doesn't mean much if a gringo says lower class Brazilian girls are easier than middle class American girls if he hasn't experienced lower class American girls, who may be the easiest of all.

With the exception of Luke, I had talked to four guys who banged a Brazilian girl. A common pattern was that they had to give the girl money for a cab or bus back home. These guys will go home thinking

Brazilian girls are easy, pushing the stereotype onto other Westerners, when the fact very well may be that only poor Brazilian girls are easy.

The next day Paula took me to "Posto 9" on Ipanema next to the big coconut tree, the most popular slice of beach in Rio where all the beautiful people pack themselves so close together that it's impossible not to meet your neighbors after a short time sunbathing. Paula's company was pleasant and laid back, lacking the sort of drama that usually dominates my friendships with women. My time increasingly went to her, Joana, and their friends instead of Luke. He was my buddy but with all his mates around I was the third wheel. It was hard to get him alone besides for *açaí* runs.

For a week it was almost like Paula and I were in a relationship with the daily calls and hang outs. All that we didn't do was have sex. I never made a move. If she was interested in me at all it was definitely lost when she rather suddenly began talking about other guys she had been involved with.

VI

I was able to convince Luke to leave his boys behind in the hostel and get a head start with me at a club called Casa Do Matriz. We walked from our hostel towards the main street to catch a cab when a loud *BOOM* rocked the street. We instinctively stepped back and covered our heads. Forty feet away pieces of plastic rained on a bus stop and a small cloud of smoke rose from what used to be an orange trashcan. The handful of people who witnessed the explosion continued as they were, not bothered by what I guess was a homemade bomb. I doubt anyone called the police because little orange pieces of plastic laid on the street for days. If this happened in my neighborhood there would be a terrorist investigation and a one mile radius sweep for evidence and clues as residents would cry for beefed up law enforcement. New laws would be passed to give police more power to prevent such a heinous criminal act.

Casa Do Matriz was low-key, with small rooms upstairs that made it feel more like a house party than a club. There was a game room with classic arcade games, a living room with sofas, a dark room with popular American music, and even a merchandise room that sold clothes and CDs. I didn't notice any gringos but it was just a matter of time until they arrived drunk.

Luke and I settled on the strategy of ten, where we'd do at least ten approaches each before going home. I did that in Córdoba to help force myself to talk to girls until I eased into a natural talkative state. On this night I made it to two.

I saw a petite girl leaning alone against the wall. She wore a black cocktail dress that started right above her breasts and ended at the meatiest part of her thighs. Further down she had on four-inch black high heels that revealed freshly painted toenails. Her eyes were gigantic globes that moved slowly, and she had a satisfied, unaffected smirk on her face as she twirled a small plastic straw in her *caipirinha*. Even though her skin only had a hint of tan, her body language and dark hair and eyes made it obvious to me she was Brazilian. I took a gulp of my beer and slid next to her, stopping three feet away.

"Let me guess, you are from Brazil?" I said.

"Yes I am from Brazil."

"Very nice. I'm really good at guessing where people are from. There are so many countries I could have guessed, you know, but I felt a very strong Brazilian vibe." Her smile showed she understood my sarcasm. It's hard for people to pick up sarcasm in a second language unless they know it well.

"Where are you from?" she asked, still mixing her drink.

"United States. I'm a gringo."

"Why are you in Brazil?"

"Well it's part of a big trip that started in Ecuador, traveling around trying to find the meaning of life and what not. The master plan was to visit every country in South America, but I think I'm done with that and am just going to hang out in Rio because it's a nice place. Plus I'm addicted to *açaí*."

"You've probably seen more of South America than I have."

"I've seen more of South America than I have of my country."

I went on a little spiel about the countries I had visited and she seemed interested, but I wasn't sure because she looked at her drink as much as me. A part of me seemed like she was killing time until her boyfriend arrived.

"What's your zodiac sign?" she asked.

"Zodiac? What's... oh, astrology. I'm a Gemini." The only reason a girl would ask this is to see if the alignment of the stars would allow the relationship to proceed. (It unnerves me when a man asks me for my sign.)

"That's interesting."

"Why is that interesting?"

"Geminis have two personalities, the good and the bad, and they're often fighting with each other." She gave me a squinted stare, as if trying to analyze my being.

"Yeah that's true. My dark side is pretty... dark. I keep it locked up because I want to fit into society and be normal."

"I like you," she said, holding eye contact. I was taken aback and didn't know how to respond. It's only been a few minutes since we started talking.

After five long seconds I responded. "I think you're cool." I was quickly disgusted at myself for not being able to properly match her affections. We exchanged names and gave each other a stiff American handshake. Her name: Mariana. She told me she works as a stage actress.

A little later she said she had to use the bathroom. Nightmare visions of all the previous girls who didn't return filled my head—girls who couldn't possibly have shown more interest in me short of stroking my junk in front of everybody. I assumed Mariana wasn't coming back so I wouldn't get my hopes up. I was so tired of disappointment.

By now Luke's friends and other gringos from hostels around the city arrived by the vanload and turned the party into a dick fest. Luke wasn't having much luck and seemed to give up well before number ten. I told him to keep pushing but there was no motivation—he had a 16-year-old begging him for sex and the girl from Lord Jim's wanted another hotel rendezvous.

She came back.

We hit the small dance floor and gradually the distance between us narrowed. I'd get close and while she wouldn't turn her head away completely, she'd move back enough to make it difficult to kiss her. She would smile every time to show me she was in control. She gyrated her body in a way that only a girl who knows samba can, her large ass bouncing and rotating in spellbinding patterns.

I leaned against the wall with my legs spread partially apart to be closer to her short height. I wrapped my arms around her and breathed in her scent, a mix of floral perfume and sweat. The room was hot and humid. I bent down to kiss her cheek, and then, unable to help myself, I grabbed her head with my hands and held it in place to kiss her on the lips, lightly. She kissed back and for a minute only our lips touched, barely rubbing against each other. She put her head town and kissed my neck, coming up to my ear, and I opened my eyes and watched the dance floor, the people moving to house music. My eyes closed again and I explored her body with my hands. I moved my head back down to kiss her on the lips, this time rougher. I grabbed her forearms and pulled her in close so that our bodies were pressed against each other, and then she pulled away and started dancing, and all I could do was lean there against the wall, dazed, my head hanging off to the side. On and off throughout the night she'd come closer to kiss and touch, and I had trouble playing it cool, concealing my interest. I was ready to give anything to have her.

Earlier in the night I talked to a tall girl for a short while, but she ditched me to go dance with her friend. Now she was staring at me. I felt uncomfortable, even bad for her, as if Mariana and I were having sex and she was the uninvited guest I discovered in the closet with a box of tissues. I wondered if she wished it was her instead of Mariana.

At some point Mariana told me she had her own studio apartment, the first girl I met in South America who didn't live with family. I drooled at the possibility of sex in a place where I wasn't being charged by the hour, only for it to end with a gruff voice on the other end of the telephone line telling me to zip my pants and get the fuck out. My first attempt to get her home didn't have the response I was hoping for. I said, "Let's go." That's my deal sealer. It always works. She responded with "Where?" I've never gotten that answer so I just stood there twiddling my thumbs, confused.

I waited another hour, when I was about ready to explode. If she wasn't having it I'd have to go back to the hostel toilet with mental images of her body and take care of myself there.

"Let's go."

"Okay," she replied.

Turns out she came with two other friends, who didn't mind at all that I was leaving with her. We got into the cab and when I was right about to tell her that I wanted to make sure she gets home safe, she asked me if I wanted to spend the night with her.

Her studio apartment was in Flamengo, a dicey area of town near Copacabana. Her room was cozy and simple with very little decoration or furniture, just a desk and a shelf packed with books and antique looking bottles filled with various natural herbs and remedies. Stuck in the frame of a mirror near her bed was an Indian-looking man with a gigantic afro. He was a guru, she said, a master of alternative medicine. There were also a couple old photos of her before she chopped off her hair, a symbolic shedding of a recent failed relationship. I was the rebound—the black dress was bait. I moved aside the nine pillows on her bed and laid down. She dimmed the lights.

"Am I moving too fast for you?" she said.

God no!

"No, I'm fine," I said, raising my eyebrows. I needed to have her body on top of mine, vibrating in a way I'd never experienced or thought possible. I took off her clothes. Her body and face were so perfect. I've never been with a more beautiful girl.

VII

In Rio there are four soccer teams: Botofogo, Vasco de Gama, Fluminense, and by far the most popular, Flamengo. Their red and black alternating stripped jersey is worn by 10% of Rio's population at any given time. I went to a Flamengo game and was part of the singing, jumping and chanting that reminded me of the soccer game I saw in Buenos Aires, the only difference being that Brazilians were much harder on their team. It was the first game of the season, but by the second half they were already booing Flamengo's performance (the score was tied at 0-0). The Argentines wouldn't stop rooting for theirs even when defeat was imminent, but then again Flamengo did end up winning.

After the game I met up with Paula, Joana, and their friends at a restaurant for dinner. A hunk of semi-cooked beef was brought out on a hot plate powered by propane. I peeled away individual slices from the log mass and fried them to my liking. I was told that South Korea has a similar dish.

"What's this?" Paula said, pointing out a line of red dots on my hand and forearm.

"Oh they're just bedbug bites. They take about a week to go away."

When I went back to the hostel I looked in the mirror and saw them on my neck and body as well. The next day there were twenty more spots. There was no way they could have happened in just one night. Two other guys in my room had a similar rash though theirs was much worse with breakouts of large infected boils on their torso. The only part of my body spared was my face. The hypochondria kicked in.

Scabies.

There was no doubt about it, and not only did I have scabies but I gave it to Mariana. I told Luke about the rash and he told me not to jump to conclusions. A reasonable thought from a reasonable man, but I ignored his advice and went back to the computer to browse health sites and become a scabies expert. And just when I was beginning to enjoy my first week in Rio without any health issues besides dizziness from the rabies vaccine and ongoing stomach growling, cramps, gas, and borderline diarrhea.

I went to Lord Jim's that night to meet up with Mariana. We sat at a table upstairs and chatted for a bit until there was a long pause.

"Mariana there is something I have to tell you."

"You're married?"

"Hah, no. I have a, uh… rash. Look." I showed her my arms and she touched the red spots. "I think it's from the bedbugs in my hostel… but I'm not sure." I braced for her to freak out and make an excuse about how she had to return home to organize her music collection.

"I have something for that at home. It itches, yes?"

"Like crazy."

"I'm sure it's nothing. Don't worry about it baby."

Huh? Why didn't she freak out about it? An American girl would have told me "good luck with that" or "ew gross" and to call her when it goes away.

"I'm thinking of going to Bahia for a couple days," she said. "I'd like to make it up there. I don't know if Rio is going to be my last stop or not yet."

"If I go, would you like to come with me?"

"Of course."

Doesn't she know that she is showing too much interest and not playing by the rules? Doesn't she realize she's giving me the "upper hand?" With her obvious displays of affection I was able to relax, no longer having to consciously regulate the amount of attention I gave out like I did with other girls. I didn't have to play the game and could just be myself. I love how we barely knew each other but had already passed that awkward stage where we're feeling each other out and debating if there is enough substance or not to continue.

After two drinks we went back to her place. She lit a couple of scented candles and disrobed. I did the same and she took pictures of me, ones that would prevent me from ever having a career in politics. In bed all she wanted to do was please me. I hit the jackpot. I found a girl blessed with beauty who cares. It took me just a week in Brazil to find what I could never find in seven years back home. There was no thought in my mind nagging me to do better like has always been the case.

My rash was noticeably worse in the morning, now covering most of my torso, though it was hard to notice with all my body hair. I ruled out bedbugs. Not only was it definitely scabies, but it was impossible I didn't pass it on to Mariana. She gave me an herbal anti-itch ointment from an unlabeled bottle that helped with the itching.

I found a dermatologist on the internet and went straight to the office without making an appointment. After only ten minutes of waiting, I saw the doctor, a very old man who spoke fluent English with no accent. With his white hair and beard and pink skin I couldn't tell if he was American or Brazilian. I took off my shirt and he examined all the bumps.

"This is an allergic reaction, most likely due to some sort of insect," he said.

"Right now I'm staying in a hostel that has a lot of bedbugs."

He smiled and nodded his head up and down. "That would be it."

"Are you sure it's not scabies?"

"This is definitely not scabies."

Hallelujah! He said the rash would be gone in a week and prescribed me an anti-itch cream and steroid pill. The last time a doctor told me something would be gone in a week was a year prior, when I broke out in hives after an allergic reaction to antibiotics. The hives stayed with me for three months.

I suspected the visit was going to be expensive because of the free coffee and gourmet chocolates in the waiting room. It turned out to be more expensive than a visit to my American dermatologist. Mariana later made fun of me for going to the most expensive dermatologist in Brazil.

I asked to move out of the 24-bed dorm room because of the bedbug problem, and they offered to clean my pack and launder my clothes to prevent the bugs from spreading to my new room. I emptied the contents of my pack into a garbage bag. They took my empty backpack and an hour later the receptionist came to my new room holding a freezer Ziploc bag of fifty condoms, give or take. I forgot to take it out of my pack's zipper compartment. I couldn't help but feel embarrassed—it was just so many condoms. I'm sure she thought I was a sleazeball that came to Brazil for a sex vacation.

The steroid and cream did very little and I couldn't sleep. I went on the internet and out of hypochondriac boredom I did a search for the drugs I was taking. Turns out that the steroid reduces a person's immune system and the chance they'll develop active immunity against rabies while taking the vaccine. It said so right there on some animal department web site. It warned its workers to notify a health professional if taking both at the same time. It was my fault that I forgot to tell the dermatologist, but it reinforced the idea that I shouldn't see South American doctors unless my life was in imminent danger.

I stopped taking the steroid pill and applying the useless cream and went back to using Mariana's concoction. The next day it was time for my fourth rabies shot. I began to recognize the hospital staff. It was just a matter of time until they invited me to family barbecues.

I picked the date of my last shot in two weeks as a new beginning of good health.

VIII

Things were moving fast with Mariana. She wanted to talk on the phone daily and see me every other day. She was everything I wanted in a girl, but I was hesitant to get any closer, for reasons I still do not understand. It definitely wasn't to chase other girls, whether in the hostel or out in the bars.

After the initial high of meeting Mariana settled down, my mind drifted to home. I knew that if I had a chance to get and stay completely healthy it would only happen there. Down here it would just be one thing after another. I never imagined I'd be in Rio having a great time with new friends and an amazing girl only to think about how much I wanted to leave it—all because of health reasons! No, that's not entirely true—I did miss my sister and our jokey times together. I missed spending time with buddies in bars I thought I hated but now would love to hang out in. I missed my parents and watching my little brothers grow up, especially my youngest brother who probably has learned hundreds of new words since I left. I fought hard against the urge to return, knowing it would probably fade like all the previous times.

I went to Mariana's apartment and she opened the door in a long white summer dress. She had on perfume and just a touch of makeup. Her hair, still wet from showering, was held back with bobby pins.

"Where are we going?"

"Nowhere," she said. "Let's stay in tonight." She put more effort staying in than many girls I've taken out on dates.

We had a relaxing night together watching a Portuguese movie, talking in bed. We made love, not sex. She needed me to look her in the eyes and tell her how I felt about her before she was ready. I didn't have to lie.

I had the feeling that I was somehow going to fuck things up. In the past I preferred being alone, fantasizing about a happy relationship than actually having that relationship, because one takes work and commitment and sacrifice and the other doesn't.

IX

My travel alarm rang at 8am. It was time to meet up with Paula and Joana for a *bloco*, the street block party that is a big part of the yearly Carnival celebration. This particular *bloco*, one week before the official start of Carnival, was on a hill in Santa Teresa near the famous Christ Redeemer statue.

Blocos were introduced somewhat recently in the past decade to add more life into a celebration whose main focus was the famous costumed parade. Or it could be in response to the vibrant Carnival in Bahia (Salvador), which is now known as the "less touristy" way to get out sinful urges before the arrival of Lent.

We arrived at the scene of an antique streetcar stuffed with a band playing horns and drums. People of all ages and colors wore simple costumes—guys with joker hats and girls with butterfly wings and tiaras. The streetcar started its journey after a couple hundred people gathered, singing and dancing to Carnival songs 90 years old. The crowd swelled and followed through narrow neighborhood streets as residents came out of their houses, clapping and singing along. The Skol flowed, supplied by a dozen vendors trailing the crowd with their styrofoam thermoses.

We followed the streetcar for a couple miles until it stopped to take a break in a small square, so partiers could focus on talking, drinking, kissing, and eating barbecued sausage sold from makeshift grills. And then the car started moving again to return back to where it started. For Paula and Joana the *bloco* was like a high school reunion—they kept running into old chums they studied or worked with.

A big part of Carnival fed to Americans is one of sex and vice, but it wasn't obvious in this *bloco*. It was mostly singing, dancing, and hanging out with friends. While there was kissing I'd bet most of it was by existing couples. Paula summed it up nicely when she said hooking up is a "consequence" at the *blocos*, like how vomiting is a consequence of partying on the weekends. Joana chimed in to remind me that this *bloco* was just a warm up and the ones during Carnival were bigger and crazier.

After the *bloco* we went to eat and drink some more. I felt so fortunate that Paula and Joana brought me into their circle to have the "insiders" experience of Brazil, with not a single drunk Australian in sight. Even my Portuguese tutor called to invite me to another *bloco* with her friends. I got to thinking about the warmth and friendliness of Brazilians when two other people popped in my head: the hostel girl and Marcelo.

At the hostel there was always a skinny nine-year-old girl hanging around, the daughter of a hostel cook. She loved to introduce herself to gringos and ask questions about where they were from, often joking and making funny faces to get a laugh. The first time she saw me I was reading a book alone. Completely fearless, she walked up to me and asked what my name was. She stuck her tiny hand out and I gave it a shake with my thumb and first two figures. She ended the conversation by saying "It was nice to meet you!" Whenever I saw her after that she'd yell out *"Todo bem?"* ("Everything alright?") with a thumbs-up sign (the thumbs-up sign was safe in Brazil). If I was sitting down she'd pat me on the back. I found her more interesting than the other people at the hostel and would go upstairs into the restaurant hoping she was there to exchange pleasantries with me. If she wasn't there then I was disappointed and kept an eager eye out for her arrival. She genuinely liked making other people happy, which in turn made her happy. She made me feel like a sociopath for turning on whatever charm I thought I had only when I wanted something.

Marcelo worked at the juice bar nearest the hostel, and my favorite when it came to *açaí* (they put just a little bit of *guarana* that prevented the drink from tasting too tart). Rio had hundreds of juice bars and they all worked the same way: after ordering a drink the guy manning the counter yells through a little hole to a man in the closet-sized kitchen, who spits out the drink in two or three minutes. If you look closely, from time to time you can see the juice-maker wipe sweat off his brow with his hand, and I'm sure a drop or two of that finds its way into the drinks to give juices from different bars their own distinct flavor. Besides juice, the bars sell light snacks like pastries, pizza, and balls of rice with mystery meat. You could subsist entirely on eating at juice bars if you wanted to.

Marcelo knew I was a gringo and loved that he could practice his English on me. In short time he greeted me with a huge smile, a crushing handshake, and a roaring "ROOSH BUDDY!" Sometimes it would just be a genial *"Todo bem?!"* with his thumb hanging in the air. He'd shout my juice order slowly and loudly so that each syllable of Portuguese could be clearly made out. I'd stick around the bar with my large *açaí* and when the crowd thinned enough, Marcelo would write English phrases on napkins and ask me what they meant. In Spanish and Portuguese I'd do my best to explain, but often it was a tough game of charades until his eyes lit up and I could tell he understood. The only time I ever failed him was when he showed me the phrase "In God we trust." He must've gotten his hands on American money.

He worked at the juice bar six days a week, standing on his feet all day for a basic wage, but was always in a more positive mood than I was. He made me wonder why I wasn't more like him, in the same way the little hostel girl made me want to be more friendly, in the same way Mariana, Paula, and Joana made me want to be more generous and kind, and in the same way Beppe made me want to be more spirited. Compared to his more serious partner working the cash register, Marcelo's energy was so addictive that even when I wasn't hungry for *açaí* I'd go out of my way to swing by, say hello, and give a thumbs-up. I considered asking him to come out with me and let me buy him a drink, but I chickened out in the end, thinking we were too different. I should have at least tried.

X

Room rates quadrupled for Carnival. I checked into a cheaper hostel that instead of having bedbugs had all-around piss poor living conditions: broken toilets, soiled mattresses, toilet paper that was the consistency of construction paper, filthy floors, drunk staff, and rooms so overbooked that people slept on the floor. I had to time my sludgy dumps to right after the maid cleaned the bathrooms or else I'd have to wade in a half-inch of grey water.

In fits of rage an ill-tempered English guy in the hostel would yell, "I'm tired of living out of a bag!" and all I could think was, "I hear you brother." The desire for comfort was becoming too great. I started researching airfares home, the first time I had done so.

I told Paula about Mariana. She made fun of her name and asked me questions to see if she was a prostitute or not. At a restaurant the day before, Paula was infuriated after waiting fifteen minutes for our meal to arrive, storming out and refusing to pay for the drink she had. Then she complained to her friends about how indecisive they were. There is always a root cause of such moodiness and after some prodding on my part it came out that she's tired of Rio, the place and the people. She sang the praises of São Paulo and how much better the restaurant service is and how much more datable the men are. I warned her, saying how I was in Rio pining to go back to a place only six months ago I'd do anything to get away from.

It seems like as soon as I get what I want, I adjust to it quickly and then begin to ache for something else, convinced that that something else will solve the problem. The cycle keeps repeating and my life has become about chasing this ideal of happiness or contentment, when the ability to be happy or content is either inside me or not. If I can't find happiness in my own backyard, with my friends and family, my own culture and language, my comfortable routine, and most importantly my health, then I don't know how I'll find it somewhere else. There is an exception: nature. Some start a relationship with nature, far away from home, and find that it trumps relationships with people. But if you're not a nature lover and the bulk of your happiness does come from the company you keep, you'll feel very empty when your airplane lands in a place where you have no one, and when for months the only people you do care for leave your life as soon as they come in.

I couldn't stop obsessing about going home. I imagined riding a wave of happiness upon my triumphant return, until the reasons that pushed me to South America in the first place would come back again. I'd adjust to my stomach problems and be the same person, with the same ache. Then I'd kick myself in the ass and wish I stayed longer. I'd wish I did a homestay to become fluent in either Portuguese or Spanish, or that I did a better job of pursuing deeper connections with those I met. I knew all this but I didn't care. I didn't want to see another South American doctor, step foot in another dirty hospital. I didn't want to get on another bus. I didn't want to travel anymore. I thought about how ending it with Carnival would be a way of going out on top. And by on top I mean not permanently damaged. As a last ditch effort to stay I tried to reconnect with one of my favorite pleasures—hanging out at cafes and reading books. But it was hard to find good English books and cafes in Rio had waiters that gave me a weird look if I stayed too long. For three days I'd go to a café to study Portuguese for an hour and then leave. Back home I would hang out in the coffee shop for six-hour stretches.

I booked the ticket home. Mistake or not, I was ecstatic. Twelve more days and I'd be back in my dad's basement. I emailed a couple friends to tell them I was coming home. Their universal reaction was, "Why so soon... did something happen?" As if traveling through South America for six months wasn't enough.

I was so happy that I went out alone. It was two days before the official start of Carnival. Luke had already left for Bahia. I waited in line of a club behind two American guys who were complaining loudly in English about the previous bar they visited that asked them to pay a $40 exit charge. It was an obvious scam but they paid anyway. They said they already tried to buy their way into this club by offering bribes to the bouncers, but it didn't work and they were tired of waiting. I asked them how long they had been in Rio. "This is our first day." I told them to relax but it was no use.

One of them started yelling about the people being let in before him and how much Rio "sucks." When they finally got inside the velvet rope they started quoting amounts of money to the bouncer to be let in immediately. I'm sure they got eaten alive in Rio and went home complaining about how thieving Brazilians are without ever coming to the conclusion that they made themselves too much of a target. I made it quietly to the front of the club where I was asked to pay a $30 cover charge. I ditched and went to another club in Copacabana called Help, infamously known for being nothing more than a place where gringo men can pick up Brazilian prostitutes. I was simply curious.

The club was decorated like a cheesy '70s disco with shimmering globes and neon lights. The cover charge was steep ($20), but the beers were cheap. It was nothing like what I thought it would be, of gringos going up to girls and ask "How much?" Instead it was almost like a normal club—the men had to talk to the girls with basic getting-to-know-you conversation and buy them drinks to break the ice. They'd chat to the girls for ten minutes or more only for the conversation to usually end, which told me that it took a while for price to be discussed. Since the prostitutes also had to pay cover, they weren't bottom of the barrel, the type who sniffs glue in alleyways and fucks anything for a couple dollars. They could be more choosy about the men they take back to hotel rooms. It was surprising to see the prostitutes doing some of the rejecting.

I saw a prostitute with a Carnival mask approach a group of five gringos. The gringos flirted back with her for a bit and then one went to slide the mask off her face. He gave a disgusted look like he just took a bite of blood sausage and then slid the mask back on while pushing her face away. Him and his friends erupted in laughter and the masked prostitute soldiered on. Then I witnessed the nerdiest, meekest gringo in Rio walking arm-in-arm with a stunning woman who towered six inches over him. Even though he was paying I was still jealous. I left after that and walking to the hostel I put my latest theory to the test. I believed I was less likely to get robbed if I didn't have a shirt on because it would put me on a level closer to the criminal. A man who was about to rob me might hesitate when he seems I'm similar to him in appearance. I didn't get bothered on the way home, but I can't fully say it was because of that.

XI

On the day before Carnival I went to see *I Am Legend* with Mariana. I was waiting for her in the movie theater lobby when she walked in. Other guys stopped what they were doing to watch her. She has a model walk where she switches her ass with enough power that even her short hair sways back and forth. She keeps her nose up in the air and gives off a vibe that she doesn't give a damn, but it's only her public shell. In private she's more like a delicate flower, and I savored the dichotomy. She gave me a kiss and insisted on paying for the tickets but I stopped her. "You paid for the cab here," I said.

"It's okay baby I can pay."

"No I got it. You can buy me an *açaí* after."

I wore a necklace I bought at a handicraft market that had dark wooden beads the size of large grapes. She expressed her approval and said I was turning into a *carioca*, a Rio native. After the movie we went to the nearest juice bar and she bought me a large *açaí* and a small one for herself.

"I'm leaving tomorrow for a week," Mariana said. "I'm staying with a friend in Niterói. I don't like the city during the Carnival. It's too crowded and dirty."

"How many Carnivals have you stayed for?"

She thought for a few seconds, resting her hands on my thighs. "At least ten since I was little."

"Honestly I'm not that excited about it myself, but I feel like I have to experience it at least once."

"No you'll like it. It's fun if you've never done it before."

A little time passed and I just came out with it.

"So Mariana... I booked my ticket home. I leave in a week and a half."

"Oh." She withdrew her hands and looked down to her small *açaí*.

"Thing is I really want to stay. I love Rio and the food and the people, and I really like you of course, but I just have to go back. My body feels horrible and I need to get better." She just nodded. A minute later she brought up the movie and told me she liked it, mentioning that the actress was Brazilian.

We finished our *açaís*. "Do you want to come over?" she asked. "Only one thing is it's that womanly time for me."

"Hmm. How about some other time?" I thought there would be no point of spending the night with her if we couldn't have sex.

"You don't want to come over?"

"I mean it would be torture to lay next to you all night and not, you know, do anything."

She gave me an abrupt hug goodbye, walked onto the street, and got into a cab. Back at the hostel I laid on my disgusting bed to sleep, and like a bolt of lightning it hit me: I betrayed her. I was a stupid fuck. I ripped out all her petals and crushed them with my shoe.

XII

Once Carnival arrived the Brazilian population was diluted by massive amounts of gringos who came only for the celebration. Vendors were out in full force selling Carnival accessories and restaurants advertised new specials that were higher in price than before. Heavy inebriation was the rule. To someone who got used to the normal Rio lifestyle, I didn't care much for the changes, and understood why Mariana wanted to get away from it.

My hostel offered free Carnival parade tickets, but I did my research and noticed they were in the nosebleeds. I wanted to get up close to see the costumes and the insane jiggling of the female samba dancers. Seats with good views started at $165, but if I waited until the end of Carnival for the championship parade, where the winning samba schools celebrated their parade victory with an ensemble performance, the cost was half. I went with that even though I was told the energy from the performers would be lower since nothing would be on the line.

There are two types of *blocos*: camera safe and not camera safe. On the official start day of Carnival my first *bloco* was the latter, in the center of town with a crowd that descended from the *favelas*. After a quick ten minute tour with my hands protecting my pockets, I got right back in the subway to meet up with Paula in a nicer part of town for a camera-safe *bloco*. While packed in the procession, dancing along with my friends, Skol in hand, I realized how much worse Carnival would be if I didn't know anyone. I wouldn't know which *blocos* to pick and there would no one to tell me what the Carnival songs meant. And I definitely wouldn't know that the cloudy white liquid in plastic bags shaped like condoms were *caipirinhas*. For foreigners who come alone, I don't see how Carnival can mean anything more than getting drunk with a strange crowd.

At night the clubs were mostly empty because everyone was recuperating from the day's drinking. Why pay for expensive cocktails after you've been partying since the morning on plentiful cheap Skol? What a rude awakening for a horny gringo to come to Carnival ready for nonstop sex only to encounter large joyous crowds singing and dancing! I overheard an American phoning home in an internet café to say how he is experiencing the biggest and best party of his life, yet I couldn't help but notice his screen was full of amateur teen porn.

On the fourth day of Carnival I went to another *bloco* with the girls, this one in the rain. In front of a stage, thousands of people danced in a black mixture of beer, urine, rainwater, and mud. Unlike everyone else, I was more concerned about my shoes getting dirty than having a good time. I couldn't party anymore. I couldn't pour another swallow of beer down my throat. I stood there with a fake smile on my face.

After the *bloco* Joana gave me a ride home and asked me what, if anything, I was going to take home from my trip.

"The realization that I'm hypochondriac," I said.

"Come on be serious."

"I am being serious! I thought I had malaria, rabies, and scabies. Oh and dengue fever too."

"Okay what else?"

"Actually I don't think I'll know until after I go home, but I have a feeling I will remember the people more than the places. The memory of you and Paula will be a lot stronger than, say, Sugar Loaf mountain, as pretty as it is."

"When you return home don't be surprised if it feels like you traveled through a time machine."

"What do you mean?"

"Well you've changed, but your friends haven't. They won't be able to identify with your experiences, like when you struggled through Peru and Bolivia while sick. And how could they? They'll want to do the same things you were doing when you left, but your interest in those will be less because you're a different person."

"But I don't feel different," I said.

"No, you are."

XIII

It felt like a man died in my digestive system and was coming out of my ass in various states of decomposition. In denial that I needed to change my diet, I insisted on daily doses of pizza, greasy *empanadas*, and *falhado do queijos*, heavenly butter and cheese pastry bombs that left me full for hours. Every visit to the bathroom was like Christmas morning as a kid when I was surprised at what I got. A part of me believed things would magically get better when I returned home, and that the past six months would be erased with my favorite foods—peanut butter and jelly sandwiches, Fuji apples, my dad's beef kebabs, and my stepmom's rice stews, but I knew it would be a long road ahead to normalcy.

I checked out of my shithole hostel for a new one in Ipanema. It was clean and had a few pretty girls, especially an upper-class Brazilian girl who had a novel English accent from living in London, but I had no will to flirt.

I got an email from Beppe telling me he was in town. Two days later we met at a bar across the street from Emporio. He brought along an older Brazilian woman who wanted to sleep with him and a gay *carioca*, who was friends with his host.

The gay man remarked that even though homosexuality seems open in Rio, it's not something you want to advertise because of potential violence. He was educated, the son of an architect, and was very interested in talking about politics and economics. He told me in Brazil 10% of the population owns 75% of the wealth, and that rich Brazilians are not taking advantage of the vast resources bestowed from the land by investing money back into the economy. I nodded along to encourage his thoughts on the matter while Beppe talked with the Brazilian woman.

With Beppe around all of a sudden I felt motivated to hit on girls. Alone and sick I am nothing, but with a fun friend a switch comes on and the machine inside me whirls into action. I easily approached a group of four girls who walked by our outside table. It was going well until the father of one pulled up in a car to pick them up, and we all concluded they lied to us when they said they were eighteen.

I asked Beppe the question I'd been sitting on for a month: "Have you ever had any acting or stage performance experience?" His photos were still burned in my mind, those poses and facial expressions.

"Actually I studied acting," he said.

"I knew it!"

"How'd you know?"

"Your picture poses are just too perfect. Remember at the New Year's party when you were flying around like an airplane and dancing with that pot? That should have come across as goofy, but I was thinking more about how to copy them and dance with potted plants myself."

"I only do those things to make myself photogenic since I don't think I look good in photos."

"No I think you're already photogenic. Those crazy arm movements and faces make your photos even better."

With the older Brazilian woman firmly attached to his arm, I asked him for tips. He instructed me to avoid looking at the lens when a photo is being taken and experiment with different arm poses until I find ones that work for me.

The night came to an end after three beers. Every other bar was empty. It was the last night of Carnival so the gringos were packing their bags and the *cariocas* were home resting from a week of drinking and dancing. The Brazilian woman took him home and I returned to the hostel to practice arm movements in front of the mirror. He had sex with two other girls since our time in Punta del Este. I swear all he does is smile and make jokes.

RIO DE JANEIRO

Luke gave me a surprise call when he came back from Bahia's Carnival. He had one day left before his flight back to Australia. I bought him a *falhado do queijo* and met him in Copacabana at our juice bar, where I gave Marcelo one last thumbs-up. Luke was the one who introduced me to my first *açaí*.

We walked to the beach and sat next to a vendor selling Brazilian flag sarongs. Both of us already owned one. The sun was out and joggers passed by us every few seconds.

"I really like Rio and how relaxed it is," I said, "but our time in Córdoba was more fun."

"Yeah thanks to the Predator. He planted the seed. It's funny how much work we had to put in for those girls there, and then we come here and root within a few days."

"I can't get over how girls can be so different just one country over. And then you look at girls from the U.S., Australia, Ireland, and England and they're basically the same."

"I don't think the girls in Argentina would've been hard though if we stayed in the same city for a couple months and made lots of friends."

"Yeah it seems like social circle is the way to go there. Hey remember when Ethan blew it for you guys when he puked on the patio?"

"That idiot! Those girls were cute too."

"You know, combine the personalities of Brazilian girls and the beauty of Argentine girls and I think you have the perfect girl."

"I hear that's how the girls in Colombia are."

"Weird, I heard that too." A vendor with a board of handicrafts walked up to us and asked if we wanted to buy anything. We politely declined. "I wonder if it's going to be hard to date American girls again."

"Well if they are like Australian girls then probably."

"I'll just have to find the Brazilian hangouts in D.C."

"It won't be the same. They'll be the exotic ones there, not you. They won't be as friendly."

"That's true."

A short time later it was time for him to go and I gave him a hug and wished him luck. We vowed to meet again in South America, but I knew deep inside that I would never see him again.

XIV

I called Mariana. Though she was short on the phone she agreed to see me. I was craving raw fish so I told her to meet me at a sushi bar in Ipanema. While we waited for our table I apologized for how I acted, that I was stupid for not wanting to spend the night with her.

"I felt used, that you wouldn't want to be with me unless there would be sex." I cringed. She did nothing to deserve feeling that way.

"No it's not like that. My head is messed up, I think from the rabies vaccine. I wasn't thinking right."

"I thought it was over and we were only going to be friends."

I grabbed her hand and said, "I never want to be just friends with you."

Dinner was quiet and we went back to her place. In bed she was tense and stiff. Because she didn't expect us to have sex she didn't fantasize about it during the day (for her sex is a multi-hour process). We fell asleep early. In the morning she bought me an *açaí* breakfast. I gave her a tight embrace goodbye before leaving. There was less emotion than I thought there would be.

My cab driver took the scenic beach route on my way back to the hostel. Only two nights remained. The radio station was set to American love songs. Damien Rice's "Blower's Daughter" played as Copacabana beach flew by on my left. I don't think I was in love with Mariana, but I was just now starting to care. I'm slow and stupid and selfish but I'm not a monster. Maybe our relationship would play out only after a couple months, but now in this cab I'm wondering when I'm going to meet a girl like her again. I had to see her one more time.

I spent the afternoon at the market buying gifts for my family, such as Brazilian flag sarongs, soccer jerseys, and *açaí* soap. I went out with Paula and Joana and their friends to a club, but my stomach wasn't feeling well and I left after only an hour. I gave a last goodbye to the girls, telling them I'd return some day. I told Paula not to be so down on Rio. "You're lucky to live here," I said.

The next day was the Carnival championship parade. It was a wonderful manmade spectacle with painfully detailed costumes and floats full of creativity. The half-naked dancing women were a nice bonus, but the best energy came from the crowd itself, who sang along with the songs. (Each samba school had one song and it played nonstop in a loop during their respective forty-five minute processions, making the lyrics easy to memorize.) Floats ranged from a pirate ship firing phantom cannonballs to a forest full of men dressed up as leafy trees. One float represented life and death with a skeletal corpse that would rotate to reveal a chubby pink baby. The older ladies in the stands encouraged me to dance and helped me find a better view even though I was much taller than them. Everywhere in Rio the people made me feel welcome, like I was one of them.

I got my fifth and final rabies vaccine shot in the arm. The allergic reaction from the bedbugs were gone, and though my stomach was grumbling, I bought one last *falhado do queijo*. I called my sister to make sure she was picking me up at the airport. I cleaned out my pack in the hostel courtyard with rubbing alcohol just in case there was a bedbug who wanted to travel home with me.

XV

Mariana showed up at the hostel, getting double takes from the Australian guys lingering by the front desk. After a light dinner at a vegetarian restaurant, she gave me a card with an artist's drawing of a pale brown mountain. The moon was asleep on the mountain and in the background was a swirling turquoise sky dotted with yellow stars. She wrote a note inside:

Roosh, baby,

I'm glad we met. I don't know exactly what I should write for you in my poor English. I hope you can take with you to the

A DEAD BAT IN PARAGUAY

U.S.A. the new eyes of a foreigner. The eyes of a child. I hope we meet again, though I imagine we will be more different than now. Be with my love and friendship, wherever you go.

Love,
Mariana

I had thought this trip would clear my mind and wrap all my doubts and questions of life into a nice little box wrapped with a bright red ribbon. I thought it would make me happier or more fulfilled, or at least make it clear what my next step was. Instead I didn't know what I was going to do when I returned home, which wasn't even my home. I started to think it didn't matter—life was going to drag me along like a rag doll anyway. The best I could do is keep my head up so it doesn't bash on the concrete.

South America chewed me up and now was spitting me out, humbler, weaker, and more confused. The past six months was a different way of living, yes, but still living. The human experience doesn't change. Pain, disappointment, humiliation, shame, failure, illness, intimacy, friendship, pleasure, happiness, love. Notes may sound sharper in the hands of a different musician, but they don't change.

Mariana walked me back to my hostel and instead of getting right into a cab she said she was going to take a walk. I held her for a long time, fighting back tears and wiping hers, and then let her go. I watched her walk down the dark street until she passed under a large tree and disappeared. I stepped into my hostel's front yard and slammed the steel door shut behind me.

EPILOGUE

I

"So how was the Northeast?" Paula asked.

"It was just like you said—poor, but with great beaches. I went to Fortaleza, Natal, Pipa, Recife, Salvador, and Vitória. I liked Vitória the most because I swear I was the only gringo there."

"Vitória? Only businessmen travel there."

"Exactly. I'd go to a club and guys would come up to me and say, 'Hey, you're the gringo, right? I heard you talking outside in English.' I'd ask questions about how to get girls, just to make them feel like they were teaching the gringo something. The girls didn't really care, though, and would brush me off. After my last trip, I kind of thought I'd be more welcome by the women if there were no other gringos around, but I guess that's not always the case. Overall I had a fun time and believe it or not, nothing bad happened!"

"Don't say that," she said. "Now something bad will happen. Do you want to get another beer?"

She looked just like I remembered her from when she and her friends had showed me around Rio while I was dealing with my health and mental problems. I initially had planned to stay in a hostel in Ipanema, but she insisted that I crash at her place for a few nights.

In Vitória I ended up staying with a guy who worked at my hotel. He didn't have a guest bed or sofa, so I had to buy a $40 foam mattress. I hoped it would last the week, but after the first night the foam flattened until it felt like I was sleeping directly on the floor. When Paula told me she didn't have a mattress, I reluctantly rolled and tied the piece of shit up with rope and hauled it to Rio by bus. I'm certain other Brazilians thought I was homeless because I hadn't shaved for a few weeks.

Paula and I caught up on things in the bar by Copacabana's beach. I arrived two hours prior and for the last half of the bus ride my stomach was grumbling loudly, but I wrote it off as a bad case of gas. Not once in the past seven months, the first six spent in Colombia, had I gotten a stomach illness. During my last trip I had learned to cook most of my meals and limit the street food, but in the last month I had gotten cocky and started eating from the street again. At the Vitória bus station I ate an odd-tasting *coxinha de frango*, a deep-fried chicken and cheese ball that was neon orange on the inside. I figured it contained a kind of cheese I hadn't had before.

There wasn't a whole lot to tell Paula about the previous seven months. In Medellín, I had written a new book, studied Spanish, and put a lot of energy into sleeping with Colombian women. It included going to the university to hang out in the common areas to ask girls for help with my Spanish. Instead of being the old guy in the club, I was the old guy in school, but thankfully girls like men around 30 years old. I made a couple new friends, dated a really nice girl who pokes me every now and then on Facebook, and played blackjack in the casinos. Life was good, easy, and most importantly of all, cheap.

Colombia had spoiled my return to Brazil because it competed so well on many fronts, including quality of life, cost of living, and women. I had held Brazilian women on a magic pedestal for a long time after my return to the States, but now Colombian women were almost there with them. Picking one over the other would come down to a matter of personal taste because I doubt different men who have experiences with both would consistently arrive to the same conclusion.

My stomach continued to churn as Paula gave me updates on her life and her new boyfriend. I started sweating and figured I could squeeze my ass cheeks together for another half hour before using the bathroom at her place, but it's amazing how the human digestive system can move at the speed of sound when it wants to. I finally excused myself to visit the bar's restroom.

The lone toilet was covered with drops of urine and the toilet paper was out, so I quickly grabbed a dozen paper towels from above the sink, put four on the seat, and sat down. My body shook with a tremendous explosion as the entire contents of my bowels ejected in less than three seconds. There was a loud "bloo-bloop" sound and then, just like that, it was over. I lifted my ass to take a peek at what was underneath and thought, "That wasn't so bad."

We left the bar soon after and went back in her place, where I had to go again. The only problem was that her bathroom was inside her room, only six feet from the bed. There was nothing I could do to mask the embarrassing ass explosion sounds, not even a dinky ventilation fan. Over the next ten hours I had to go to the bathroom at least fifteen times while Paula slept. Poor girl—I'm sure she thought I was shitting on her head. My anus became so abraded and raw from all the wiping that it felt like I had been sodomized with a Brillo pad. During brief moments of sleep I crossed my legs, for fear that I'd accidently shit on my foam mattress.

Two days later, after a few meals of rice and potatoes, I was fine again. No fever, no lingering pain, and no constant gas. No five-month ordeal like last time.

"Whenever I see you, you're sick," Paula said, shaking her head. "Maybe you should see a special doctor."

"I was healthy the past seven months, I swear!" She probably thinks I was a premature baby and now have to deal with some type of lifelong immune system disorder.

Not wanting to impose, after three nights at her place I checked into a hostel and began looking for an apartment.

II

I called Mariana. She picked up on the second ring. I started talking in English without saying my name, to see how long it would take for her to know it was me. It only took a couple seconds.

"It's so good to hear from you," she said.

"Guess where I am right now."

"Rio de Janeiro."

They say you can tell when someone is smiling or not on the phone, and I like to think she was during our conversation. We chatted for a few minutes and made plans to hang out in two days.

Over the previous 23 months I had thought of her often, but I didn't overdo it. I didn't think of her as the solution to my problems and I'd stop myself if I wandered into any girlfriend fantasies. It's true that she had rarely popped in my head when I was seeing a new girl, but after the dust had settled and I was alone again, I'd remember our time together and wonder if it was the real deal or not. Was I romanticizing a short relationship made intense by what I was going through my last time here, or was she really the one?

Now that I was back in Rio, I had trouble holding back. I got excited. For the next day, all I could do was think about what our reunion would be like. Should I pick her up when we hug? Should I go for the kiss right away? Should we end up in a club after a drink or two at a quiet bar? Should I dress up or keep it simple? Should I trim my beard or keep it a little long? I found myself thinking about things I didn't usually worry about.

We agreed to meet the next afternoon at 5pm. At first I thought she wanted to meet early because she couldn't wait to see me, but then I realized she probably had other plans later that night. I was ready to jump to the conclusion that she had another guy. After all, it had been two years. What did I expect? Was she supposed to greet me with open legs and scream, "Take me, Roosh! I've been waiting for you all this time!" Back to reality, and that reality is that a lot of time had passed, and people meet other people. Still, her having a boyfriend would destroy my plans for picking up exactly where we left off.

III

Nostalgia is a powerful thing. I had a constant smirk on my face while doing all the simple things I had done before, like getting a *folhado* at my favorite bakery, recharging my cell phone balance at the mobile shop, doing pull-ups on the beach bars in Ipanema, and eating lunch at Delirio Tropical. In Copacabana, I visited Marcelo's juice bar and was surprised to see him still working there. I walked up to the counter and before I could say anything he squinted in a flash of remembrance.

"I was here two years ago," I said.

"What's your name again?"

"Roosh."

"Rooooooosh, that's right!"

He put out his hand and gave mine a healthy shake. We chatted for maybe thirty seconds and then he went back to work. I think I was more sentimental about our relationship than he was judging by how quickly the smile evaporated from his face. I wanted him to be more than just my juice guy, but I knew he saw a dozen gringos like me every day and I was lucky he had remembered me at all.

Eventually I ran out of nostalgia. I walked around Ipanema, by the McDonald's, KFC, and expensive boutiques I'd never stepped into, then thought, "Okay, now what?" I did it. I had come back, just as I'd told everyone I would, and I was about to reunite with my girl, but the mission that had consumed my thoughts for the past two years was almost complete. I felt a little empty, and then I remembered something someone had once told me: "Sometimes wanting something is better than having it." That was probably why I hesitated in Vitória before returning to Rio. I stayed there ten days instead of three, perhaps subconsciously conflicted about the fact that I was about to finish what I set out to do. I wanted to hold on to wanting just a bit longer.

IV

I had no complaints when Mariana pushed our date back one day (because of allergies, she told me) to Saturday night, which was a more proper time for a reunion. We were supposed to meet at the subway station, but it began pouring, so she texted me her address instead. At our meeting time I stood partially hidden under a tree in front of her building, waiting for her to come out.

I stared at her for a good five seconds before she noticed me. It was a careful stare, trying to see what had changed and what hadn't. Her hair was longer—longer than mine, finally. Her body still looked great and it's wasn't obvious that she had aged two years. She smiled when she saw me hiding behind the tree. I gave her a hug, but she seemed decidedly cool, only giving me a weak embrace. The first thing she asked was where the taxi was, and when I told her I had let it go, she sounded annoyed, asking me twice why I'd done that, almost scolding me like a child. If she was happy to see me, I couldn't tell.

We decided to walk up a steep hill to some local bars in her neighborhood. She had a tiny umbrella, so we both got wet as we lost our breath climbing, and several times she criticized herself for not bringing a bigger one. She was tense and made little effort to help with the conversation. The silences were painful. We hadn't seen each other in two years, but after five minutes we had almost nothing to say. I thought either she had a serious boyfriend and was simply giving me a token meeting or needed time to warm up to me again.

When we finally settled into the bar twenty minutes later, I decided to approach it as just another date: I'd talk my ass off, tell her the interesting things I had been doing, make her laugh, and touch her more and more as the evening progressed.

"So my book is done. I finally finished it—and you're in it," I said.

"Oh, no!" She laughed.

"No, it's nothing bad. Meeting you was a good way to end the story, I think, after all the bad stuff that happened."

"What name did you give me?"

"Mariana."

"How did you pick that?"

"Well, I went on the internet and did a search for Brazilian names, and you seem like a Mariana, so I went with that."

I told her about the book, carefully avoiding its sexual theme and focusing on the friendships and cities I had visited. Mariana is the type of girl who didn't care much about my past, but I still didn't feel comfortable with her knowing about all the girls I had tried to get with before getting with her. I didn't want to trivialize our relationship by saying it was the culmination of dozens of approaches and brainstorming and effort and game. There's no romance in that.

By the second hour of our date, we had settled into a fun conversation. She opened up more, telling me about the time she had been robbed at knife-point, the traveling she had done, and the productions she had acted in. There were many moments where we relived our time together and I'd say, "I put that in the book!" Even though she had never seen the book and had no idea what filled its nearly 300 pages, she seemed pleased that she was in it. The whole time I held on to the hope that our reunion wouldn't be anything less than worthy of the two-year wait.

We moved to a sushi bar and as we walked, she hooked her arm through mine. She seemed to laugh harder at my jokes and gave me longer stares. She asked more questions, and if this had been any other date, I would have been thinking, "This is going well."

After four hours of talking, we decided to call it a night. On the walk to her apartment we held hands, but at the front door she was prepared to say goodbye and send me on my way. I couldn't let that happen.

"Can I use your bathroom?" I said. She didn't answer. Without skipping a beat, I added, "Okay well can you point me to an alley where I can go? Hopefully I won't be robbed."

She paused for a few seconds. "No, that's fine," she said. "You can come in."

I knew I'd be staying a while when she offered me a drink. I went into her room and saw that the pictures of her guru were still there, but the shelf of herbal remedies was gone.

"Where's all your medicines?" I asked.

"What medicines?"

"You know, the natural medicines you used to have in those dropper bottles."

"I think you imagined that."

"Are you sure? Because I put it in the book."

The last bit of nostalgia I had was with her and I milked it for all it was worth. I wanted the wait to be validated. I wanted to be correct that she wasn't just another notch. I had so many relationships that were meaningless that I needed this one to be real.

"The last time I was here," I said, "I was a bit messed up, I think. When I went home, I hibernated in my dad's basement and it took two months until I felt normal again. I'm telling you this because I didn't want to leave you. There's a lot of things we didn't do together."

"You didn't have time," she said.

"I could've made time. I could've stayed longer. I…"

She put her hand in mine. A few minutes later she led me to her bedroom.

V

There was a peculiar moment the next morning when I left. She gave me a kiss goodbye and said, "Take care."

"Take care?" I replied.

"Yeah, take care," she repeated. "Isn't that what Americans say?"

"Well, 'take care' is something you say to someone you're not going to see for a while. If you run into an old college friend you haven't seen in years and you chat for a couple minutes, you say 'take care' at the end. It means 'See you in a few years, maybe.'"

"Oh, no, that's not what I meant at all," she said. Then she gave me a more proper farewell as I left.

I really wanted to say that she was indeed the one, that I ended the game because of her, that we feel in love and had beautiful Brazilian babies, and that I lived out my days in a tropical country. But that wasn't the case.

Five days later we met for lunch at her suggestion. Beforehand, I debated whether I should comment on her coolness. I knew something was wrong because all the signs were there: rescheduling our date, getting annoyed at my letting the taxi go, excusing aloof behavior with a made-up illness (allergies), not inviting me back to her place, and giving me an impersonal goodbye. I remembered the first time we met, when she had asked me to come over, but the previous night I had to weasel my way in as if she was any other girl. Her kisses were also different—quicker, colder, and not as sensual. Our lovemaking was more detached. I decided to not say anything and see what would happen. Well, I didn't have to wait long.

During lunch she barely said a word. Like on our date, I talked and talked to get something out of her, but she responded with simple one-word replies. I had brought a book with me, Milan Kundera's *The Book of Laughter and Forgetting*, and the only time she really said anything was when she explained that she had liked his most famous work, *The Unbearable Lightness of Being*. Did I have to bring one of his books on every date just to get something going? Whether she was no longer interested in me or not, there is no way I can date a girl who doesn't talk to me. Disappointment set in.

We finished our meal in silence, then she said, "I have to tell you something."

I knew what was coming.

"I think we should just be friends."

I'd been dumped many times before, where things simply faded away and a girl stopped agreeing to go out with me. Maybe I would run into her later and we'd have sex again for old time's sake, but not once in seven years had a girl I genuinely liked sat me down and said she never wanted to be romantically involved with me again. The last time I had been hurt, but this time I was angry.

She was about to tell me why when two businessmen sat next to our table. She asked if I wanted to talk on the beach. I agreed. We walked without saying anything, then sat on the sand.

"You don't have to give me a reason," I said. "I don't care, whatever you want."

"No, but I *want* to tell you. When we first met, my heart was open, but I can't do this. I can't see you for two months and then have you go away again. I can't suffer like that."

Oh, god. She was giving me the excuse I had been using on girls for the past year—a spin-off of the 'It's not you, it's me' routine.

"I understand completely," I said. "If that's what you want. I knew something was wrong anyway, because it didn't feel like last time. You were colder, and from the moment you postponed our date, I knew something wasn't right."

"But I wasn't feeling well," she protested. "I had allergies."

"Look, if I was in a hospital bed, half-dying, I'd still crawl out to see you after two years. You just weren't excited. I told myself, 'I'm 100% sure she's seeing a guy,' and that's what I still think."

I looked deep in her eyes because a part of me wanted to know the real reason, even though that reason would ultimately boil down to her not wanting to see me. I needed to know if she had something else going on instead of preferring to watch *telenovelas* at home rather than spending time with me.

"He's not better than you, but he's here. You're going to leave in two months. Then what am I going to do?"

"The other night you were telling me that you were thinking about having a kid in a year or two," I said. "When a woman says that, what she really means is that she wants a child right now, and I understand that. You're at the age where you're ready to find something long-term, but I can't give you that."

"I know you can't."

"I guess the only reason we got together in the first place was because you had just broken up with someone. I was the rebound."

"Yes my heart was open then. I knew you were leaving soon and it wouldn't mean anything."

I winced and turned away, my eyes falling upon a group of guys in skimpy Speedos playing foot volleyball.

"But now it's harder, because you're staying longer, but you'll still be leaving again. You're too…" She fumbled for the right word. "Light."

"I'm sorry I'm not a Brazilian citizen. I'm sorry I can only stay a couple months at a time, but it's because I'm light that we even met. It gives and it takes, I understand that. You think this conversation we're having right now is the first time for…" I wanted to talk to her as if she was a therapist and discuss the pros and cons of living the lifestyle that I've chosen, but I stopped short and started making patterns in the sand with my book.

"And you barely kept in touch while you were away," she said. "Do you know the word *cultivar*?"

"Yes, to cultivate."

"That's what I want. Something that grows. You sent me two postcards, a couple emails, and we talked once on the phone."

"So you wanted me to call so you could ask when I was coming back, only for me to say, 'I don't know, maybe soon.' What would we have talked about? 'Hey, Mariana, I'm going out with my friends a lot and writing. Oh, yeah? Great. I can't wait to have *açai* again.'"

"Well let's be friends. And I mean that," she said. "This Saturday I'm going out dancing with my friends, and I'd like it if you'd come along and meet them."

"No, that's okay."

"What?"

"I don't want to be just friends. No, it's either all or nothing with me."

"So you don't even want to see me again?"

"We can exchange emails, and maybe have lunch before I leave the country."

She frowned and tightened her lips. Part of me felt bad for her because after all she was a girl I really liked, but another part of me was pleased that I was hurting her.

"I can't believe you don't want to be my friend. You're blackmailing me! This isn't how Brazilians do it. We keep in touch. We see each other."

"Yeah, well, I do things differently," I said flatly. "I have enough friends anyway." That was a lie. There was only one other person in Rio I could call.

"Then the only thing you really want from me is my body."

I said nothing, wondering about the question myself.

She told me that every other guy she'd ever broken up with had jumped at the chance to stay in touch and that I was being silly not to want the same. I refused to reward her decision to dump me with friendship. I wanted her to wonder if she made the right choice by letting me go. She needed to feel genuine loss. I had to inflict either pleasure or pain—nothing in between. I had to burn my bridges because it was the right thing to do.

"I think it's time for me to go," I said.

We got up and she insisted on escorting me to my hostel. On the way she continued to push the friendship idea, but I said little, thinking that I wanted her to feel what I was feeling: utter rejection.

"You really don't have to walk me back," I said, as if she was following me like a pest. At the end of the block she stopped, but I kept walking.

"Wait!" she called after me.

I stopped, looked back, and said, "Yeah?"

"Aren't you at least going to give me a hug?"

I sighed, then gave her the most awkward hug I could muster, my body leaning so far forward that only the boney tops of my shoulders touched her body. She stood on her tiptoes to give me a kiss on the cheek, but I pulled away as soon as I felt her lips make contact with my skin.

It was another goodbye, two years and two blocks away from the last one. I took three steps back and stared into her big eyes, which were glassy with tears. She smiled wanly, as if encouraging me to say something comforting, but all I wanted to do at that moment was destroy something beautiful. I raised my hand and said, "Take care."

I didn't wait for a response. I immediately turned and walked away.

VI

A couple weeks later I got into a fight with Paula's best friend, Joana, at a samba club. She had discovered my writings and tried to use them against me. The entire night I endured things like, "So when are you going to *bang* these girls?" "Are you going to learn samba so you can *bang* a lot of girls?" and "What clubs do you go to so you can *bang* girls?" I bit my lip. I didn't want to create a scene, but at the end of the night, while hailing a taxi, she said, "The night is still young enough to *bang* girls. You should stay out."

I'd finally had enough. "Can you shut the fuck up about that already. Are you going to do that all the time from now on?"

The ride home was awkward. Of course she told Paula, who cooled toward me afterward, taking days to reply to one of my text messages instead of the usual hour or less. I now had no friends in Rio.

EPILOGUE

One night about a month after Mariana dumped me, I went to Lapa alone. While walking up the stairs of the club, I ran into her. She was with her sister and didn't offer to introduce me, as if I was a distant acquaintance, so I just nodded as if to say *I see how it is* and kept walking.

She found me later and asked what had happened. "You tell me what happened," I said. "You seemed like you didn't want to talk and didn't even offer to introduce me to your sister."

"You looked upset! It seemed like you wanted to walk away from me!"

I stuck with her for the rest of the night. We sat on the couch and talked about emotions, love, and all sorts of nonsense my friends back home would have made fun of me about. Whenever I looked away, she wiped away her tears. We gently stroked each other's hands and when she stared at me, I got the feeling that she wanted me to make a commitment and say, "Baby, I'm going to live in Brazil. Let's do it!" That's what she wanted, and I felt confident that if I said those words, she would have been mine as long as our relationship could last.

I imagined how my life would be if I chose that route. I'd have to make a permanent move to Rio, and the only way to do that legally would be to get married. We'd be husband and wife, with our own little apartment in Copacabana. Three nights a week I'd cook American food, three nights a week she'd cook Brazilian food, and one night a week we'd go out. I'd support her in her career and listen to her troubles at work. We'd take trips into the Brazilian countryside to get away from the city. We'd be best friends. I'd become an English teacher or get some other job that brought in a regular income. We'd have a Little Rooshinho and I'd find out if I had what it took to be a good father. We'd outgrow our apartment in Copacabana and get a bigger one in Ipanema. I'd become fluent in Portuguese. I'd visit my family and friends in the States once a year. I'd become a family man and have a regular, pleasant life. If our marriage worked, we'd make each other happy until our last days, companions until death. Our graves would be side by side.

I remained silent.

"You were never in love with me anyway," she finally said.

Besides my gentle touches, I offered Mariana no reason to dump the guy she had just "started" dating to get with me. I made my choice, and I was ready to live with it.

We walked out when the club closed at five in the morning. When we hugged, she closed her eyes and practically dived in my chest, but she didn't let me hold her long enough to kiss her. She hopped into a cab and at that point I realized she was too sure of what she wanted to be weak for another night or two. I could accept that, but I went to bed wondering how I was going to meet another girl like her. For my remaining three months in Rio I didn't.

Those were shallow times, going out to drink and fuck random girls in my *favela* apartment while building very little of substance. There was the pretty daughter of a gastroenterologist, who spoke French and treated me well, but I just couldn't fall for her. There was a *telenovela* actress from São Paulo who was gorgeous but spoke no English and was hard to pin down. There was an Argentine girl with a magical booty who tasted like a bar ashtray. There were traveling American girls I slept with only hours after meeting. It's after these girls, ten days before I was set to leave Rio for good, that I had an overwhelming desire to see Mariana again. I didn't care if it was "bad game" to contact her or not, so I called and said I needed to see her before I left. She agreed to a date.

VII

The crowd at the champagne bar was typical: older professionals who wanted to wind down after work. We sat next to each other at a huge table that ran the length of the bar. I caught her up on my life in Rio.

"When I first came here, I fell in love with the city and imagined myself living here, but now I don't know if I'm ever coming back." I took a sip of champagne, which was extremely cold because of the salt solution the bartender had put into our ice bucket.

"Why don't you like Rio?"

EPILOGUE

"Well, it's expensive and dangerous, the traffic is bad, the nightlife sucks, there's too many gringos, it's either unbearably hot or raining, it's dirty, smelly, making friends is hard, and I don't even like the beach that much. It's like Rio was a girl who I fell hard for, but once I got to know her, I realized we didn't have a lot in common. I think it was you who..."

I paused.

"Me who what?" she asked.

"The first time I was here, you made the city better than it actually is."

"I don't believe that."

"You don't have to, but there's no reason for me to stay here now, or even to come back."

I noticed that she was touching me often and shifting nervously in her seat. I had gotten her to meet me under the guise of friendship, and while I didn't expect more, I was sure hoping for it.

"Remember that guy you told me you had just 'started' seeing?" I asked.

"Yes."

"Well, I think that was a lie. I think you invented him to make me feel better."

"No, I really was seeing a guy! But I'm not seeing him anymore."

"Oh."

"And then there was another guy."

"What?"

"But it was really quick. Very short."

"So you're not seeing anyone right now?"

"No."

"Well, good, because after this bottle of champagne you can come to my place and we can make love one last time." I smiled, but not too hard since I wanted her to believe I was mostly serious. Just testing the waters.

"Oh, baby, no." She shook her head. "Let's just be friends."

"I'm leaving in ten days—it's not like I'm asking for more. But anyway..."

"So did you meet any girls?"

"A couple, but nothing serious. After you ended it I wasn't too upset because I thought it would be easy to find your replacement, especially since I met you only a week after I arrived in Rio." I paused a moment. "But I haven't been able to find another Mariana."

She smiled, but said nothing. I asked if she was still on her allergy medication. She said she wasn't. I kept filling her glass and eventually ordered a second bottle.

I was having trouble containing my feelings and said some things I knew I shouldn't have, but it felt right and she seemed to be getting closer to me. I went with it. There was no need to lie or pretend.

"When I came back," I said, "I was ready to give us a shot, to see only you."

"I don't believe that. I know your type, going from country to country. You probably have girls in each country that you keep in touch with."

"No, well... no, you're wrong. No one I really care about," I said, searching for the right words. "The last time we talked, I got the feeling that you wanted me to make a stronger commitment, to invest more." I paused again, then asked the question that was on my mind for the past couple months. "I guess what I'm asking is... if I lived here, would things be different?"

She looked at me for what seemed like eternity and said, "Yes, they would."

I nodded, then the conversation drifted into silence. I tried to kiss her a few minutes later, but she turned her head at the last moment.

"We're only friends," she said. "Friends don't kiss."

"They don't?"

"Well, sometimes," she said softly. Then she gave me a look that said, "I'm going to be vulnerable now... please be gentle."

I approached again slowly, and when our lips touched, I felt something unusual—something electric that seemed to paralyze my body. Only my lips and mouth were alive, and they were heating up. For the next thirty seconds I felt this heat coming into my mouth, increasing in temperature with every moment. The movements of her tongue triggered flashes of white light on the back of my eyelids. My head seemed to separate from the rest of my body. The people and the music faded into the background until we were completely alone, until I processed not a single thought or sensation besides the heat in my mouth and the lights dancing in my vision. I don't know how long the kiss lasted, but she pulled away first, leaving my lips hanging in the air. It took several seconds for the sounds of the bar to reenter my consciousness and for my body to reattach itself. I looked at her, confused, as if coming out of a hypnotist's trance. I swallowed hard and began to rub my hands over my face. Then I excused myself and went into the bathroom so she wouldn't continue to see the effect she had on me.

The champagne continued to flow and like an octopus I let my hands explore her body, slowly creeping up her leg until she smacked them back down. I just wanted to have her one more time, and then we could be done for good.

Getting her back to my place took quite a bit of convincing. I had to basically sign a contract stating that she'd stay no more than fifteen minutes and that we'd only hug and kiss. Of course she couldn't help herself once she was lying on my bed, and neither could I.

When it was over, I lay on my back, staring up at the ceiling fan, trying to keep my eyes focused on one of the rotating blades, wondering how a petite Brazilian girl gained so much power over me.

I turned on my side to face her and said, "I don't see you for three months and I'm leaving, but now we're… doing things."

"Well, yes, that's why," she said softly. "This is how I protect myself. Why would I get too close to someone who's staying a short time?"

We stared at each other for a long moment, and then I said, "I love you." I didn't smile.

She laughed.

"Why are you laughing?"

"Because you're not serious."

"How do you know I'm not serious?"

"Because you're not ready!"

I saw her twice after that, once for a movie and the other for a walk through a park. Things were decidedly more friendly and nothing got past simple hand-holding or light kissing. She made a reference to having "drunk too much" the night at the champagne bar, and I got the hint. We were just friends—and there would be no additional sex.

After the park, we went for a quick *açai* and grabbed the same bus. I was emotionally numb. I wanted to get off the roller coaster ride she had put me on and if she wanted to only be friends then fine. It didn't matter anyway—I was leaving in two days. Even if she wanted to stay with me, I wasn't ready to move to Rio just for her. She was right.

I told her my stop was coming up. I looked over to her and saw tears streaming down her face, more tears than when I had first left her about two years earlier.

I had trouble understanding why she was so upset. I stared at the back of the seat in front of me until I broke the silence with, "Quero cafuné." It was a phrase she had taught me, which means, "I want to gently stroke your hair." She laughed and told me to be sure to use it on other girls.

"I guess our time was two years ago," I said.

"Yes. I was more open then."

"I'll always remember it."

We both knew I wouldn't be coming back to Rio again. I gave her a quick kiss, then pulled the cord and walked towards the back of the bus.

It was finally over for good.

For more travel stories, visit my web site:

http://www.rooshv.com

CPSIA information can be obtained at www.ICGtesting.com
Printed in the USA
LVOW102134281211

261504LV00001B/99/P